A meeting of the Defense Appropriations Subcommittee, July 1969. Senators Symington (ex officio), Ellender, and Russell question Air Force Generals

UNUSED POWER

*The Work of
the Senate Committee
on Appropriations*

STEPHEN HORN

UNUSED POWER

*The Work of
the Senate Committee
on Appropriations*

THE BROOKINGS INSTITUTION
Washington, D.C.

196980

Foreword

Until recently, the congressional appropriations process has largely been overlooked by students of Congress. When it has been examined, attention has usually focused on the work of the House Committee on Appropriations rather than its Senate counterpart. The Senate committee, however, has a crucial role to play in considering the executive budget, presidential and agency recommendations, and the appropriation bills. What the role of Senate Appropriations is now and what it ought to be, how the committee functions now and how it might meet its responsibilities better, are the subjects of this study.

The work reflects the author's experiences and observations as the legislative assistant from 1960 to 1966 of Senator Thomas H. Kuchel of California, a member of the committee. Dr. Horn prepared the volume while a senior fellow at the Brookings Institution from 1966 to 1969. During that period he interviewed or corresponded with all members of the committee and its staff who served during the Eighty-ninth Congress (1965–66). The Institution and the author are grateful to the senators and staff members who gave freely of their time in assisting this study.

Several persons read the manuscript and made helpful suggestions. They include George A. Graham, director of Brookings' Governmental Studies Program while this work was in progress; James L. Sundquist and Charles B. Saunders, Jr., of the Brookings staff; Jerry Landauer of *The Wall Street Journal;* and Joseph Cooper of Rice University. In addition, Gilbert Y. Steiner, the present director of Governmental Studies at Brookings, and Herbert Kaufman, a senior fellow, reviewed Chapter 6. Bailey Guard, a senior staff member of the Senate Committee on Public Works, commented on the Prologue. The author wishes to express his appreciation to all of them, as well as to Heather Adams, who provided many needed public documents, and to Richard D. Hupman, the Librarian of the United States Senate, and his staff, who were cooperative throughout the study. Ellen Joseph edited the manuscript and Helen B. Eisenhart prepared the index.

The views expressed in this work are those of the author and do not necessarily represent the views of the staff members, officers, or trustees of the Brookings Institution.

KERMIT GORDON
President

June 1970
Washington, D.C.

Contents

Tables

Tables (*continued*)

Figures

UNUSED POWER

Prologue: The Setting

A Markup Session

It is shortly before ten o'clock on a spring morning in 1966. In the two buildings that house the Senate offices in Washington, D.C., a number of hearings are about to begin. Hoping to witness a klieg-lit investigation that has been on the front pages of the nation's newspapers for over a week, two hundred potential spectators line up outside the caucus room in the Old Senate Office Building. Outside Room 1223 of the New Senate Office Building, however, only a small group of people quietly gathers. Several are lobbyists, with interests varying from the construction of an agricultural experiment station to the presence of Nasser's army in Yemen; a few are legislative liaison officers from executive departments; the others are reporters. A slightly stooped, smiling octogenarian, walking stick in hand, slowly works his way toward them. They murmur, "Good morning, Mr. Chairman," as Democrat Carl Hayden of Arizona, chairman of the Senate Committee on Appropriations, pushes open the heavy walnut door marked "executive session" and disappears within.

Entering Room 1223 Hayden joins colleagues who, as members of the Committee on Appropriations, are among the most powerful figures in the United States Senate.[1] While other Senate committees

1. See Appendix A for a table of data about the 1965–66 members of the Committee on Appropriations, including their committee, party, and Senate positions.

can influence only some of the programs administered by the vast federal establishment, this committee has the opportunity to exert a continuing impact on all of them. At this time in 1966 eight of the twenty-seven members[2] are also chairmen of legislative committees; one is Democratic leader of the Senate; another is assistant Republican leader. Two others are the chairman and the secretary of the Republican Conference. Hayden himself, who has been a member of the committee since 1927 and chairman since 1955, is president pro tempore of the Senate, and fourth in line to the presidency of the United States. His record of continuous congressional service—beginning in the House of Representatives in 1912—is unequaled in American history.

In the familiar setting of the committee room, Hayden takes his seat at the massive thirty-foot table where the members are placed according to party and seniority. On the chairman's left is ranking Republican Leverett Saltonstall, a former governor and for over two decades a senator from Massachusetts. Saltonstall would be chairman if his party had a majority in the Senate. Now, having decided not to seek reelection, less than a year of his Senate career remains. Milton Young of North Dakota, next in seniority among the Republicans, will shortly become the ranking minority member. On Hayden's right is Richard Brevard Russell of Winder, Georgia: leader of the southern bloc, skilled parliamentarian, a member of the committee since he entered the Senate on January 12, 1933. Second in service on the committee (and its next chairman after Hayden's retirement at the end of 1968), Russell scrutinizes roughly half of the proposed expenditures in the annual federal budget as chairman of the Subcommittee on Defense Appropriations.

To Saltonstall's left, in descending seniority, are the places of the other Republican committeemen, who represent states from the East, Midwest, and West. On Russell's side the South is heavily represented. Of the nine senior Democrats, only Hayden and Warren Magnuson of Washington are not from the South, a situation reflecting that region's long dominance in the congressional wing of the Democratic party. The nine junior Democrats, however, approach the regional diversity

---

2. During 1967–68, Appropriations had twenty-six members: seventeen Democrats, nine Republicans; in 1969, total membership was reduced to twenty-four: fourteen Democrats, ten Republicans.

of the Republicans, and even include two Democratic liberals, one from the Midwest and one from Texas—both of whom were seated years after some of their more conservative brethren made it.

Room 1223 is a congenial place. While the chairman and early arrivals await some of their tardier colleagues, a casual atmosphere of fellowship prevails even among political antagonists. Many committeemen are keen ideological opponents but warm personal friends. One or two senators move around the room lining up support for an amendment they plan to offer to the appropriation bill that the committee will consider in the next few hours. A legislative assistant at a telephone in the corner calls the office of an absent member to secure a proxy should his senator need it. Several senators check in with the chief clerk to help provide the quorum of fourteen needed to report the bill, and then go to other meetings scheduled for the same time or to their offices to meet with staff or constituents or to confront their full desks.

When a quorum has been recorded, Chairman Hayden bangs his gavel and states curtly: "The committee will be in order. A quorum is present. The chair will now hear a report from the subcommittee chairman on the bill which is before us." A few subdued conversations continue until the chairman whose bill is scheduled for consideration begins to summarize his subcommittee's recommendations.

Before the members as they listen are mounds of printed material: the bill passed by the House, with the subcommittee's suggested changes; the subcommittee's proposed report; the thick brown-covered volumes of the testimony taken at hearings before the House Appropriations subcommittee that originally reviewed the bill; and the somewhat thinner green-covered volumes composed of the Senate subcommittee hearings. Each senator also has before him the bill's "sideslips"—a bound, printed volume prepared by the subcommittee staff showing for each item the appropriation for the previous year, the budget estimate recommended by the President for the coming fiscal year, and the allowance granted by the House of Representatives in the bill under discussion. The sideslips also contain excerpts from the annual budget, Senate hearings, letters to the committee, and the language of amendments proposed by various senators and interest groups. Staff-prepared tables, with up to a dozen columns and often hundreds of line items, enable a senator to trace and compare at a glance the increases and decreases in the President's budget as a result of House and Senate subcommittee action. Finally, there is available, too, the report containing the House committee's recommendations on the bill. Prepared in the first instance to meet the needs of the House of Representatives, this lengthy report is also designed to give the executive agencies guidance as to how the funds should be expended.

As the presentation unfolds, members frequently interject a query. The subcommittee chairman responds and, on occasion, looks to his ranking Republican for a nod of confirmation. The summary completed, the committee is ready for business. In the give and take of the markup that follows, an item of $100 million is disposed of within two minutes while an appropriation for $10,000 uncorks a long argument. Regions compete, philosophies clash, but partisan diatribes seldom are heard. Decorum prevails and only rarely is a table pounded. Sometimes a roll call occurs, but usually—as befits a gentleman's club within "the most exclusive club in the world"—a consensus is reached after the contending parties are accommodated with a word revision here and a dollar change there.

The committee hopes to complete its work and report the bill out favorably before noon, when the Senate is usually called to order. Should the markup not be completed in the morning, however, the chairman will probably arrange an afternoon session in the committee's ornate Capitol suite so that members will be near the chamber while the Senate is in session. There, if necessary, a five-minute recess can be called while the members cram into a small elevator that lifts them one floor to the Senate chamber where they can respond to a quorum or roll call.

When the last item has been approved and the bill ordered reported, "Mr. Hayden," as Senate style goes, adjourns his committee. The subcommittee chairman calls in the waiting representatives from the news media. A department liaison officer hurriedly notes the essential decisions made by the committee—contemplating all the while which senator his cabinet superior can approach with a floor amendment to restore the funds cut from an "essential" program. As the news conference begins, senators scatter to other engagements or to the Senate floor, knowing that the work their committee has just completed constitutes the final detailed scrutiny the appropriations measure faces on its way to becoming law.

The Budgetary Process

The work of the Senate Committee on Appropriations is one part of the continuous and interacting budgetary process that involves both the executive and legislative branches.[3] Within a few hours or at most a few days after the full committee's markup session on a measure, the committee's report and its proposed amendments to the House bill, prepared by the staff on behalf of the subcommittee chairman, are filed with the Senate and printed. Then the bill is scheduled by the Senate leadership for floor debate. After debate, possible revision, and passage, the measure as amended by the Senate is returned to the House of Representatives, which may accept it but almost always prefers instead to go to conference where representatives from both Senate and House Appropriations Committees work to resolve any differences. Finally, after both houses have approved a single version, the bill is sent to the President for his approval.[4]

Preceding the committee's seemingly casual markup session—and providing the basis for the decisions reached there—are many long hours of work by a small group of subcommittee members and professional staff from both parties. There are hearings, usually in public or open session, that may have taken a week or several months; subcommittee markup sessions, usually closed, that may have lasted a few hours or several days; and uncounted private meetings held with department officials, lobbyists, and interested citizens. And preceding these efforts are thousands of man-years of work before the budget requests ever reach the Senate.

Well over a year before Senate consideration, budget items first clear numerous hurdles within the bureaus and departments, and then

3. Useful books on various aspects of the appropriations process are Richard F. Fenno, Jr., *The Power of the Purse* (Little, Brown, 1966); John S. Saloma III, *The Responsible Use of Power* (American Enterprise Institute, 1964); Arthur Smithies, *The Budgetary Process in the United States* (McGraw-Hill, 1955); and Aaron Wildavsky, *The Politics of the Budgetary Process* (Little, Brown, 1964).

4. A President seldom vetoes an appropriation bill. Between 1789 and 1966 approximately forty appropriation bills were vetoed. Congress overrode the President on ten of the forty. Eight of the ten were public works appropriation bills. See *Presidential Vetoes*, List of Bills Vetoed and Action Taken Thereon by the Senate and House of Representatives, 1st Congress through the 86th Congress, 1789–1961, Compiled by the Senate Library (Government Printing Office, 1961), pp. 3, 10–11, 197, and *passim*.

within the Bureau of the Budget, which coordinates the preparation of the executive budget for the President. Civil servants, scientists, lobbyists, generals, admirals, budget examiners, cabinet officers, and President may all be involved in the tug-of-war over a single item. The latest techniques of operations and systems analysis, and studies detailing benefit-to-cost ratios may be utilized.

As the calendar year nears a close, program priorities are decided. Economists issue last-minute projections of federal revenues for the fiscal year (July 1 through June 30) still six months away. Decisions become final and the dollar amounts are forwarded to the Government Printing Office to be printed as the annual Budget of the United States—a closely guarded document until it is submitted by the President to Congress in January. Then the spotlight turns on the House and Senate.

While Congress considers the myriad requests and seeks to comprehend programs that involve billions of dollars, the executive budget machinery continues its steady pace. Daily judgments affect expenditures. The funds already appropriated are apportioned and program needs constantly evaluated. Congressional budget experts maintain an active interest in these executive activities, particularly when funds they have fought to appropriate in excess of a presidential request occasionally find their way into budget reserves and remain unspent. Throughout the year requests to reprogram appropriations for other purposes are submitted by the executive branch to the chairmen of the House and Senate Committees on Appropriations for their approval. Sometimes a bill is sent to Capitol Hill to cover deficits in on-going programs (deficiencies) or to request funds for new programs authorized by Congress since the last regular appropriation was considered (supplementals).

In all of these endeavors the Senate Committee on Appropriations plays an essential role. Its functions have largely been overlooked or slighted in the literature concerning the congressional appropriations process because by tradition, though not by constitutional mandate, appropriations bills originate in the House.[5] Traditionally, too, although this practice has begun to change in recent years, the Senate committee does not begin its consideration of an appropriations request until the House has completed its work on it. Nevertheless, substantial

5. See Appendix B, "The Origination of Appropriation Bills, 1787–1861."

power resides in the Senate committee, both because its parent body is an equal partner in a bicameral legislature and because it is the final examiner of all budget items. While the committee's decisions are ultimately subject to ratification by the Senate (and, if they are to stand, eventually by the House in agreeing to a conference report and by the President in approving an appropriation bill), by tradition it has for all practical purposes substantial leeway in what it can do.

Woodrow Wilson once wrote, "It is not far from the truth to say that Congress in session is Congress on public exhibition, whilst Congress in its committee-rooms is Congress at work."[6] A major strength of the American Congress in terms of its own power is its standing committee system. The British House of Commons—long looked to by some political scientists as the epitome of legislative enlightenment—is increasingly recognizing the virtues of a standing committee system that can develop its own subject-matter expertise, scrutinize in greater detail executive proposals and actions, and provide a forum where administrator and legislator can face each other in a free exchange without the government falling. Standing committees did not appear full grown with the adoption of the Constitution and the meeting of the First Congress in 1789. In both House and Senate, special committees were created during the early years to review the President's message and to deal with particular policy problems. By 1816, following similar action in the House, the Senate created a system of eleven standing committees, including one on finance that had jurisdiction over both revenue and appropriation bills. In 1867, again following the House, a separate Senate Committee on Appropriations was established.

This committee has fulfilled various purposes. There is still more it might do. Almost all federal programs—including numerous grant-in-aid programs to the states—must pass muster here. Members of the committee have the chance, by discussion and by vote, to modify or even change drastically the direction of government policy. The Senate Appropriations Committee is a place where the authority and power of the legislative branch come to a focus on specifics. It is a place where presidents, programs, senators, and interests can be tested.

How effective the committee is depends on the will, desires, and

6. Woodrow Wilson, *Congressional Government* (Meridian Books, 1956), p. 69.

mode of operation of the senatorial participants. The study that follows will explore various aspects of committee and subcommittee life: assignments to the committee and its subcommittees, the formal structure, the unwritten rules, and the information-gathering and decision-making processes. The competence and role of the professional staff will also be examined. So will relations with the House Appropriations Committee and the executive branch. The purpose is to explore how the work of the committee—whether one believes this work should be mainly budget scrutiny, policy formulation, or administrative oversight—could be performed with greater effectiveness, given Congress and the Senate as they now exist.[7]

A study of the Senate Committee on Appropriations is important not just because the committee is the principal vehicle through which the Senate fulfills its constitutional responsibilities with regard to appropriations. Nor is such a study important merely because the work of the committee has largely been overshadowed by the role of its House counterpart, or because some of the most powerful men in the Senate are numbered among its membership. By evaluating the committee's present and potential use of its powers, it may be possible also to judge whether Congress can hold its own in the constitutional system and whether the Senate can hold its own in the congressional system—particularly in the appropriations process.

7. This study is based in substantial measure on a detailed examination of the Senate Committee on Appropriations during the Eighty-ninth Congress (1965–66). In 1966, twenty-three of the twenty-seven senators on the committee submitted to interviews which averaged over an hour in length. The four remaining members responded to various questions in writing. Five ex officio members of the committee discussed their unique role. Nineteen members of the professional staff, three former staff members, fourteen other Senate staff members, and several lobbyists and administration officials were interviewed for from one to five hours each.

CHAPTER ONE

The Members

Harold Lasswell once noted that political science "is the study of influence and the influential" and "the influential are those who get the most of what there is to get."[1] The members of the Senate Appropriations Committee aptly illustrate this epigram.

Motivation

Students of the Senate and members alike are well aware of what has been described as the caste system that ranks some committees ahead of others in terms of desirability and prestige. Donald R. Matthews, a political scientist, plotted all switches in Senate committee assignments from the Eightieth through the Eighty-fourth Congresses (1947–56). He found that senators display "both consistency and agreement in their choice of committee posts" and that each committee tends "to lose members to those ranked above it while tending to gain members from those ranking below." While admitting that the pattern is by no means perfect, Matthews concluded, "There is sufficient agreement in committee preferences to say that the committees are clearly stratified."[2]

1. Harold D. Lasswell, *Politics: Who Gets What, When, How* (McGraw-Hill. 1936), as reprinted in *The Political Writings of Harold D. Lasswell* (The Free Press, 1951), pp. 295, 309.
2. Donald R. Matthews, *U.S. Senators and Their World* (University of North

Continuing Matthews' analysis, and applying his format, Table 1–1 portrays the net gains and losses of each Senate committee for the Eighty-fifth through Eighty-ninth Congresses (1957–66). A high degree of comparability and consistency in senatorial preferences is evident in the two decades. In both decades, Foreign Relations, Appropriations, Finance, and Armed Services were the most prestigious committees.[3] Foreign Relations, which gained two senators from Appropriations in the 1947–56 decade, was clearly first for the earlier period, which encompassed the dramatic days of the Marshall Plan, Greek-Turkish aid, the North Atlantic Treaty, and the Korean war. The Committee on Appropriations, with a total of twenty transfers during the period 1957–66 for a net gain of sixteen, seemed to have the lead during the later period. Indeed, during the 1960s members of Appropriations were almost unanimous in considering their committee "Number 1 in the Senate." As one member who was also chairman of an active legislative committee commented: "The membership is the proof of the pudding. I'm seventh in the Senate in seniority and seventh in seniority on the Appropriations Committee. All the senior members of the Senate who want to be on the committee are on the committee."

The reasons members have given for requesting assignment explain why the committee stands so high—and provide enlightenment about the context in which members approach their responsibilities. Members made clear in discussing the subject in 1966 that on Appropriations they feel they "are at the crucial point where [they] can direct the activities of government for good or ill," because "no matter how much you legislate, the main ingredient is money and whatever type of program you have, its success is dependent on adequate financing." One senator who had served on both Agriculture and Foreign Relations stated: "What happens in those two fields is determined more by Appropriations than by the policy-formulating legislative committees

---

Carolina Press, 1960), p. 150. See his section, "The 'Committee Caste System,'" pp. 148–52, for an explanation of the methodology involved.

3. There was also agreement in both periods on the four lowest committees: Government Operations, Rules and Administration, Post Office and Civil Service, and the District of Columbia. In the later period Labor and Public Welfare rose from eleventh to eighth place—perhaps reflecting the increased activity of the committee in handling major Great Society programs. Banking and Currency fell from eighth to thirteenth. The Committee on Aeronautical and Space Sciences, created in 1958, was quickly established as a "glamour" committee.

of the Senate." Members also feel that under "present methods of operation, despite the Committee on Government Operations, the effective oversight which can be carried on is at the appropriations level. It is more effective when . . . dealing with an agency to get them at the point where they are asking for money."

Table 1–1. Net Gain or Loss in Senate Committee Memberships through Changes in Assignment, 1957–66

Committee	Appropriations	Foreign Relations	Finance	Armed Services	Judiciary	Aeronautics and Space	Commerce	Labor and Public Welfare	Agriculture	Public Works	Interior	Government Operations	Banking and Currency	Rules	Post Office and Civil Service	District of Columbia	Net totals
Appropriations		−1	+1	+2	0	—	+2	+2	+3	+2	—	—	+3	+1	+1	—	+16
Foreign Relations	+1		—	+1	−1	+1	+1	—	+4	+1	+1	+3	+1	—	+1	—	+14
Finance	−1	—		—	0	—	—	+1	+1	+2	—	—	+1	+5	+1	—	+10
Armed Services	−2	−1	—		—	—	+1	+2	+1	+2	+1	+4	+1	+1	—	—	+10
Judiciary	0	+1	0	—		—	+1	+1	—	+2	+1	—	+1	—	+1	+1	+9
Aeronautics and Space	—	−1	—	—	—		+1	+1	—	−1	—	+3	+1	+1	+1	—	+6
Commerce	−2	−1	—	−1	−1	−1		—	+2	+2	+1	+2	+2	+2	—	+1	+6
Labor and Public Welfare	−2	—	−1	−2	−1	−1	—		−1	+2	0	+1	+2	+2	—	+2	+1
Agriculture	−3	−4	−1	—	—	—	−2	+1		+3	—	+1	−1	—	+1	—	−6
Public Works	−2	−1	−2	−2	−2	+1	−2	−2	−3		+2	+1	—	+3	+2	—	−7
Interior	—	−1	—	−1	−1	—	−1	0	—	−2		0	—	−1	+1	+1	−5
Government Operations	—	−3	—	−4	—	−3	−2	−1	−1	−1	0		+2	—	+1	+1	−11
Banking and Currency	−3	−1	−1	−1	−1	−1	−2	−2	+1	—	—	−2		+1	+1	+2	−9
Rules	−1	—	−5	−1	—	−1	−2	−1	—	−3	+1	—	−1		+2	+2	−10
Post Office and Civil Service	−1	−1	−1	—	−1	−1	—	—	−1	−2	−1	−1	−1	−2		+2	−11
District of Columbia	—	—	—	—	−1	—	−1	−2	—	—	−1	−1	−2	−2	−2		−12

But this control over the country's purse strings, with its concomitant power over programs and agencies, is attractive to only a few members primarily because of national policy interests. Most desire Appropriations first of all because of what membership can do for their state. As one legislative assistant pointed out: "A senator can get control over a far greater spectrum of things that affect his state than he would on a legislative committee. . . . He can prove how valuable he is to his people." Committee members strongly concur in this view. A senior Democrat who had observed members of the committee for many years stated: "A senator seeks Appropriations because of the opportunity it gives him to press the needs of his state." A younger Democrat agreed: "It is obvious. Here on Appropriations is where the money is. It is the clearest pipeline to your state." A senior Republican, who looked on Appropriations as composed of "have" and "have not" senators—defined as those from states that pay the taxes and those from states that use the taxes—said that "the great desire to get on Appropriations generally comes from senators who represent states which are not paying the bills." Those senators from the wealthier states also have an interest, however: they want to recoup some of what their citizens contribute to the Treasury. As one senator from a rapidly growing state put it: "There are so many things for which the federal government has total or partial responsibility—such as navigation, flood control, office buildings, Veterans Administration hospitals, agricultural experiment stations—that Appropriations is the only place where these things are affected."

Such opportunities for constituency service have obvious political advantages. The comment of an Appropriations member about his colleague, Republican Karl Mundt of South Dakota, makes this clear: "Mundt, for example, can work for the Indians. It is not big money, but it is small matters that the committee will allow. It makes him look good politically back home." Both Democrats and Republicans on Appropriations are convinced that the well-informed citizen feels it is important for his state to be represented on Appropriations and consequently wants to keep a senator there regardless of his party.

Some senators aim for a seat on the committee from the day they enter the Senate because their predecessor had been on it and had made its significance known. Indeed, one senator observed that he wanted to get on the committee not simply for what the "good folks" in his state thought he could do for them in Washington, but also to protect himself from the "bad folks": "The money power structure in my state has its hands in the federal treasury up to its armpits and I want them to think I might be able to turn off the faucet."

For a senator whose party is in the minority, membership on Appropriations with its bipartisan tradition is especially helpful politically. With the opportunity to write important Senate legislation largely closed to him by the majority party, membership on Appropriations provides him with the opportunity to perform constituent favors—and to secure publicity. Each endeavor might seem a small one, but the cumulative effect over a six-year term can be substantial.

Membership is not an unmixed political blessing, however. Members share the belief that constituents sometimes expect too much from them. Remembering that the Bureau of the Budget had failed to recommend two appropriations that were important to his state, one senator worried: "The voters expect me to restore these items and maintain them in committee and in conference. I'm not sure that I'll be able to do it. If I can't there will be real trouble back home." In a campaign, senators and staff believe mention of Appropriations alone does not communicate much. As one member observed, unless a senator's specific subcommittee achievements are stressed, Appropriations "doesn't ring a bell with the voters since they don't really know what it is." And while senators recognize that through their work on Appropriations they can help their people more over a long period of time, and gain more publicity, than through work on a legislative committee, they doubt that this is of much practical value in a crucial aspect of election politics—raising campaign contributions. "Appropriations is not a field that helps private business as much as it helps government programs. The recipients of Appropriations aid really don't have much money to give," declared a Democratic legislative assistant who had been active both in the work of the committee and in his senator's campaign. Most Appropriations members believe that service on other committees such as Commerce, where "you are regulating the very existence of the interests," is more productive of contributions.

Nonetheless, most members agree that the advantages of serving on the committee greatly outweigh the disadvantages. It is not just the state benefits that count. For the senator who wants "to be a force in government and not just a cipher," as one put it, the complete education in the workings of the government that serving on Appropriations provides is considered a significant advantage. Membership also gives a senator leverage with the executive agencies, a legislative assistant commented. Because of membership on the committee, a senator is able to "cut across all agencies and apply pressure to the most sensitive areas. Through the budget process the senator gains attention, even though he might hesitate to use pressure. He expedites inquiries. He knows the exact guy to talk to."

Even more important to most senators is the leverage within the Senate itself that membership confers. Senators are well aware that by being on the committee they are in a position to help their colleagues and thus to increase their own effectiveness and advance themselves in the Senate's power structure. For a senator who wants his voice heard by his colleagues, Appropriations' relative power and prestige among Senate committees is of great value. As one Republican who had been consigned to two committees without national scope remarked, "The Senate couldn't care less about what my previous committees did, so I looked for a committee with the widest breadth and influence. Appropriations was just such a committee."

As with most human choices, the motivations for choosing Appropriations are a complex mixture of the obvious and the subtle, the lofty and the crass. Perhaps the sometimes elusive factors of state and national interests, power and prestige, were most succinctly summarized by one longtime committee staffer: "They want to be around when they're cutting up the pie."

Getting on the Committee

How does a senator get on Appropriations once he has chosen membership as his goal? Rule 24 of the Standing Rules of the Senate provides that "unless otherwise ordered" the Senate as a whole shall proceed by ballot to appoint the chairman of each committee and then by one ballot the other members of that committee. The practice is for the party leaders to submit a resolution containing the appointments to each committee. The Senate can overrule these slates, but with rare exceptions it does not.[4] Each party prefers to control its committee assignments rather than permit appointments for both parties to be made by the majority. The number of seats to be filled on the committees is specified in Rule 25. The party ratio is usually worked out by the two leaders but finally determined by the wishes of the majority party. They attempt to assure, with varying degrees of

---

4. For a few examples of occasions when the Senate has interfered, see George Goodwin, Jr., "The Seniority System in Congress," *American Political Science Review*, Vol. 53 (June 1959), p. 413.

success, that the party representation on each committee reflects the party representation in the Senate. In making their committee assignments, both parties consider seniority a prime factor, but especially for Democrats, seniority is not everything.[5]

The Role of the Democratic Leader and Steering Committee

For Senate Democrats, committee assignments are determined by the Democratic Steering Committee. The views of the party leader are especially influential, however. He appoints and chairs the Steering Committee, and while his Steering Committee appointments nominally are subject to confirmation by the Democratic Conference, in reality they are his handpicked choices. The Conference usually meets once at the beginning of a Congress to select its floor leadership and permit the party liberals a few hours of protest. Then it adjourns to let the Steering Committee apparatus supposedly responsible to the Conference go its own way. The result, of course, is perpetuation of party control in the Senate by the most senior members, and especially the senior southern conservatives. Former President Lyndon B. Johnson of Texas, for example, when Democratic leader from 1953 to 1961, made appointments to the Steering Committee without recourse to the Conference at all.

With the upsurge in the fortunes of the urban Democrats, however, there has been increasing unrest at these traditional practices. In 1961 the newly elected party leader, Mike Mansfield of Montana, was faced with efforts by the Conference to have members of the Policy and Steering Committees elected. When he threatened to resign if this succeeded, the Conference instead approved a motion giving it the right to confirm or challenge leadership appointments. It also instructed the Democratic leader to make his selections for the Steering Committee with due regard for both the philosophical views and the

5. What this has meant in relation to membership on Appropriations is illustrated in the following comparison, based on continuous service, of committee party seniority with Senate party seniority for members of Appropriations in the period 1965–66 (the first of each pair of figures denotes party rank in the committee, the second denotes party rank in the Senate):

Democrats: Hayden (1, 1); Russell (2, 2); Ellender (3, 3); Hill (4, 4); McClellan (5, 6); Robertson (6, 10); Magnuson (7, 7); Holland (8, 9); Stennis (9, 12); Pastore (10, 16); Monroney (11, 17); Bible (12, 24); Byrd (W. Va.) (13, 35); McGee (14, 42); Mansfield (15, 21); Bartlett (16, 34); Proxmire (17, 31); Yarborough (18, 30).

Republicans: Saltonstall (1, 3); Young (N. Dak.) (2, 4); Mundt (3, 6); Smith (4, 7); Kuchel (5, 11); Hruska (6, 13); Allott (7, 16); Cotton (8, 12); Case (9, 15).

geographic distribution that exist within the party.[6] While the extent
to which these instructions have been followed has been a sore point for
urban liberals, the complexion of the Democratic Steering Committee
has changed in recent years, although much more slowly than the complexion of Senate Democrats as a whole.[7]

The Democratic leader, if an active one, usually tries to resolve in
advance conflicting desires for assignments in order to avoid rancor
among the brethren and argument within the Steering Committee. But
when conflicts cannot be worked out, the members of the Democratic
Steering Committee are faced with choosing between colleagues, a
painful task made even more painful when such decisions cannot be
hidden behind a strict rule of seniority.

The lack of strict seniority in recent Democratic committee appointments is due to the so-called Johnson Rule, first implemented when
Johnson became minority leader during the Republican-controlled
Eighty-third Congress. At that time he made certain that two of the
four new Democratic senators elected despite Dwight D. Eisenhower's
1952 landslide received choice committee assignments, which ordinarily
would not have gone to any but the most senior members. Thus Mike
Mansfield was placed on Foreign Relations, while Stuart Symington
of Missouri, a former secretary of the Air Force, was assigned to Armed
Services. The Johnson Rule, simply stated, was that every new Democrat in the Senate ought to have at least one good committee assignment
before a more senior Democratic senator had two. The tradition had
been for most senators to go through years of apprenticeship on less
desirable committees while they waited for their senior colleagues on
the choice committees to retire, resign, meet defeat at the polls, or die.
And with senators, as Thomas Jefferson observed of executive branch
appointees in the early years of the republic, few died and none
resigned. The Johnson Rule also meant that a powerful party
leader supported by the Democratic Steering Committee would have

6. *New York Times,* Jan. 5, 1961.

7. In 1953, when Johnson became Democratic leader, there were fifteen senators
on the Democratic Steering Committee, of whom seven were from the South, three
from border states, two from the Southwest, one from the Midwest, and two from
the East Coast. In 1966, while there were still seven from the South, the committee
had been enlarged to seventeen members and also included four from the Southwest–
mountain state area, three from the Midwest, and three from the East. The majority
leader (Mansfield) served as chairman. Russell B. Long of Louisiana, as majority
whip, and Senator George A. Smathers of Florida, as secretary for the Democratic
Conference, were ex officio members with vote.

an opportunity to reward his friends and to punish his enemies. Mr. Johnson was never one to shy from the use of power.

Of course, Johnson's committee assignment practices were not completely new in the Senate. In 1933, for instance, Richard B. Russell, now chairman of Appropriations, won appointment to the committee on his first day in the Senate. As the dynamic young governor of Georgia, Russell had received national attention before his election to the Senate. When he took the oath of office in 1933, the Democratic leader of the Senate, Joseph T. Robinson of Arkansas, routinely asked him his committee choices. Russell replied: "Appropriations." The majority leader explained that there were quite a few senators ahead of Russell waiting to get on that committee, and the freshman senator responded that if he could not be on Appropriations, he did not want to serve on any committee. Robinson went away from his conversation with Russell thinking that Russell's answer was a threat (which it was not) to join forces with Democrat Huey P. Long of Louisiana, who had accused Robinson of being "a tool of the interests" and had resigned from all his committees. Some of the press had already compared Russell's progressive governorship with Long's. A day later Robinson returned to say he had worked it out. So Russell was appointed to Appropriations.

It was the Eighty-sixth Congress that provided Democratic leader Johnson with the greatest opportunity to apply his committee assignment policy. The first issue confronting the Senate in 1959 was that of amending Rule 22, the so-called filibuster rule. To avoid a fight, Johnson worked for a "compromise" that would require two-thirds of those present and voting, rather than two-thirds of those elected, to invoke cloture. For those who were looking for an out, this face-saving device was made to order. The fact was conveniently forgotten that on key cloture votes, such as those pertaining to civil rights, usually *all* senators were present and voting even if they had to be brought in on stretchers.

The senator from Texas prowled the floor and the cloakrooms in search of what he fondly referred to even then as a "consensus" for the "Johnson rules change." In one pocket the majority leader carried a list of available committee assignments, and in the other he carried a list of how senators might vote on his rules proposal. When confronted, senators were informed of both lists in a friendly way and were asked first how they planned to vote on the rules change. A new senator, or even one with some seniority, who desired a choice committee assignment found that strange things happened on the way to the Democratic Steering Committee if his answer did not please the majority leader. Few so answered.

The Johnson revision of Rule 22 passed on January 12 by a vote of 72 to 22. Senators Estes Kefauver of Tennessee, A. S. Mike Monroney of Oklahoma, Alan Bible of Nevada, Robert C. Byrd of West Virginia, Thomas J. Dodd of Connecticut, and Gale W. McGee of Wyoming were all appointed to the Committee on Appropriations on January 14, after Johnson had secured Senate approval to increase the membership from 23 to 27. All had voted for the Johnson rules change. Byrd, Dodd, and McGee had just been sworn in and were the beneficiaries of the Johnson Rule on committee appointments.[8]

Since the unusual appointments of Byrd, Dodd, and McGee in 1959, only one Democrat with less than four years of Senate service has been appointed to the Appropriations Committee, the others having been senators from six to ten years. Nonetheless, the Johnson Rule has meant that seniority is not—if it ever was—the single decisive factor in gaining a seat on a prestige committee.

A Case Study of the Democratic Selection Process in 1963

In a Senate of 100 individuals, all of whom are equal in vote but many of whom are unequal in power, it is to be expected that occasionally a senator might view some of his colleagues and their aspirations with a certain hostility and be in a position to do something about it. Such an opportunity might be available particularly to members of the Democratic Steering Committee. Yet the comments of a conservative Democrat from the South are fairly typical:

> On the Steering Committee you try to do the best you can. I voted for some to serve on Appropriations when I completely disagreed with their philosophy. However, I thought they were entitled to the seat. You can't act from

8. McGee, a professor of history at the University of Wyoming, had been aided by Johnson in 1958 when he was actively working for the Democratic ticket across the nation—and possibly for the presidential nomination two years away. In a speech at Casper, Johnson publicly declared, "If you send me this professor, I promise he'll be on the Appropriations Committee." Wyoming did, and McGee was selected when the Democratic Steering Committee met; indeed, Appropriations was McGee's only choice. Other senators, including three possible presidential candidates in 1960, John F. Kennedy of Massachusetts, Hubert H. Humphrey of Minnesota, and Stuart Symington, were not so lucky. Johnson was said to have been pressured by each of them for a spot on Appropriations. As one of the senators who was appointed explained: "I was not running for President."

narrow prejudices. The people in their state who have a different philosophy are entitled to be represented on those committees of Congress and you should do unto others as you would have them do unto you. I think a person's state and his seniority entitle him to that recognition and I don't think too much goes on in the sense of narrow shenanigans.

Some of the Democratic liberals believed otherwise. One was Senator Joseph S. Clark, who became a member of the Steering Committee in 1961. A reformer since his days of attempting to clean up Philadelphia from the mayor's chair, the senior senator from Pennsylvania had long been a source of irritation to the Senate establishment—the senior members in both parties and particularly southerners in the Democratic party—or, as he described it, "a self-perpetuating oligarchy with mild, but only mild, overtones of plutocracy."[9] In 1963 Clark brought into the open charges that reveal some aspects of the diverse factors entering into the Democratic committee selection process.[10]

In almost every recent Congress, until passage of the Civil Rights Act of 1964, when cloture was finally invoked and strong equal opportunity legislation adopted, the opening days of the Senate featured a wrangle over changes in Rule 22. Southern Democrats, afraid that allowing majority rule to shut off debate would bring a rash of civil rights legislation, dug in. They were joined by senators from the less populous states who regarded the Senate tradition of relatively unlimited debate as a bulwark against what the larger urban states might enact in the House. The argument over the rules brought other business—including committee assignments—to a standstill. If the party leader was so inclined, the delay provided leverage for him and a majority on the southern-oriented Democratic Steering Committee[11] to elicit support for or against particular proposals in return for favorable committee assignments.

The year 1963 was no exception to the pattern. On January 14, after the President's State of the Union message, the various proposals to

9. Joseph S. Clark and other senators, *The Senate Establishment* (Hill and Wang, 1963), p. 22. This is a reprint of Senator Clark's remarks in the Senate on Feb. 19, 20, 21, and 25, 1963.

10. The Steering Committee normally functions in secrecy. The minutes are never made public, even those dealing with committee appointments a half-century before. There is a general understanding not to reveal the votes that take place. Usually, the only staff member present when the Steering Committee meets is the Democratic floor secretary.

11. In 1963 in the Senate the South accounted for 31 percent of the total Democratic membership. However, on the Steering Committee seven of the fifteen senators, or 46 percent, were from the South.

change Rule 22 were submitted to the Senate. On February 7, the forces favoring a rules change mustered a majority (54 to 42) but not the two-thirds of those present and voting needed to invoke cloture and shut off debate. The Senate then voted to adjourn since it was clear that those opposed to any rules change would continue to filibuster. After this, on February 14, the Steering Committee met and determined committee assignments. Clark, who participated in the meeting, felt that the assignments had been made "in a manner which entrenched the control of the establishment over the committee structure of the Senate."[12] Following the meeting he asked party leader Mansfield to call a Democratic Conference to review the Steering Committee's decisions. Mansfield turned him down. Clark then took the matter to the Senate floor for an airing, as Mansfield described it on February 19, of "our dirty Democratic linen in public...."[13]

Clark spoke to the Senate on February 19, 20, 21, and 25. In his opening speech he filed notice of a motion to amend Rule 25 of the Senate in order to enlarge the membership of the Committee on Appropriations by two seats, from twenty-seven to twenty-nine, and both Finance and Foreign Relations by four seats each, from seventeen members to twenty-one—proposals that the Steering Committee and Democratic Conference had rejected. Clark then went on to charge that the Steering Committee had denied several Democrats "committee seats to which by seniority they were entitled," adding that these members were "facing bitter and possibly uphill odds in their efforts to get reelected to the Senate next year." He said that on nine committees seniority was ignored and the requests of senators who were up for reelection in 1964 "were overriden, and Senators having far less seniority, and not required to face the electorate for another six years, were given choice committee seats, seats which rarely in the past have gone to freshmen Senators."[14] Clark noted that ten Democrats had applied for the two vacancies on Appropriations, including (besides Mansfield, who clearly was entitled to the first vacancy), in order of seniority, Ralph Yarborough of Texas, William Proxmire of Wisconsin, Clair Engle of California, E. L. Bob Bartlett of Alaska, Philip A. Hart

12. Clark, *The Senate Establishment*, p. 14.

13. Clark, *The Senate Establishment*, p. 56. See also *Congressional Record*, Vol. 109, Pt. 2, 88 Cong. 1 sess. (1963), p. 2563.

14. Clark, *The Senate Establishment*, p. 36. See also *Congressional Record*, Vol. 109, Pt. 2, 88 Cong. 1 sess. (1963), p. 2558.

of Michigan, Frank E. Moss of Utah, Edward V. Long of Missouri, Daniel B. Brewster of Maryland, and Daniel K. Inouye of Hawaii. The second seat was filled by Bartlett, although Yarborough and Proxmire were ahead of him in seniority and Engle was equal to him.

At this point an archcritic of the seniority system seemed to be praising its merits. But Clark's thesis was clear. Paul Douglas, also a longtime gadfly of the Senate leadership, spelled it out during the ensuing debate:

> As I examine the committee assignments I am compelled to ask whether a certain pattern seems to emerge—namely, that seniority is disregarded in a significant number of cases of Senators who vote to restrict the filibuster and to apply a more rigid cloture rule, and that such Senators are passed over, in favor of Senators who vote to maintain the filibuster and to oppose more stringent cloture. Am I correct in this?[15]

Mansfield denied the charge, naming nine senators who had received most of what they wanted from the Steering Committee and arguing that seven of them had favored changing the filibuster rule. Douglas, far from satisfied, suggested that an analysis of the appointments be made. Clark agreed to look into the matter. The next day, February 20, Clark summarized his findings:

> Mr. President, one who analyzes this statement for the purpose of determining the ultimate facts will see that eight nonfreshman Senators who opposed a rules change submitted eligible bids for new committee assignments. Seven of the eight got new assignments. Six of the eight got new assignments which represented their first choice. Fourteen nonfreshman Senators who favored a rules change applied for new assignments. These were men who had voted for cloture. Five of the fourteen got new assignments. Only one got the committee of his first choice, and that was the majority leader.[16]

Mansfield saved his rebuttal for February 25, before the Senate voted on the various Clark amendments. He began by wryly noting that for Clark the organization was equitable when those who agreed with Clark received committee appointments and inequitable when those who did not agree with him received such appointments. "In the last analysis," the Democratic leader continued, "the responsibility rests with the conference to see that equity is done, for the steering com-

---

15. Clark, *The Senate Establishment*, p. 65. See also *Congressional Record*, Vol. 109, Pt. 2, 88 Cong. 1 sess (1963), p. 2565.

16. Clark, *The Senate Establishment*, p. 101. See also *Congressional Record*, Vol. 109, Pt. 2, 88 Cong. 1 sess. (1963), p. 2670.

mittee and the leadership are but its creatures." (Mansfield, however, had refused to call a meeting of the Conference, as Clark requested following the Steering Committee meeting, so that it could assert its "responsibility.") Seeking to answer the Clark-Douglas charge of discrimination, Mansfield observed that of the nine newcomers who received their choice of committees, seven had favored changing Rule 22. As for Appropriations, the Democratic leader added:

> This committee is perhaps the most heavily balanced on the southern side. Some suggestions were made that another southern or southwestern Senator be named. On geographical terms, this made no sense. I voted for the Senator from Wisconsin [Proxmire] to fill the vacancy. A majority of the steering committee chose the Senator from Alaska. It was a good choice. Neither of our new States has had representation on the Appropriations committee, and it is about time that they were given such consideration.[17]

Presumably, therefore, the Steering Committee had acted to improve regional representation. But by ignoring the requests of Proxmire and Yarborough, the Midwest continued to be the most underrepresented region on Appropriations and the Democratic liberals also remained underrepresented.[18]

In the roll calls that followed, the Clark proposal to increase the size of the Finance Committee was defeated 68 to 17. His attempt to increase the membership on Appropriations was defeated 70 to 12. All of Senator Clark's votes came from those who had supported a change in the cloture rule. A handful of these senators probably had the fate of medicare legislation uppermost in their minds. But the overwhelming defeat indicated that most senators, whether liberal or conservative, simply believed that committees with much more than seventeen members were unmanageable.

The Steering Committee battle in 1963 also emphasized an unwritten rule of committee appointment: no two senators from the same state, regardless of their party affiliation, should serve on Appropriations at the same time. The issue was clearly put before the Democratic Steering Committee by the application of Senator Clair Engle. An expert on western water problems and author of several major California reclamation projects, Engle, who was four years into his term, saw a difficult re-election campaign ahead of him in 1964. Thus he renewed his request for a seat on Appropriations, which he had sought since coming to the

---

17. *Congressional Record,* Vol. 109, Pt. 3, 88 Cong. 1 sess. (1963), pp. 2920–21.

18. Proxmire did receive a seat on the committee later in 1963, and Yarborough was appointed in 1965. In the interim Engle had died.

Senate. Thomas H. Kuchel, his Republican colleague from California, was already on Appropriations, however, having been selected in 1959. Kuchel, as ranking Republican on the Senate Committee on Interior and Insular Affairs, would soon be engaged in a long and complicated battle with Appropriations chairman Hayden over the water rights of existing Arizona and California projects on the Colorado River. At issue was Hayden's dream to authorize for Arizona a vast reclamation–public power project costing well over one billion dollars. For eleven years the two states had been litigating the water rights of the lower Colorado before the Supreme Court of the United States. In 1963 a final decision by the court was imminent. Once that was available, Hayden planned to renew the effort for the Central Arizona Project, which had interested him since before 1918. He was not prepared to see a second Californian get on Appropriations at that time, if ever. He insisted that as a matter of representation no state should have two senators on Appropriations. Engle's bid was eliminated.

The Republican Appointment Process

With the Republicans, seniority tends to be an almost absolute rule in committee assignments.[19] Perhaps one reason is that the Republicans have long been in the congressional minority and have not had to face the pressures confronted by a Democratic leader in finding choice committees for a large following. A member of the Committee on Committees, the Republican equivalent of the Democratic Steering Committee, remarked: "We go by strict seniority. This makes it easier than for the Democrats, who are using other factors than seniority, and prevents a lot of the wheeling and dealing which goes on there."

For most of this century the Republican Conference, to which the Committee on Committees reports, has had a rule that a senator could not serve on both Appropriations and Finance. Following the Johnson precedent and at the recommendation of a special committee headed by Senator Jacob K. Javits of New York, the Conference agreed that beginning in 1965, Republican appointments to Appropriations, Armed Services, Finance, and Foreign Relations would have to meet a criterion other than seniority. Freshman Republicans would have their choice on one of these four committees before a more senior Republican secured a second appointment to one of them. The Repub-

19. See note 5, p. 15, for a comparison of committee party ranking with senate party ranking for 1965–66 Appropriations members.

licans, like the Democrats, have tried to avoid placing two senators from the same state on a committee, although because of the scarcity of openings there have been exceptions. Unlike the Democrats, they have long aimed for a reasonable regional and ideological balance on their Committee on Committees and have made a practice of almost completely changing its membership every two years.

What role, if any, do interest groups play in helping a senator get assigned to Appropriations or in keeping him off? Senators on both party selection committees agree that few interest groups become involved in Appropriations appointments and those who make such an attempt do not have much effect. This is not true of assignments to the legislative committees, however. One longtime Republican participant in the Committee on Committees discussions stated that although he had never known of interest group activity on an Appropriations appointment, "they become extremely active when selections for Commerce or Finance are under consideration." Where one vote might tip the scales for or against revising the oil depletion allowance or for or against revising the Taft-Hartley Act, an assignment becomes a "life or death" matter, and lobbyists actively seek assignments for "friendly" senators.

Staying On: The Plight of the Junior Member

It is not enough for the junior members to get on Appropriations; they also have to stay on. While seniority largely determines the former, it is the party ratio in the Senate that definitely decides the latter. The hazards of being eliminated from the committee by the changing political tide are not limited to Democrats, as Senator Javits discovered in 1963, or even to liberals, as the conservative Virginia Democrat A. Willis Robertson found out a decade and a half earlier.

In August 1962 Javits was appointed to fill a Republican vacancy on Appropriations. An active, articulate progressive, his presence on the committee was looked upon with disfavor by the southerners who dominated the upper echelon of the committee and the inner workings of the Democratic party in the Senate. Later that fall, the New Yorker won reelection by more votes (983,094 over his Democratic opponent) than any senator in the country. He did it in a year that, with the Cuban missile crisis, was generally unkind to Republicans. The GOP Senate contingent dropped from thirty-six to thirty-three and Democratic strength rose from sixty-four to sixty-seven. When

Congress reconvened in 1963, the Democratic Steering Committee changed the party ratios on some committees but left them unchanged on others, with the result that Javits was the only senator eliminated from a committee assignment. Republican leader Dirksen was added to the Committee on Finance, where the party ratio remained unchanged and extremely unrepresentative. One cynical observer commented: "Whenever the establishment wants to make an exception to the rule, they do it, as in the case of Dirksen. If they don't want to make an exception, they invoke the seniority rule, or the party ratio, or something, as in the case of Javits." The *Baltimore Sun* of February 15 asserted: "Liberal sources contended that Javits was ousted from the important Appropriations Committee, where he was the lowest ranking Republican member, because he fought for a rules change to make it easier to shut off filibusters."

Senator Richard B. Russell, one of the most prestigious figures in the Senate and a key member of both the Steering Committee and Appropriations, defended the action on the Senate floor on Februray 19.[20] Russell contended that there was nothing unusual in a senator's being dropped from Appropriations by a shift in the party ratio. He cited the case of Senator A. Willis Robertson, first appointed to the committee in January 1949.

At that time, Appropriations had twenty-one members—thirteen Democrats and eight Republicans. Robertson bumped Republican William F. Knowland of California, who had been on the committee for two years. When death brought a change in party composition during 1949, Robertson lost his position to Knowland, having served only until July 26, as the committee ratio became twelve Democrats to nine Republicans. Robertson was appointed for the second time in 1950, when the committee ratio—again reflecting a shift in the makeup of the Senate—was changed to thirteen Democrats and eight Republicans. There he stayed for a year, only to lose the seat once more in early 1951, when the committee ratio was again readjusted to eleven Democrats and ten Republicans. He was appointed to the committee for a third time four months later, as the committee ratio became twelve Democrats to nine Republicans.

Russell concluded his remarks about the effects of shifts in the party ratio by noting that in his judgment Appropriations was "too large at

20. See *Congressional Record,* Vol. 109, Pt. 2, 88 Cong. 1 sess. (1963), pp. 2538–41 for the full text of the exchanges recounted in the following paragraphs.

the present time to do effective work." He had no doubt that "in the near future, as the tide of politics changes or as nature takes its toll of the members of the committee, the Senator from New York [Mr. Javits] will reappear on the committee."

There were other charges to answer, however. Citing a newspaper column that quoted "well-informed sources" as saying that "the quid pro quo [for not changing the Senate Finance ratio] for the southern Democrats . . . was Senator Dirksen's agreement not to join the Senate liberals in the fight to modify rule 22, the filibuster rule,"[21] Russell denied that Dirksen had ever approached him regarding the committee ratios. Russell did recall, though, that Mansfield had told him Dirksen "was exceedingly anxious to increase the Appropriations committee," and that Russell had told Mansfield he would "oppose vigorously increasing the committee," because the Committee on Appropriations "of all committees is too large." Dirksen then joined the debate and denied discussing with Russell an assignment to the Finance Committee in conjunction with the fight over changing Rule 22.

Toward the end of debate on the Clark amendments on February 25, Mansfield supplied additional evidence about who was responsible for Javits' removal from Appropriations. In attempting to refute the charge that "a calculated job of 'bumping' . . . had been done," Mansfield stated:

> I have said on the floor that had the minority leader been prepared to favor enlarging the Finance Committee, the majority leader would have been prepared to support the enlargement of the Appropriations Committee so that the Senator from New York might have kept his seat. So if there has been any bumping, the responsibility does not rest on this side of the aisle.[22]

But Senator Dirksen had assured Javits over the previous weeks that he was trying to work out something with Mansfield to save Javits' seat on Appropriations. Dirksen's first concern, however, had apparently been Dirksen, a not unnatural state of affairs for any senator. He had wanted the seat on Finance because the fight over medicare and major tax legislation would center in that committee. In terms of its impact on the Senate decision-making process, Dirksen's appointment to Finance, which was closely divided ideologically, had much

21. Rowland Evans, Jr., "Senate Conservatives Score on Double Play," *Washington Post*, Feb. 16, 1963.
22. *Congressional Record*, Vol. 109, Pt. 3, 88 Cong. 1 sess. (1963), p. 2920.

greater significance than Javits' removal from Appropriations.[23] Never asked during the debate was why, if the Democrats could tolerate underrepresentation on the Finance Committee, where the eleven to six ratio was considered an adequate reflection of their better than two to one control of the Senate, they could not continue to accept the seventeen to ten ratio on Appropriations, especially when changing that ratio resulted in the only removal of a senator from a standing committee.

Thus even though a party may follow seniority in appointment, a committeeman may be removed as a result of a shifting party ratio or a leadership deal that readjusts some of the committee balances and not others. In 1967 Javits regained his seat on Appropriations. For four years he had been excluded from the committee, until the Republican electoral gains in 1966 again provided him with the opportunity for appointment.

Who Gets On

Once selected, do the members of the Appropriations Committee prove to be substantially different from senators as a whole?[24] As might be expected, a committee with prestige and power attracts senior senators—in both age and service—and, as the preceding section has shown, the selection process favors giving them membership.

23. Arthur Krock, close to the southern leadership of the Senate, wrote in his Washington column dated Feb. 16, 1963, that President Kennedy and his staff had made a vigorous attempt to enlarge the Committee on Finance. When the move failed, Mansfield, in Krock's judgment, simply undertook the "loyal assumption of full responsibility for the unsuccessful effort to pack the Senate Finance Committee to improve the prospects of Kennedy's proposed new tax legislation" even though the Democratic leader was not actually responsible. Krock stated that a dozen or so White House legislative agents at the Capitol were very busy lobbying for the committee packing with members of the Democratic Steering Committee before they rejected it, 10 to 5. Arthur Krock, "A Presidential Policy of Prudent Invisibility," in the *New York Times* (western ed.), Feb. 18, 1963.

24. Data concerning the age (as of 1965), educational attainments, and occupational backgrounds of members is from *Congressional Quarterly Weekly Report,* Vol. 23 (Jan. 1, 1965), pp. 25–26, and *Congressional Directory,* 89 Cong. 1 sess. (1965), *passim;* information concerning the dates of appointment to the committee is from the records maintained by the Senate Committee on Appropriations and can also be found in relevant volumes of the *Journal of the Senate of the United States of America* and the *Congressional Record.* Data on voting participation is from *Congressional Quarterly Weekly Report,* Vol. 23 (Nov. 12, 1965), pp. 2308–09.

In 1965, for example, the eighteen Democrats and nine Republicans who then made up the committee averaged sixteen years of Senate service compared with an average of ten years for all one hundred senators. They averaged sixty-three years in age, compared with fifty-eight years for the Senate as a whole. Democrats on the committee had served in the Senate an average of seventeen years; the Republicans, fourteen. Even though four of the eighteen Democrats became members of the committee during their first year in the Senate (Carl Hayden, Richard B. Russell, Robert C. Byrd, and Gale W. McGee), most Democrats—because of southern electoral longevity—had waited an average of almost six years before being appointed. The typical Republican, whose committee assignment was determined by a more rigid seniority rule, had a shorter time to wait—slightly more than four and a half years.

In a Senate with two-thirds of the members schooled in law, two-thirds of those on Appropriations had a similar background, although one of them (Byrd) acquired his law degree at night after he became a member. But primarily the committee members' background and occupation was in politics—twenty of the twenty-seven members had experience in state and local elective office (four as governors). Fourteen of the twenty-seven served in the House of Representatives before their election to the Senate. In comparison, in the Senate as a whole in 1965 sixty-four senators had experience in state and local elective office (nineteen as governors); forty-three senators served previously in the House. Committee members were experienced at all levels of the federal system. And the committee contained the intellectually bright as well as the politically wise: eight members had Phi Beta Kappa keys, several held advanced degrees, and a few were on university faculties prior to election.

It can be assumed that a committee of senior members consists of those with a political base relatively free from the changing tides of national presidential politics. Two of the 1965 members (Hayden and Russell) were members before the New Deal of Franklin D. Roosevelt began in 1933. Eight others came on before the end of the Fair Deal of former Senate colleague Harry S Truman. All were in the Senate during the New Republicanism of Dwight D. Eisenhower and the New Frontier of John F. Kennedy. All but one served on the committee prior to Lyndon Johnson's presidency.

For most senators on Appropriations, the Senate is their life. They stay in Washington and do their work. As one indication of this characteristic, in 1965 both Democrats and Republicans on the committee participated in Senate roll calls more than the typical member of their party as a whole. That year the Senate Democrats averaged 84 percent participation and the Senate Republicans 87 percent. However, eight of the eighteen Democrats on the committee participated in 90 percent or more of the 1965 roll calls, as did six of the nine Republicans. One Republican, Senator Margaret Chase Smith of Maine, was the only senator to be present and to vote on every roll call in 1965.

How Appropriations members voted on these roll calls gives a good indication of the committee's ideological makeup.[25] The first session of the Eighty-ninth Congress, in 1965, was the initial year of the presidentially proclaimed Great Society, which saw the passage of a myriad of legislative proposals, most old, some new. On the whole, the Democratic senators on the committee supported President Johnson's program slightly less than did Senate Democrats generally. The difference can be explained primarily by domestic policy issues—the voting rights legislation, in particular, was consistently opposed by the senior southern Democrats on Appropriations. Few differences occurred over foreign policy. The nine Republicans on the committee tended to support President Johnson 5 to 6 percent more often than all Senate Republicans on both foreign and domestic issues, and more often than either the average Democrat on Appropriations or the average Democrat in the Senate.

When measured in terms of support for a larger role for the federal government, the average Democrat on Appropriations tended to be less enthusiastic than the average Senate Democrat. The average Republican on Appropriations, on the other hand, supported a larger role for the federal government than his Republican colleagues in the Senate. Republican support on the committee for a larger federal role was still much smaller than that of Democrats either on Appropriations or in the Senate. Yet no Republican on Appropriations opposed expanding federal responsibilities on all twelve test roll calls selected by *Congres-*

25. *Congressional Quarterly* has developed various indices to aid in analyzing the roll call behavior of individual legislators; these include presidential support or opposition (Nov. 26, 1965, pp. 2387–91); support for a larger or smaller federal role (Dec. 3, 1965, pp. 2417–21); party unity or party opposition (Nov. 5, 1965, p. 2247); and support or opposition for the conservative coalition of southern Democrats and Republicans (Nov. 12, 1965, p. 2306).

sional Quarterly, although one Democrat did. Seven of the eighteen Democrats on the committee, however, consistently favored expanding the responsibilities of the federal government on each of twelve test issues, whereas only two Appropriations Republicans supported an expanding role for the federal government on as many as eleven roll calls.

As the above statistics suggest, the composition of the committee affirmed the maxim that the differences within each party are greater than the differences between the two major parties. Both Democrats and Republicans on Appropriations generally gave less support to the majority position of their party than did their colleagues in the Senate. Each party had on Appropriations only one of the six senators who had the highest "party unity" score in the Senate. However, both parties had three of their six lowest "party unity" senators on Appropriations. The nine southern Democrats on the committee were generally more conservative than southern Democrats in the Senate as a whole, while the nine Republicans on Appropriations usually opposed the conservative coalition of southern Democrats and Republicans more than the average Senate Republican. Some of the northern Democrats on the committee, especially those from the western mountain states, supported this conservative coalition on some issues. All Republicans but one on the committee, however, supported the coalition more often than any of the nine northern Democrats on the committee.

Regional Imbalance

A senator's region is important in determining his outlook on public issues. While America has become primarily an urban society, there are still vast areas of the country where special needs require different types of governmental action. If senators from a region become entrenched on Appropriations, benefits can flow more in their direction than in another.

Given the constitutionally unrepresentative nature of the Senate—with each state limited to two senators regardless of the size of its population—some regional and population imbalance can be expected. In 1965, the twenty-seven senators on Appropriations, each from a different state, came from constituencies with a total population of 88 million, or 46.1 percent of the national population of almost 191 million. The representation was fairly evenly divided among states with differing levels of population: there were five of the first ten states

Table 1–2. Regional Representation on the Senate Committee on Appropriations, 1965–66

Region	Total number of states in region	States represented on committee	Percentage of total number of states represented	Total population in region	Population represented on committee	Percentage of total population represented
North Central[a]	12	4	33	53,610,000	6,932,000	12.9
Northeast[b]	9	5	55	47,051,000	14,506,000	30.8
South[c]	16	10	63	58,413,000	40,139,000	68.7
West[d]	13	8	62	31,502,000	26,239,000	83.3
Total	50	27	54	190,576,000	87,816,000	46.1

Source: U.S. Bureau of the Census.
a. North Central: North Dakota, South Dakota, Nebraska, Kansas, Minnesota, Iowa, Missouri, Michigan, Wisconsin, Illinois, Indiana, Ohio.
b. Northeast: Maine, New Hampshire, Vermont, Massachusetts, Connecticut, Rhode Island, New York, Pennsylvania, New Jersey.
c. South: Delaware, Maryland, West Virginia, Virginia, North Carolina, South Carolina, Georgia, Florida, Kentucky, Tennessee, Alabama, Mississippi, Arkansas, Louisiana, Oklahoma, Texas.
d. West: Hawaii, Alaska, Washington, Oregon, California, Nevada, Arizona, Utah, Idaho, New Mexico, Colorado, Wyoming, Montana.

in population represented on Appropriations, five of the second ten, four of the third ten, seven of the fourth ten, and six of the last ten. On a regional basis, as Table 1–2 shows, the West and South were overrepresented and the Northeast and North Central regions under-represented, in that order. With only four senators on Appropriations, the twelve-state North Central region, stretching from Ohio to North Dakota, was the most underrepresented both in states and in population. The four senators came from states with only 12.9 percent of the regional population of 54 million. The five senators from the nine-state Northeast, with 47 million people, came from states with a total population of less than 15 million. On the other hand, the sixteen-state South had ten senators from states totaling 40 million people out of a regional population of 59 million. The most overrepresented area, however, was the West (defined as that region from Montana down through New Mexico and west to include Alaska and Hawaii). In 1965, eight senators representing 26 million people sat on the committee from this thirteen-state area of 32 million.[26]

26. Population figures are based on the estimate for July 1, 1964, prepared by the U.S. Bureau of the Census. The figures have been adjusted to exclude the District of Columbia from the South since the nation's capital is not represented in the Senate. U.S. Bureau of the Census, *Current Population Reports,* Series P–25, No. 324, "Estimates of the Population of States: July 1, 1964" (Jan. 20, 1966), p. 12.

Table 1–3. Percentage of Time Each State Has Been Represented on the Senate Committee on Appropriations, 1867–1966

State[a]	Percent	State[a]	Percent	State[a]	Percent
Arizona (46)	85	South Carolina	46	New York	27
Maine	85	Washington (34)	44	Pennsylvania	22
Wyoming (62)	82	Maryland	42	Connecticut	21
Virginia	73	Missouri	42	Michigan	21
Oklahoma (42)	71	Nevada	40	Nebraska	21
New Mexico (38)	70	Tennessee	39	Texas	21
New Hampshire	61	West Virginia	39	Wisconsin	20
Louisiana	59	Arkansas	38	Idaho (12)	16
California	58	Rhode Island	38	Mississippi	15
Alaska (4)	57	Alabama	37	New Jersey	14
Colorado (51)	57	Kansas	37	Montana (10)	13
Georgia	56	Utah (24)	34	Vermont	13
Illinois	53	Oregon	33	Delaware	12
North Dakota (40)	52	Florida	30	Ohio	10
South Dakota (40)	52	Kentucky	29	Indiana	4
Iowa	51	North Carolina	29	Hawaii	0
Massachusetts	49	Minnesota	27		

a. Numbers in parentheses are actual years a state has been represented since statehood. These data are given only for states admitted since 1867.

Historically, the West has been represented on the committee to a greater degree than any other region. Table 1–3 shows that only in the West have over half (or eight out of thirteen) of the states had senators on the committee at least 40 percent of the time since 1867. Although the North Central region was underrepresented in 1965, over the last century five of the twelve states in that region were represented on Appropriations for at least 40 percent of the time. In the South, it was six of sixteen states; in the Northeast, it was only three of the nine states. As the American people moved westward, need for internal improvements and federal assistance in taming the frontier increased. Few committee assignments were more helpful than Appropriations. From the plea to establish military posts to protect settlers against hostile Indians in bygone days, to the current quest for vast reclamation and hydroelectric power projects, the demands by westerners have been successfully pressed on Appropriations.

* * *

Although constituency and personal considerations are uppermost in a senator's decision to seek an assignment to the Committee on Appropriations, long-existing institutional processes and practices determine whether he finally receives it. Ideologically, the committee is not greatly unrepresentative of the parent chamber. Although the Democratic membership is more conservative—especially on domestic matters—the Republican contingent is more moderate than its overall Senate membership. The committee, however, is unbalanced geographically. With a lessening of strict seniority as a criterion for appointment in both parties, it would not be unreasonable to hope that the Northeast and North Central regions might in time receive more recognition than they now have.

Providing its members with the opportunity to get something for their constituencies and also to secure recognition from their colleagues, Appropriations stands at the apex of the Senate committee structure. It is truly a committee sought by those who are and want to be influential. But can it be more than a collective grab bag where each senator seeks a share of the federal largess? An examination of some of the formal and informal factors of committee life might aid in answering that question.

CHAPTER TWO

Committee Life:
The Operating Structure

The Chairman

The chairmanship of Appropriations can be a powerful position—given a determined occupant who retains reasonable support from his colleagues on the committee and in the Senate. There is no job description setting forth the chairman's duties. Although various statutes and rules do require the chairman of Appropriations, like the chairmen of other standing committees, to be responsible for certain activities, what he does depends largely on tradition and inclination. By law, he fixes the compensation of the professional staff, approves the vouchers to pay the expenses of the committee and its subcommittees, and endorses the accounts of committee members and employees itemizing their use of foreign currencies in travel abroad. He is required to report promptly to the Senate any measure approved by his committee and to take the necessary steps to bring the matter to a vote. So much for the statutory mandate.

The chairman, of course, presides over the full committee and determines when it shall meet. Unlike other standing committees, Appropriations does not have to fix regular weekly, biweekly, or monthly meeting days for the transaction of its business. If a chairman desires, he has unusual leeway in timing committee activity. Although the committee as a whole is authorized to appoint the necessary staff by majority vote, actually the chairman works out staffing needs in

34

consultation with the chief clerk, the various subcommittee chairmen, and the ranking minority member. Formally, the chairman votes last in a full committee markup, but how active he is in leading the committee along particular policy lines and participating in the markup discussion can vary widely. Perhaps the chairman's greatest opportunity to exert influence on Appropriations actions, if he is so inclined, is through his position as the communications center for committee activity.

In the important matter of subcommittee assignments and jurisdiction, the chairman is a creature of the seniority system and is bound by it. Once a member has been assigned or a subcommittee established, there is little the chairman can do to change what has been done. He cannot pull bills from subcommittee to full committee for a hearing because traditional subcommittee autonomy is too great. But as leader of the committee's majority, he is not simply a clearing house for automatic assignments. The chairman can favor the expansion of some subcommittees, and not others, and then let seniority work its will, thus aiding or hindering those members next in line. He can see that a new subcommittee is established to meet a particular institutional or individual need. And—especially upon becoming chairman after a change in party control—he can see that a subcommittee is not created in the first place. For example, in order to avoid the "economy" mentality so prevalent in House Appropriations consideration of foreign aid bills, Senator Hayden simply never established a foreign aid subcommittee since it would probably have been dominated by the more conservative senior members; instead, until 1969 foreign aid appropriations were considered by the full committee, which had a sympathetic majority for the program. (After Hayden's retirement, a Subcommittee on Foreign Operations was established with five Democratic and three Republican members.)

Since Appropriations is a committee of influential men where seniority has primarily determined who receives the chairmanship, it is not surprising that by the time a man reaches the pinnacle of committee power he is also an integral part of the Senate power structure. The last four chairmen, for example, have also been president pro tempore of the Senate, a position usually reserved for the senior senator in continuous service in the majority party. Nonetheless, the chairman of Appropriations is only first among a number of equals. While the scope and complexity of the committee's work has determined much of his role, so has the power and independence of his committee colleagues, especially the subcommittee chairmen. Unlike subcommittee chairmen on House Appropriations, those on Senate Appropriations often have an independent power base—usually the chairmanship of a major legislative committee, sometimes a leadership position in the Senate, and occasionally both. No doubt at times the age of a chairman has also played a part in limiting his role, as Carl Hayden's tenure epitomized. "But," a longtime staff member pointed out, "even if Carl Hayden were twenty years younger he would not have told Maggie [Senator Warren G. Magnuson, the chairman of the Subcommittee on Independent Offices] what to do on airports. Neither did [Chairmen] Bridges or McKellar before him."

While there have been few differences in power, there have been sharp differences in the purpose and style of the various chairmen who have presided over Senate Appropriations since the Second World War. Republican Styles Bridges of New Hampshire, establishing and expanding the professional staff during the Eightieth Congress, attempted an overall look at the budget. "He would hammer away all the time," recalled a Democratic subcommittee chairman. Members were urged to reconcile their differences and then stick together on the floor. The committee was smaller then, and the numerical division of the parties was close. There was greater urgency for committee unity. Both Democrats and Republicans who served with Bridges during his 1947–48 and 1953–54 chairmanships remember him as a "senator's senator," "a vigorous chairman," a "skilled" and "clever" politician, "considerate but firm," and "strong."

The tenure of Democrat Kenneth D. McKellar of Tennessee, who presided for a brief period in 1946 and between 1949 and 1952, was quite different. Many senators viewed his reign as chairman with less than fondness. In failing health, McKellar was variously described by senators as "hotheaded," "vindictive," and "obstinate." Senators would cringe with embarassment when McKellar clashed with the equally crusty and autocratic House chairman, Democrat Clarence Cannon of Missouri. The result was that Hayden, as the next in line, and Bridges, as ranking Republican, usually managed to accomplish much of the committee's work behind the scenes. Even in his dotage, however, McKellar fought vehemently and effectively for the needs of Tennessee. Eventually the voters in his own party repudiated him in the 1952 Tennessee Democratic primary and Carl Hayden, following the two-year Republican interlude under Bridges, took up the chairmanship that he was to hold for the next fourteen years.

Guy Cordon of Oregon, a Republican senator who served on Appropriations for a number of years with Hayden, is credited with the most succinct summary of that chairman's legislative skill: "Carl Hayden has smiled more money through the Committee on Appropriations than any other senator has gotten by valid argument." Some of the many descriptions of Hayden volunteered by senators and staff include "sweet," "respected," "faithful to his duties," and "easygoing." His colleagues recognized that Hayden slowed with age, but they were amazed at his capacity not only "to remember what happened fifty years ago but also what happened yesterday." Although Hayden was as vigorous in the pursuit of projects for Arizona as McKellar was for those of Tennessee, he did not "punish" members who disagreed with him. He was also content to let senators other than himself have the limelight. A staff member who had worked for and observed Bridges and McKellar, as well as Hayden, noted: "Hayden doesn't give a damn if he gets on the front page of the *New York Times*. He cares only for Arizona."

Hayden's live-and-let-live philosophy meant that the desires of each subcommittee chairman went largely unchallenged. Commanding affection, Hayden gave the subcommittee chairmen latitude and authority, thereby avoiding any resentment or revolt by ranking members against centralized direction, a situation that has occurred on a few congressional committees. Such decentralization was welcomed by the subcommittee chairmen, who served as barons within their own principalities, and also by the staff, who performed as junior peers of the realm. Nonetheless, many of his most aggressive subcommittee chairmen and colleagues believe that the lack of direction resulting from Hayden's easygoing nature and tolerance was harmful in the long run to the decisiveness and power of the committee. Several senators in 1966 were outspoken in their belief that any quest for an overall review of executive branch activities would be submerged by the members' narrow program interests, which had been allowed to dominate the committee's processes. One senior senator commented then:

> The chairman has passed his peak. He had a fine knowledge when he was active. A lot depends on the chairman. Over the years the power has shifted to the chairmen of the subcommittees. My interest as a subcommittee chairman is secondary to my interest in seeing that the committee has a head.

It is true that the committee had to branch out in subcommittees because of the tremendous volume of work. But you need a tight, hard-hitting staff of competent men and there is no driving force. There is also no reconciliation of the different budget requests within the committee. An active chairman should have close liaison with subcommittee chairmen.

Hayden's retirement from the Senate early in 1969 brought Richard Russell to the chairmanship. At the time of this writing, shortly after the changeover, there seems to be little difference in the committee under Russell. Some staff members suspect that Russell has not yet been able to bring about the changes he would like in committee practices.

The Subcommittee System

The basic unit of the Senate Committee on Appropriations is the subcommittee. On the diligence, interest, and whim of the subcommittee's chairman, members, and staff rests the extent to which the Senate will fulfill its responsibility to scrutinize the appropriations requests submitted by the executive branch. As one staff member, intrigued by the power of the subcommittee, correctly noted: "The Senate gives power to the full committee and the full committee gives honor to the work of the subcommittee."

The Senate Committee on Appropriations has fourteen subcommittees that usually conduct formal, public hearings: Agriculture and Related Agencies; Defense; Deficiencies and Supplementals; District of Columbia; Foreign Operations; Independent Offices; Interior and Related Agencies; Labor and Health, Education, and Welfare and Related Agencies; Legislative; Military Construction; Public Works; State, Justice, and Commerce, the Judiciary, and Related Agencies; Transportation, which was added in 1967; and Treasury and Post Office and Executive Office. A fifteenth group, unlisted until 1969 and meeting only in closed session, reviews the activities of the Central Intelligence Agency (CIA).

While most of these subcommittees parallel those of House Appropriations, there are a few differences reflecting the special needs of the Senate committee. As mentioned earlier, matters relating to foreign operations, considered by a separate subcommittee in the House, were until 1969 reviewed in the Senate by the full committee sitting as a subcommittee. This assured domination by moderate forces, and since the foreign aid appropriations bill usually came up late in the session, it expedited consideration by avoiding a stage in the committee's internal clearance process. A second difference is that supplemental appropriation bills are handled by the regular subject matter subcommittees in the House but by an overall supplemental subcommittee in the Senate. This system could create difficulties since, no matter how able the colleague, regular subcommittee chairmen resent giving up review of "their" programs to another member merely because additional appropriations have been recommended. The Senate's separate Supplemental Subcommittee, which was established in 1962, overcomes this problem by basing its membership solely on the chairmen and ranking minority members of most of the regular subcommittees. Before the retirement of Hayden and Democrat Lister Hill of Alabama in 1969 there was a third difference between the House and Senate committees: in Senate Appropriations the Public Works Subcommittee was divided into three panels—one on Army Civil Functions, on which all subcommittee members served, and two smaller panels, one to consider Atomic Energy Commission–Tennessee Valley Authority requests (under Hill's chairmanship), the other to consider Bureau of Reclamation–Interior Power Marketing Agencies items (under Hayden's chairmanship).

Senate Appropriations' CIA Subcommittee is a special case. In the late 1950s, because of overlapping membership, the senior members of the Senate Armed Services Committee and of Appropriations informally merged the two separate subcommittees that had reviewed the activities of the Central Intelligence Agency since its inception in 1947.[1] The appropriations decisions made by the CIA Subcommittee are not ratified by the full committee. In keeping with the nature of the sub-

---

1. In 1966 the merged group totaled seven senators, with two, Russell and Saltonstall, serving as representatives from both Appropriations and Armed Services. Two more, John Stennis of Mississippi and Margaret Chase Smith of Maine, were also on both committees but were designated only from Armed Services. Membership was on the basis of seniority. In both 1956 and 1966, the Senate by a margin of 2 to 1 rejected attempts to create a formal standing committee to oversee the activities of the CIA and the other intelligence agencies. Such a committee would have included representation from Foreign Relations as well as from Armed Services and Appropriations. By 1968, however, three senior members of Foreign Relations—Democrat J. William Fulbright of Arkansas, Republican Bourke B. Hickenlooper of Iowa, and Democratic leader Mansfield—were serving "by grace and not right" (as one committee aide noted) on the informal joint group.

ject, no formal hearing records are kept. In a sense this subcommittee, whose existence was not even admitted on Appropriations' annual printed list of subcommittees until 1969, although Armed Services did list it, is the most powerful unit of the full committee.

Evolution of the Subcommittees

Like the standing committees, subcommittees have evolved because they provide a useful framework for conducting the Senate's business. As early as 1880, thirteen years after the Senate Committee on Appropriations was established, the accepted method of operation was by subcommittee. The subcommittees of that time reflected the concerns of an America of a different era. While there were no subcommittees on Foreign Operations or Labor, Health, Education, and Welfare—vital governmental fields of the mid-twentieth century—there were subcommittees for Fortifications, Indians, and Pensions (the latter a particular concern of the Grand Army of the Republic). Other subcommittees included Legislative, Sundry Civil, Post Office, Army, Military Academy, Naval, Consular and Diplomatic, and Deficiencies. In 1881, a separate subcommittee for the District of Columbia was added, and in 1882, one for Agriculture.

In 1887, the Committee on Appropriations listed its River and Harbor Subcommittee as consisting of members of the Senate Committee on Commerce—a legislative committee. This was tacit recognition of the fact that neither Appropriations nor its predecessor, Finance, had ever been able to secure jurisdiction over the politically important pork barrel bills that appropriated federal funds for dams and channel improvements. The existence of this subcommittee foreshadowed a development that had already occurred in the House of Representatives and would be consummated in the Senate by the turn of the century: the dispersal of major appropriation bills to legislative committees.

By 1913, the first year of Woodrow Wilson's administration, the subcommittees on Senate Appropriations were reduced to six: Deficiencies, Diplomatic and Consular, District of Columbia, Fortifications, Legislative, and Sundry Civil. The diffusion of appropriation bills among various legislative committees had been in effect for a decade and a half. With the adoption of the Budgeting and Accounting Act of 1921 and the submission of revised appropriation bills by the President in 1922, Congress reversed this process of diffusion. A consolidated and strengthened Senate Committee on Appropriations resulted.[2] From 1924 until the Reorganization Act of 1946 took effect and further strengthened the committee, Senate Appropriations basically had ten subcommittees. During the Republican Eightieth Congress, in 1947, other subcommittees were added, in particular the Subcommittee on Labor–Federal Security, which became the Subcommittee on Labor-HEW with the creation of a new cabinet-level Department of Health, Education, and Welfare during the first year of the Eisenhower administration in 1953.

In 1955, with the return of Congress to Democratic control, Clarence Cannon, then House Appropriations chairman, rearranged the scope of several subcommittees. A firm believer in functionalism, Cannon assigned related programs to a single subcommittee even though they were scattered throughout various government departments. He was convinced that such a reorganization would prove helpful to Congress not only in securing uniformity among comparable programs but also in achieving some balance of priorities in the actual allocation of funds. For example, Cannon moved the Bureau of Reclamation and major Department of Interior power marketing agencies (such as the Bonneville Power Administration) from the Interior to the Public Works Subcommittee. Cannon, besides being chairman of the full committee, also ran Public Works. In addition, he assigned to his subcommittee the Atomic Energy Commission and Tennessee Valley Authority budgets, which had been handled by Independent Offices. Review of the various federal electric power policies and operations was thus located in a single unit of House Appropriations.

While Senate Appropriations might have continued the previous subcommittee arrangements, to do so would have caused confusion, with several Senate subcommittees possibly considering an appropriation bill that had been developed in a single House subcommittee. The result would have been a chaotic conference with the House—and these conferences were already difficult enough. Therefore, the Senate, as it had done so often in the past, simply conformed to the structural changes made by House Appropriations. But since senators do not relinquish power willingly, those who had been responsible for

2. For the background of these changes in the power of Appropriations, and the price the committee paid for reconsolidation, see the section on ex officio membership later in this chapter.

a particular matter simply shifted with it to the new subcommittee in order to maintain control.[3]

Other changes have taken place since then. Following a House Appropriations rearrangement in 1955, a separate subcommittee for the Department of Commerce and Related Agencies was established. Again following House Appropriations, this was disbanded in 1961 and review of Commerce Department appropriations was returned to the State-Justice Subcommittee. This change left Democratic Senator Spessard L. Holland of Florida, who had been chairman of the Commerce Subcommittee, without a chairmanship until 1962, when a separate Deficiencies and Supplementals Subcommittee was created and he assumed the chairmanship. In 1959, Democratic Senator Dennis Chavez of New Mexico secured approval to establish a separate panel within his Defense Subcommittee to handle the military construction budget. (The year before, the House had created a separate subcommittee for Military Construction.) The work of the new unit greatly relieved the pressure on the Defense Subcommittee since the panel's recommendations went directly to the full committee for approval. In 1963, Military Construction formally became a subcommittee, although it had been publishing separate hearings and functioning independently since 1961. In 1967, after the establishment of a cabinet-level Department of Transportation, a Transportation Subcommittee was created. Thus, over time the subcommittee structure of the Appropriations Committee has changed and grown, reflecting changes in the nature of society, executive changes in appropriations procedures, the establishment of new federal departments, rearrangements by House Appropriations, and even upon occasion the needs of a "deserving" senator.

Getting on a Subcommittee

The reasons for a senator's choice of a particular subcommittee are little different from the reasons for his choice of a full committee: he wants to help his state, he needs leverage, he seeks power. In getting

3. No one, for example, was going to remove reclamation matters from Carl Hayden's purview—reclamation was too important for the state of Arizona. Although Hayden was already chairman of the full committee, and in addition chairman of the Interior Subcommittee, he met the House move by establishing and taking charge of a Public Works panel to review appropriations for the Bureau of Reclamation and various Interior power marketing agencies. Similarly, Lister Hill, who had handled TVA matters as a member of Independent Offices, continued his scrutiny as chairman of a newly established Public Works panel charged with responsibility for AEC-TVA matters.

a subcommittee assignment a senator's own desires are important, but the controlling factor almost always is seniority in committee service.[4] This is especially true of the subcommittee chairmanships. In 1947, when the Republicans assumed control of the committee for the first time since 1933, Styles Bridges, the new chairman, met with the Republican committee members in his office. He asked each senator in order of seniority: "What do you want?" When two colleagues sought the same subcommittee chairmanship, seniority decided it. When the Democrats regained power in 1949, Kenneth McKellar went through the same ritual. In 1953, Bridges, again chairman, repeated the process. Hayden did the same with the Democratic comeback in 1955, allocating subcommittee chairmanships according to seniority in the full committee.

Changes in the chairmanship of the Defense Subcommittee make a good case in point. In 1955, Richard B. Russell rejected an opportunity to become the chairman, preferring to retain the chairmanship of the Agriculture Subcommittee, where he was proud of the work he had done to revitalize farming by emphasizing research and new methods. As a result, Senator Chavez became chairman of Defense. By 1962, Chavez was seriously ill, and Defense subcommittee member A. Willis Robertson of Virginia had become acting chairman. After the death of Chavez on November 18, 1962, Chairman Hayden, following seniority, first contacted Russell in his search for a new subcommittee chairman. Russell expressed interest but wanted to think it over. Several other senators in descending order of seniority were also approached in case Russell remained unwilling to take the job. Russell did accept, however, and gave up his chairmanship of the Agriculture Subcommittee. Senator Robertson, who had been acting chairman during Chavez' illness, was never contacted in the exploratory period because he did not have sufficient full committee seniority.

The few exceptions to the seniority rule in selecting subcommittee chairmen are usually made with the consent of those to whom the positions would have gone on the basis of seniority. Upon Democratic

4. There is an important difference between Senate seniority and committee seniority. The allocation of parking permits, office space, and other institutional prerogatives is based on one's length of continuous service in the Senate, regardless of party. Committee seniority is based on the continuance of an individual on a committee and in a party, as Senator Wayne Morse (Republican, Independent, and, until defeated at the polls, Democrat from Oregon) found out when he left the Republican party during the 1952 election and lost his committee assignments. See Ralph K. Huitt, "The Morse Committee Assignment Controversy: A Study in Senate Norms," *American Political Science Review*, Vol. 51 (June 1957), pp. 313–29.

leader Lyndon B. Johnson's appointment to Appropriations in 1956, he immediately became chairman of the Subcommittee on State, Justice, the Judiciary, and Related Agencies. This had been the chairmanship held by Harley M. Kilgore of West Virginia, whose vacancy Johnson filled. Those senior to Johnson, such as John L. McClellan of Arkansas, Holland, Stennis, and Earle C. Clements of Kentucky, stepped aside.

Exceptions also occasionally occur with regard to subcommittee membership. Here the persuasive powers of a majority leader can be overriding. When Mike Mansfield, Johnson's successor, was appointed to Appropriations in 1963, he was soon assigned to the Defense Subcommittee, although Bible, Byrd, and McGee outranked him in committee seniority. Mansfield argued that because he was a candidate for reelection in 1964, membership on the Defense Subcommittee was vital to him, and the three Democrats yielded to the wishes of their leader.

As has already been noted, the emphasis on seniority in both subcommittee memberships and chairmanships greatly limits the power of the full committee chairman. It would be a break with tradition for the chairman of Senate Appropriations to assign newcomers to whatever subcommittees he pleased, to transfer a senior member from one subcommittee to another, or to abolish a subcommittee in order to prevent a majority member from assuming the chairmanship. Yet, on occasion, that is exactly what has happened in House Appropriations, where the chairman is not as rigidly bound by the norm of seniority. In the Senate, breaks with tradition seldom occur unless they are supported by most of the subcommittee chairmen.

RELATIVE PRESTIGE AMONG SUBCOMMITTEES. Since seniority plays such an important role in subcommittee assignments, the choices available to most newcomers on Appropriations are limited largely to the less desirable subcommittees. Like the committees of the Senate, the subcommittees of Appropriations are ranked hierarchically by the members, with a high degree of consensus among members of both parties as to the most prestigious and least prestigious subcommittees. This hierarchy is demonstrated by the relative difficulty of securing initial appointment to the subcommittees, the seniority of their membership, and their holding power in keeping members from leaving for other subcommittees.

Table 2–1, which presents the number of newcomer appointments to each subcommittee during the period 1955–66, reveals that Defense

Table 2–1. Difficulty in Securing Appointment to Senate Appropriations Subcommittees for New Members, 1955–66, by Party

| Degree of difficulty | Democrats (16) | | Republicans (9) | | Agreement between both parties |
	Subcommittee[a]	Number of new members appointed	Subcommittee[a]	Number of new members appointed	Subcommittee[a]
Most difficult	Defense	1	Defense	0	Defense
	Independent Offices	1	Public Works	1	Public Works
	Public Works	2	Legislative	1	
			State-Justice	2	
			Interior	2	
Moderately difficult	Military Construction	3	Military Construction	2	Military Construction
	Legislative	6	Commerce	2	Agriculture
	Labor-HEW	6	Agriculture	5	
	State-Justice	8	Independent Offices	5	
	Agriculture	8			
Least difficult	Interior	10	District of Columbia	7	Treasury–Post Office
	Treasury–Post Office	11	Labor-HEW	8	District of Columbia
	District of Columbia	13	Treasury–Post Office	9	
	Commerce	12			

a. The Commerce Subcommittee existed from 1955 to 1961; the Military Construction Subcommittee began in 1961. Their placement in the table is based on the assumption that the same rate of appointment would have continued if they had existed for the whole period. The Deficiencies and Supplementals Subcommittee is not included since it was not organized until 1962 and has consisted almost exclusively of subcommittee chairmen and ranking minority members.

and Public Works were the most difficult assignments to secure for newcomers in either party. Two subcommittees that were moderately difficult for newcomers in both parties to join were Military Construction and Agriculture. The least difficult for both Republicans and Democrats were Treasury–Post Office and the District of Columbia.

For the other subcommittees, there are notable differences between the parties. In Independent Offices and State-Justice, unusual attrition accounted for the differences. Few vacancies among Democrats occurred on Independent Offices. Because of its wide range of activity, most of the senior Democrats stayed, and when vacancies developed, members of other subcommittees transferred over, leaving room for only one newcomer. For the Republicans, even though there was some transferring by senior committee members, electoral defeat or death made five initial appointments possible. In the State-Justice Subcommittee, the opportunity for initial appointment was greater for newcomer Democrats because of the higher turnover among members of their party already serving on the subcommittee.

The difference in initial assignments to the Legislative Subcommittee reveals an interesting divergence between the parties. This subcommittee is charged with reviewing the budget for the Senate and the House of Representatives (although comity between the bodies usually leaves the expenses of one house unchallenged by the other), the Architect of the Capitol, the Library of Congress, the Government Printing Office, and other activities under the jurisdiction of Congress. It is concerned with the details of running the legislative establishment—details about which all senators and their staffs hold strong opinions and that consequently are difficult to deal with. In the years between 1955 and 1966, the Democrats put six new members on the subcommittee while the Republicans appointed only one. The makeup of the subcommittee itself was indicative of its different status for each party. It was chaired in 1966 by Mike Monroney, who ranked eleventh on the committee in terms of seniority but who had an interest in the workings of Congress because of his membership on the two major reorganization committees since the Second World War. The other Democratic members, however, were the three lowest in seniority. The Republicans, on the other hand, included Senator Saltonstall, the chairman of the Senate Republican Conference as well as ranking Republican on the full committee; Milton R. Young, secretary of the Republican Conference and second ranking Republican on the full committee; and Thomas H. Kuchel, Senate Republican whip and middle ranking Republican on the committee.

Initial assignments to the Interior Subcommittee also showed a wide variation between parties. It was among the least difficult appointments for a Democrat and among the most difficult for a Republican. There was a great increase in the Democratic representation from the West during this period (for the western senator, Interior is a "bread and butter" subcommittee).

The statistics for two other subcommittees deserve mention for the ideological differences they reveal between the two parties. From 1955 through 1961 there was a Commerce Subcommittee to which newcomer Democrats had no difficulty in securing an assignment. In fact, every Democratic newcomer during the period 1955–61 was assigned to

Commerce. For the Republicans, with closer ties to the business community, it was a moderately difficult initial assignment. With the Labor-HEW Subcommittee the reverse was true. Democrats had moderate difficulty securing an initial assignment; for Republicans, the competition was not keen and appointment was almost mandatory, as all but one of their nine newcomers during the period were assigned to Labor-HEW.

Table 2–2 demonstrates the relative prestige of subcommittees in terms of the average seniority, by party, of its 1966 membership. According to this criterion, Democrats and Republicans agreed on the relative prestige of seven of the twelve subcommittees. The Subcommittees on Deficiencies and Supplementals and on Defense were the most attractive for both parties. Agriculture, Military Construction, and

Table 2–2. Attractiveness of Appropriations Subcommittees on the Basis of Seniority of Membership in 1966, by Party

Degree of attractiveness	Democrats		Republicans		Agreement between both parties
	Subcommittee	Seniority score[a]	Subcommittee	Seniority score[a]	Subcommittee
Most attractive	Deficiencies and Supplementals	6.58	Legislative Interior	2.66 3.33	Deficiencies and Supplementals
	Defense	6.64	Deficiencies and		Defense
	Independent		Supplementals	3.50	
	Offices	6.66	Defense	3.66	
	Public Works	7.50			
Moderately attractive	Agriculture	9.40	Military		Agriculture
	Labor-HEW	9.50	Construction	4.00	Military
	State-Justice-		Independent		Construction
	Commerce	9.66	Offices	4.66	State-Justice-
	Interior	10.55	Agriculture	5.00	Commerce
	Military		Public Works	5.00	
	Construction	10.86	State-Justice	5.20	
Least attractive	Treasury–		Labor-HEW	7.00	Treasury–
	Post Office	11.20	Treasury–		Post Office
	District of		Post Office	8.00	District of
	Columbia	13.00	District of		Columbia
	Legislative	15.50	Columbia	8.50	

a. The seniority score represents the average seniority of the subcommittee members, using their ranking on the full committee. Democrats were marked from 1 (most senior) to 18 (least senior); Republicans, similarly, from 1 to 9.

Table 2-3. Attractiveness of Appropriations Subcommittees on the Basis of Switches between Subcommittees, 1955–66, by Party

Degree of attractiveness	Both parties — Subcommittee[a]	Net	Gain	Loss	Democrats — Subcommittee[a]	Net	Gain	Loss	Republicans — Subcommittee[a]	Net	Gain	Loss	Agreement between both parties — Subcommittee
Most attractive	Public Works	+13	14	1	Public Works	+8	8	0	Public Works	+5	6	1	Public Works
	Defense	+11	11	0	Defense	+7	7	0	Commerce	+5	5	0	Defense
									Defense	+4	4	0	
Moderately attractive	Commerce	+4	8	4	Agriculture	+2	2	0	State-Justice	+2	3	1	State-Justice
	State-Justice	+3	7	4	Independent Offices	+2	4	2	Military Construction	+2	2	0	Military Construction
	Military Construction	+3	6	3	State-Justice	+1	4	3	Agriculture	0	0	0	Agriculture
	Agriculture	+2	2	0	Military Construction	+1	4	3	Interior	0	1	1	
	Independent Offices	0	8	8	Labor-HEW	+1	3	2					
Less attractive	Interior	-1	3	4	Interior	-1	2	3	Legislative	-1	2	3	Legislative
	Legislative	-2	5	7	Legislative	-1	3	4	Independent Offices	-2	4	6	
	Labor-HEW	-3	5	8	Commerce	-1	3	4					
Least attractive	Treasury–Post Office	-11	2	13	Treasury–Post Office	-7	1	8	Labor-HEW	-4	2	6	Treasury–Post Office
	District of Columbia	-13	2	15	District of Columbia	-8	1	9	Treasury–Post Office	-4	1	5	District of Columbia
									District of Columbia	-5	1	6	

a. The Deficiencies and Supplementals Subcommittee is not included since it was not organized until 1962 and has consisted almost exclusively of subcommittee chairmen and ranking minority members.

b. Initial appointments to subcommittees or additions to subcommittees when no subcommittee was given up are not included in this tabulation.

State-Justice had some attraction for both parties, and Treasury–Post Office and the District of Columbia Subcommittees were viewed as least attractive. With the remaining subcommittees, the same factors of attrition seemed to be involved as affected initial appointment. The greatest contrast was found in the Legislative Subcommittee. Legislative was the most attractive for Republicans and the least attractive (even more so than the District of Columbia Subcommittee) for Democrats. The high standing for the Interior Subcommittee among Republicans reflected the fact that several of the senior Republicans on the committee were from the West—traditionally Republican territory until the Democratic sweep of 1958—whereas most of the Democratic westerners were new to the committee in the last decade and thus low in seniority. In contrast, Public Works, which appropriated funds for the nationwide activities of the Army's Corps of Engineers, had appeal not only for westerners but for senators from all sections, including the South. Since most senior Democrats on Appropriations were from the South and on Public Works, the subcommittee was most attractive in terms of seniority.

The analysis in Table 2–3 of the switches made during the period 1955–66 is helpful in revealing subcommittee prestige as well as in emphasizing differences between the parties. Since frequently a senator simultaneously gives up membership on two less desirable subcommittees to accept one or two more important appointments, no direct relationship can be ascertained as to movement between specific subcommittees. However, net shifts (gains minus losses) over a period of time are somewhat indicative of the relative prestige of a subcommittee. Both parties agreed on the relative standing of eight of the twelve subcommittees, with Public Works and Defense attracting both Democrats and Republicans to a greater degree than the other subcommittees.

If the results of the analyses of initial appointments, seniority of membership, and switches in assignment are combined, it is clear that there is very wide agreement among Democrats and Republicans on the relative standing of the various Appropriations subcommittees. The most prestigious are, as has been noted, Defense and Public Works.[5] In the next group are Agriculture, Military Construction, and

5. As was noted on Tables 2–1 and 2–3, the Subcommittee on Deficiencies and Supplementals is excluded since it was not established until 1962 and has been composed almost exclusively of subcommittee chairmen and ranking minority members. By the criteria used in the analysis, it would automatically appear as the most prestigious subcommittee.

State-Justice. Least prestigious are the Treasury–Post Office and the District of Columbia Subcommittees.

With such a variation in subcommittee prestige, it is likely that there will be a difference in the degree of enthusiasm with which newcomers assigned to the less prestigious subcommittees approach their work. As Chapter 4 on the information-gathering process will explain, there are also substantial differences in the work loads of these subcommittees and in the participation of the membership. Since senators give up less desirable assignments as soon as possible, there is little opportunity to develop and retain subject matter expertise on some subcommittees. Consequently, less prestigious subcommittees soon become the almost exclusive fiefdoms of their chairmen.

The ex Officio Member

A unique structural aspect of the Senate Committee on Appropriations is the inclusion of ex officio members from legislative committees who may participate in deliberations and vote. Appropriations has twenty-seven ex officio positions in all, six on the Public Works Subcommittee and three each on seven other subcommittees. As Table 2–4 illustrates for 1965–66, these positions are filled by three members each from eight legislative committees (the three from the Armed Services Committee sit on both the Defense Subcommittee and the Military Construction Subcommittee). There are no ex officio members on House Appropriations or on any other committee in either body.

The responsibilities of ex officio members are specified in the Standing Rules of the Senate. In the case of the Subcommittees on Agriculture, Defense, District of Columbia, and Military Construction, ex officio members are free to vote on all issues. On the others, participation is more narrowly defined. Senators from the Space Committee are limited to aeronautical and space activities in Independent Offices. In the case of Public Works, ex officio members from the Committee on Public Works are restricted to rivers and harbors items and ex officio members from the Joint Committee on Atomic Energy are limited to atomic energy matters. In State-Justice, ex officio members represent the Committee on Foreign Relations only on diplomatic and consular items. Treasury–Post Office ex officio senators from the Committee on Post Office and Civil Service are eligible to participate solely on post office

Table 2–4. Ex Officio Members from Legislative Committees to Senate Appropriations Subcommittees and Panels, 1965–66

Ex officio members	Legislative committee	Appropriations subcommittee or panel
Allen J. Ellender (D–La.) Olin D. Johnston (D–S.C.)ᵃ George D. Aiken (R–Vt.)	Agriculture and Forestry	Agriculture and Related Agencies
Harry F. Byrd (D–Va.)ᵇ Stuart Symington (D–Mo.) Strom Thurmond (R–S.C.)	Armed Services	Defense Military Construction
Thomas J. McIntyre (D–N.H.) Joseph D. Tydings (D–Md.) Winston L. Prouty (R–Vt.)	District of Columbia	District of Columbia
Clinton P. Anderson (D–N. Mex.) Stuart Symington (D–Mo.) Bourke B. Hickenlooper (R–Iowa)	Aeronautical and Space Sciences	Independent Offices (on aeronautical and space activities only)
Patrick V. McNamara (D–Mich.)ᶜ Jennings Randolph (D–W. Va.) John Sherman Cooper (R–Ky.)	Public Works	Public Works Panel on Army Civil Functions (on rivers and harbors items only)
Clinton P. Anderson (D–N. Mex.) Albert Gore (D–Tenn.) Bourke B. Hickenlooper (R–Iowa)	Joint Committee on Atomic Energy	Public Works Panel on Atomic Energy Commission–Tennessee Valley Authority (on atomic energy items only)
J. W. Fulbright (D–Ark.) John J. Sparkman (D–Ala.) Bourke B. Hickenlooper (R–Iowa)	Foreign Relations	State, Justice, and Commerce, the Judiciary, and Related Agencies (on diplomatic and consular items only)
Olin D. Johnston (D–S.C.)ᵃ Jennings Randolph (D–W. Va.) Frank Carlson (R–Kans.)	Post Office and Civil Service	Treasury–Post Office–Executive Office (on post office items only)

a. Senator Johnston died on April 18, 1965. He was replaced on Agriculture and Related Agencies by James O. Eastland (D–Miss.) and on Treasury–Post Office and Executive Office by Daniel B. Brewster (D–Md.).
b. Senator Byrd resigned from the Senate on November 10, 1965. In 1966, he was replaced on the Defense and the Military Construction Subcommittees by Henry M. Jackson (D–Wash.).
c. Senator McNamara died on April 30, 1966. He was replaced on the Public Works Panel on Army Civil Functions by Stephen M. Young (D–Ohio).

items. Despite these limitations, however, during subcommittee markup there is some leeway based on a senator's expertise.[6]

No party ratio for the three ex officio members from a legislative committee is specified, but the division has invariably been two from the majority and one from the minority. The Senate Rules authorize only one of the three ex officio members to participate in any conference held with the House on the regular annual appropriation bill to which they are assigned. While no provision is made for inclusion of the ex officio members in conferences on supplemental appropriations bills, they occasionally do participate—especially if the supplemental is limited to one department.

The origin of ex officio membership on Appropriations provides a useful insight into the varying degrees of power the committee has held within the Senate and illustrates the fact that no matter how powerful a committee may become, the Senate as a whole is more powerful—if it exerts its will. Like many Senate Rules, ex officio membership was the product of historical happenstance and a desire for mutual accommodation. It was the price the Senate Committee on Appropriations had to pay in 1922 when it recovered its jurisdiction over all appropriation bills—a jurisdiction that had been divided among the legislative committees in the late nineteenth century when the Senate followed the action taken by the House of Representatives in curbing the power of its most aggressive committee.

The Taming of House Appropriations

In the two decades following the Civil War, the power of the House Committee on Appropriations grew to awesome proportions. Under the chairmanship of Samuel J. Randall, a Pennsylvania Democrat who was speaker of the House from 1876 to 1881 and Appropriations chairman in 1875–76 and from 1883 to 1889, the committee reached its peak and its nadir. The strong-willed Pennsylvanian used his prerogative in scheduling appropriation bills for immediate House considera-

6. For example, when Democrat Robert S. Kerr of Oklahoma was an ex officio member from the Senate Committee on Public Works to the Public Works Appropriations Subcommittee, his aggressiveness and his power within the Senate establishment enabled him to transcend the restriction to rivers and harbors items only and engage in battle in a markup session on matters of reclamation policy as well. Although some regular members resented his forays and his acid tongue, few tangled with the "uncrowned King of the Senate" who—though he was not chairman of either—was the most powerful man on both the Committee on Finance and the Committee on Public Works.

tion to block legislation that was distasteful to him. The resentment of the legislative committees steadily increased.

From the dawn of the standing committee system in the House, there had been a struggle for jurisdiction over the river and harbor appropriation bill and other measures related to internal improvements. As waterways competed with roadways and railways with waterways, this strife intensified. In April 1876, the Commerce Committee secured House permission to have the river and harbor appropriation bill recommitted to it without reference to Appropriations. Within a few days, Commerce brought the bill back to the House and, under a suspension of the rules, secured its passage.

In April 1879, Appropriations members failed in their attempt to change the rules of the House to require that three-fourths rather than two-thirds of the members present vote affirmatively to suspend the rules in order to pass a general appropriation bill. A change in rules was secured, however, by the powerful Commerce chairman, Democrat John H. Reagan of Texas, which granted the Commerce Committee the privilege long held by Appropriations of reporting the river and harbor bill at any time in the session. Democrat Joseph C. S. Blackburn of Kentucky, a leading member of both Appropriations and Rules, then submitted to the House a complete revision of the rules. The Committee on Rules agreed with Blackburn that all appropriation bills should be referred to one committee, Appropriations. When the House debated the proposed changes in early 1880, Reagan again secured for Commerce the privilege of reporting the river and harbor bill. Then the western farm and Grange representatives won an amendment granting the Committee on Agriculture the power to appropriate funds for the Department of Agriculture. Every member of Appropriations fought the second diminution of their control, but when the roll was called in March 1880, the rural representatives had won, 133 to 102. It was the beginning of the end. In December 1885, the House Committee on Rules—seeking to curtail Randall's power—reported, and the House adopted, a new rule that completed the crippling of House Appropriations; with this change, the Army, Consular and Diplomatic, Indian, Military Academy, Navy, and Post Office appropriation bills were removed.

The Senate Follows Suit

Not until 1899 did the Senate follow the House precedent in distributing several of the major appropriation bills to legislative committees, although such an effort actually began in the Senate prior to the removal of the agricultural bill from House Appropriations in 1880. A growing bitterness against Senate Appropriations was evident from 1879 on.[7]

In 1883, the Senate Committee on Rules completed its extensive revision, codification, and simplification of the Rules of the Senate. Besides recommending that the river and harbor appropriation bill be given to the legislative committee, it suggested that "bills making appropriations for the expenses of the government of the District of Columbia" be referred to the Committee on the District of Columbia rather than to Appropriations.[8] These exceptions were an open invitation for other committees to advocate similar treatment. And they did so. First was the Committee on Agriculture and Forestry, whose House counterpart had been accorded such jurisdiction in 1880. In January 1884, by two votes, the Senate narrowly decided against transferring the District of Columbia appropriation bill to the legislative committee. And by ten votes, the attack of the Committee on Agriculture and Forestry was repulsed.

For another decade only sporadic attempts were made to strip the committee of some of its jurisdiction. Then in 1895, a first-term Republican maverick from Idaho, Fred T. Dubois, began the drive that was to weaken the Senate Committee on Appropriations for almost a quarter-century. He soon was joined by senators who, on the average, were little more than halfway through their first term. It was a "young Turk" revolt.

In December 1895, Dubois introduced a resolution calling for only three bills (legislative, executive, and judicial; sundry civil; and all deficiencies) to remain with Appropriations. All others were to be divided among ten legislative committees. Instead of allowing his resolution to be referred to the Committee on Rules—the graveyard of the previous proposals—Dubois arranged that the resolution lie on the table.

7. For an excellent account of the Senate during this period of strong party leadership but growing discontent, and a description of the external forces affecting the Senate as well as the leadership techniques used within, see David J. Rothman, *Politics and Power: The United States Senate, 1869–1901* (Harvard University Press, 1966).

8. *Report of the Committee on Rules Relating to the Rules of the Senate, the Joint Rules of the Senate and House of Representatives, and the Senate Manual,* S. Rept. 2, 48 Cong. 1 sess. (Dec. 10, 1883), pp. 15, 23.

Within a week Dubois called up his resolution, arguing that it gave "to the committee which, on account of its membership and duties, is most interested in a given subject the power to regulate and determine what amount of money shall be appropriated and how it shall be expended in order to satisfy the necessities and demands of the country as to this particular subject."[9] He enumerated a long series of grievances senators held against the Committee on Appropriations; among them were the adding of legislative matters to appropriation bills, clogging the Senate calendar in the closing days of a session, failing to promote the interests of the country as wisely as the legislative committees could, and agreeing to items in conference without prior consultation with the appropriate committee. Having assaulted the citadel of power, Dubois sought to assure "the foremost men of the Senate," as he called the members of the Senate Committee on Appropriations, that his effort to bury them was not the least bit personal. Republican William B. Allison of Iowa, beginning his fourteenth year as the chairman of Appropriations, sat largely silent through the discussion. After all, he had gone through this before: why give the matter more attention than it deserved by debating a first-term senator?

Two months elapsed. When the Senate leaders sought on February 4, 1896 to bring up an urgent deficiency appropriation bill, Dubois made his move. He demanded that the Senate have the opportunity to vote on his resolution. The managers of the deficiency appropriation bill protested, but the Senate, by a vote of 44 to 25, refused to proceed to consideration of the deficiency measure. By another vote, 49 to 24, it agreed to consider the Dubois resolution.

Then, for three days the Senate debated. Dubois and his supporters attacked the Committee on Appropriations for ignoring the recommendations of the legislative committees. A single committee, they argued, simply could not give adequate consideration to fourteen appropriation bills. The legislative committees might even become fiscally conservative if they were granted the responsibility to appropriate funds. A higher level of interest in budget matters would be elicited from all senators, and it would be a convenience for witnesses to deal with only one committee rather than to divide their efforts between a legislative and an appropriations committee. These were the rational arguments, but a more basic motive for the Dubois resolution

9. *Congressional Record*, Vol. 28, Pt. 1, 54 Cong. 1 sess. (Dec. 11, 1895), p. 132.

was voiced by a southern senator who hailed the attempt "to change the distribution of power in the Senate, to emancipate the Senate from the monopolistic dominance of about 20 men here who compose the two leading committees, those of Appropriations and Finance. . . . There is too much power lodged in one committee. . . ."[10] Combined with the desire to divide the power of Senate Appropriations was the dissatisfaction with the lack of representation on the committee of all sections of the country. Virginia's senior senator argued: "There is not a single Senator from the Maryland line to the Rio Grande upon the Appropriations Committee. There is not a single Senator from a cotton State . . . upon the Committee on Appropriations."[11]

Appropriations Chairman Allison, Finance Chairman Nelson W. Aldrich of Rhode Island, and a handful of other senior Republicans who comprised the Republican leadership, sought to beat back the maverick uprising. The principal argument against dispersal was that only a single committee could keep in view the condition of the federal treasury and the aggregate of all appropriations. In fact, Chairman Allison argued that Appropriations was not strong enough. He suggested that both the revenue and appropriation functions should be under one committee—as they had been prior to 1867. Appropriations senators were particularly disturbed by the seeming piety of their legislative detractors and, admitting some excesses, predicted that the legislative committees would also railroad through legislation on appropriation bills once they gained control of them. Countering the objection that their committee was too small, Appropriations senators questioned whether turning appropriation bills over to an even smaller "junta" on the various legislative committees was a reform. Certainly, they argued, such a dispersion of bills would not enhance state representation, since it was impossible for all states to be represented on each committee. Resorting to some piety of their own, they observed that appropriation bills were not to be a mere grab bag for each state and protested that the legislative committees would be too liberal in granting appropriations. Appropriations members also believed a great deal of experience would be lost by the Dubois rearrangement without any increased speed in handling appropriation bills. And they pleaded that only a single committee would not have prejudices for or against any department.

10. *Ibid.*, Vol. 28, Pt. 2 (Feb. 4, 1896), p. 1288.
11. *Ibid.*, p. 1329.

Despite the seeming willingness of the Senate to accept the Dubois resolution, by the fourth day of debate Appropriations members had gained sufficient strength to postpone impending disaster. On February 4, Dubois had won the initial two roll calls—refusing to take up the deficiency appropriation bill and agreeing to take up his resolution—by 44 to 25 and 49 to 24 respectively. But two days later, Dubois lost the crucial motion to adjourn by a vote of 34 to 29. On February 7, confusion occurred in Dubois' ranks over another motion to adjourn, with his followers voting both ways. Then, a motion to instruct the Rules Committee to report the Dubois resolution back favorably was lost by a vote of 39 to 29, and, finally, the Dubois resolution was referred to Rules by a vote of 40 to 28. As Republican Senator Joseph R. Hawley of Connecticut had noted on February 6, "every solitary" member of Rules was opposed to the Dubois proposal. Dubois, a first term senator, was simply outgeneraled on the floor by old hands such as Aldrich and Allison.[12]

When the proposal was finally adopted three years later, Dubois was no longer in the Senate. It was recommended by the Committee on Rules, considered by unanimous consent, and agreed to without debate.[13] And thus the power of the Committee on Appropriations was effectively contained.

The Reconsolidation of the Committee

With the enactment of the Budget and Accounting Act of 1921, which eliminated a hodgepodge of federal budgetary procedures and established a national budget, new titles were devised for the regular appropriation bills. The resulting consolidation once again brought before the Senate the issue of who should handle appropriation bills—a single committee or diverse legislative committees. (The House had changed its rules to give appropriations jurisdiction to a single com-

---

12. Length of Senate service was the only characteristic distinguishing between Dubois' supporters and opponents. The average service of those who supported Dubois on the final roll call on Feb. 7, 1896, was slightly over 3.6 years. Dubois' opponents averaged 10.5 years of Senate service, as did those who did not vote.

13. Neither Dubois' papers, books on the period, nor the *Congressional Record* has revealed any reason why there was no longer any opposition. Beginning Dec. 4, 1899, the appropriation bills for rivers and harbors, agriculture, the Army, the Military Academy, Indians, the Navy, pensions, and Post Offices were referred to their respective legislative committees. In July 1919, the Senate agreed to refer appropriations for the diplomatic and consular services to the Committee on Foreign Relations.

mittee before passage of the budget law.) Early in 1922, shortly after the new bill categories were adopted by House Appropriations, Republican Senator Francis E. Warren of Wyoming, chairman of Senate Appropriations, placed the matter before his colleagues. Declaring that implementation of the budget law would be incomplete if a single committee did not review appropriation measures, and that the dispersal of bills had cost the nation "unnecessarily many millions of dollars," Warren offered a solution:

> Undoubtedly the correct way—in fact, the only correct way—of working out the greatest success under the budget plan would seem to be for all appropriation bills to be built up carefully by the various subcommittees and passed upon finally by the one main full committee; and it is also undoubtedly true, in the event this course should be followed, that there could be drawn and added to the main committee members from the other committees, experienced in appropriations, thus enlarging to some extent the general Appropriations Committee.

Warren submitted an amendment to Rule 26 of the Standing Rules of the Senate to provide that "all general appropriation bills shall be referred to the Committee on Appropriations."[14]

The Committee on Rules recommended acceptance of the Warren resolution on February 15, 1922, on the ground that this change was in line with the purposes of the Budget and Accounting Act—and that the House of Representatives had already so acted. The committee, however, had amended the resolution to provide for ex officio members to serve on the Committee on Appropriations "when the appropriation bills affecting their respective committees are being considered." Ex officio members were to come from the Agriculture, Commerce (for rivers and harbors items), Foreign Relations (for diplomatic and consular matters), Military Affairs, Naval Affairs, and Post Office Committees. Indian Affairs and Pensions, which had reported appropriation bills since 1899, and on occasion even before, were not included. Their bills had been merged in the new Interior bill. The resolution prohibited Appropriations from reporting any new or general legislation in an appropriation bill "so that the various committees which have heretofore handled appropriation bills will not be deprived of their right to initiate and consider legislation. . . ."[15]

14. *Congressional Record,* Vol. 62, Pt. 2, 67 Cong. 2 sess. (Jan. 18, 1922), pp. 1322, 1325.

15. *Reference of General Appropriation Bills,* Report to accompany S. Res. 213, S. Rept. 498, 67 Cong. 2 sess. (Feb. 15, 1922), p. 2.

A six-day debate on the issue began March 1. Those favoring consolidation reiterated their view that unification was the only way to carry out the intent of the Budget and Accounting Act. If the rules remained unchanged, an appropriation bill such as that of the War Department would have to be divided and parts sent to three separate committees for consideration, with resultant problems in the Senate and in conference. Opponents and doubters were reassured that they need not fear a loss of power since the Committee on Appropriations would be prohibited from legislating. Besides, senators could amend any bill on the floor of the Senate. Rules Chairman Charles Curtis of Kansas, who was also Appropriations' fourth-ranking Republican, exhibited a degree of wishful thinking in explaining the role of ex officio members. They would "no doubt, have almost complete, if not complete, charge of the appropriations for their respective committees," he held, while serving on Appropriations. The chairman added that the Committee on Rules preferred to add ex officio members for particular bills rather "than to increase the membership of the Committee on Appropriations, say, to 25 or 26" from the sixteen senators it had in 1922.[16]

Those opposed to consolidation objected to diminishing the power of the sixty-four senators who were involved in the Senate appropriations process by virtue of their membership on certain legislative committees that had jurisdiction over particular appropriation bills. Mississippi Democrat Pat Harrison, the principal opponent of any change in the rules, rejected any shift of rivers and harbors appropriations away from Commerce to Appropriations. It would be taking power from a committee "composed of liberal-minded men in favor of river and harbor appropriations" and putting it "into the hands of a committee who would be for squeezing the very life out of those appropriations and cutting them to the bone."[17] Oregon Republican Charles L. McNary, a rising power on both Agriculture and Commerce, protested the loss of expertise that such a consolidation would bring about. Arguments against House dictation of Senate procedures were also heard. So was criticism of the lack of widespread representation on Appropriations.

Over several days, as a result of numerous divisions and roll calls, the final form of the rules change was hammered out. An amendment

16. *Congressional Record,* Vol. 62, Pt. 3, 67 Cong. 2 sess. (March 1, 1922), p. 3200.
17. *Ibid.,* Vol. 62, Pt. 4 (March 2, 1922), p. 3280.

was adopted providing that at least one of the three ex officio members would be a member of any conference committee appointed to confer with the House on a particular bill. Also agreed to was an amendment subjecting appropriation bills to a point of order if new or general legislation were proposed. House-approved bills containing legislation that were being reported out of Appropriations were not subject to this provision. Another amendment was accepted granting ex officio membership to the Committee on the District of Columbia. After a roll call defeating an attempt to specify that one of the three ex officio members must represent the minority party, it was decided that the members of the legislative committee, not the chairman, would select the ex officio members. On March 6, after rejecting an effort to eliminate the ex officio membership provision, the Senate overwhelmingly approved the rules changes by a vote of 63 to 14.

Since 1922, several attempts have been made to expand ex officio membership, but only two have been successful. In February 1951, ex officio membership was extended to the Senate members of the Joint Committee on Atomic Energy for consideration of the annual bill making appropriations for developing and utilizing atomic energy. In July 1958, the Committee on Aeronautical and Space Sciences was granted ex officio membership.

The Role of the ex Officio Member

Senator Curtis' claim that ex officio members would have "almost complete . . . charge" of the appropriations in their particular area once the Senate established a consolidated Committee on Appropriations proved to be only partially correct, even in the short run. Between 1922 and 1926 the ex officio members of several subcommittees were integrated with the regular members on the basis of seniority. From 1922 to 1933 the Agricultural Subcommittee was chaired by the senior ex officio member from Agriculture and Forestry and the War Department Subcommittee by the chairman and senior ex officio member from Military Affairs. In addition the chairman of Naval Affairs, who was ranking member of Appropriations, presided over the Naval Subcommittee. When the Democrats assumed control of Congress in 1933, however, all of this was changed. No longer did any ex officio members preside over Appropriations subcommittees.

As an examination of ex officio membership in the period 1965–66 shows, while most present-day ex officio members feel free to participate fully in the hearings and markup session of the annual appropriation bill to which they are assigned, their influence and acceptance on the subcommittees vary considerably. One active member of Appropriations—formerly ex officio from a legislative committee—commented: "I don't believe the ex officio system has worked out too well on the whole. I don't lend much weight to what ex officio members say. I look more to the regular members of the committee. On crucial votes, however, ex officio members could be and have been the balance of power in a markup session."

Members of Appropriations and their staffs note that unless the subject under consideration is controversial ex officio senators do not participate as often as they might. In 1965, of the twenty-four legislative committee members filling the twenty-seven ex officio positions on Appropriations, only fourteen appeared at any of the hearings to which they were assigned. Like all senators, ex officio members have only a limited amount of time they can give to their assignment. On the whole, however, those who do show up for both hearings and executive sessions believe that their views are respected. They know that their acceptance, as in regular committees, is directly related to their colleagues' estimate of their diligence and expertise.

Some ex officio members have pointed out that the authorization process is a loose one and the legislative committees are more concerned with general criteria than with establishing particular program or state priorities. For these senators the opportunity to participate in the appropriations process is invaluable in providing them with an insight into—and an oversight of—the implementation of the programs that their legislative committees have authorized. For instance, Democrat Allen J. Ellender of Louisiana, the chairman of the Senate Committee on Agriculture and Forestry, while a regular member of Senate Appropriations and serving as such on six subcommittees, uses his ex officio membership on a seventh, the Agricultural Appropriations Subcommittee, to oversee numerous domestic and international farm programs approved by his legislative committee.

Nonetheless some members feel that this justification of ex officio participation—one of the original arguments in its favor—has been eliminated by the overlapping memberships between Appropriations and the various legislative committees. Unlike House Appropriations, where with rare exceptions members serve only on that one major committee, all members of Senate Appropriations have other major assignments. In 1966 almost half served on two other committees; eight of the eighteen Democrats were chairmen of legislative committees; one was vice-chairman (chairman in alternating Congresses) of the Joint Committee on Atomic Energy; and five of the nine Republicans were the ranking minority members on various legislative committees. In addition, no member was on less than five Appropriations subcommittees, fifteen of the twenty-seven senators were assigned to six, two to seven, and one (Russell) to eight.[18] It is hard to escape the conclusion that in recent years the interests of the legislative committees have in fact been represented on Appropriations more through overlapping memberships than through the structural device of ex officio memberships.[19]

The Staff System

Since senators are limited by their multiple assignments in the amount of time they can give to Appropriations matters, the staff of the committee performs a substantial role in its operations. How the staff has evolved, especially in the period following the Second World War, provides some understanding of the effectiveness with which the committee has sought to fulfill its responsibilities.

Gradual Staff Growth and Increasing Professionalism

Each year budget requests have grown progressively larger and authorizing legislation more complex, while the time available for analyzing them has stayed the same. Despite this, the staff of the Senate Committee on Appropriations has continued to be relatively small. Indeed, Appropriations throughout its history has been undermanned. From a single clerk in its early years, and a chief clerk, one assistant, and a messenger during the 1890s and early 1900s, the staff evolved until by 1966 it included twenty-four professionals with a supporting clerical group of ten. Even then, however, compared with the professional staff of the legislative committees, of House Appropriations, and of the vari-

18. Members of House Appropriations also have fewer subcommittee assignments. In 1966 only four of the thirty-four Democrats on the House committee were assigned to three subcommittees. Half of the Democrats were assigned to two, as were three-fourths of the Republicans. The rest were on only one subcommittee.

19. This point may be illustrated for the period 1965–66, for example, by a comparison of data on ex officio members in Table 2–4, p. 51, with the data in Appendix A on the legislative and Appropriations responsibilities of the regular members.

ous offices within the executive branch, the committee was understaffed. But up to 1947, and including the period of the Second World War when the budget first reached $100 billion, there were only four or so professional staff members, although during the war additional staff were borrowed from the General Accounting Office and the Federal Bureau of Investigation to help with specific studies. Everard H. Smith, who was appointed to the staff in 1913 and retired as chief clerk fifty-three years later in 1965, one principal assistant, and a few other staff members handled all of the administrative detail for all of the bills.

The turning point in the development of the professional staff was the Legislative Reorganization Act of 1946 and the return to power of the Republicans, who in 1947 assumed control of both houses for the first time in sixteen years. The Reorganization Act sought to streamline the legislative branch in an attempt to keep pace with an ever expanding federal bureaucracy. It brought about a simplification of committee procedures, a reduction in the number of standing committees, and a recognition of the need for a truly professional committee staff. Section 202 (a) of the act provided for the appointment of "not more than four professional staff members" on each standing committee "on a permanent basis without regard to political affiliations and solely on the basis of fitness to perform the duties of the office." The Appropriations Committees, however, were exempted from this four-man limitation and were authorized to hire as many as each chamber would permit in approving the annual legislative appropriation bill.[20]

The implementation of the 1946 act fell on Senator Styles Bridges, who as a result of Republican control of the Eightieth Congress was the new chairman of Appropriations. Bridges, a skilled politician who dominated the Republican party in his native New Hampshire, was a

20. 60 Stat. 834. The Joint Committee on the Organization of Congress had recommended that "the full committee and each subcommittee of the Appropriations Committees of the two Houses be given 4 expertly trained staff assistants. . . . Two would be assigned to the chairman of the appropriations subcommittee and two to the ranking minority member to aid them in careful study and scrutiny of budget requests with a view to reducing any unnecessary expenditures." *Organization of the Congress,* Report of the Joint Committee on the Organization of Congress, S. Rept. 1011, 79 Cong. 2 sess. (March 4, 1946), p. 21. The Senate approved the Legislative Reorganization bill (S. 2177) with this staffing provision by a vote of 49 to 16 in June 1946. In the House it was a different story. House Appropriations Chairman Cannon objected to the staffing provision and offered a substitute, which was accepted without a fight in July and became Section 202 (b) of the final bill. The Cannon language left the staffing determination up to each Appropriations Committee.

master of legislative intrigue and an avid partisan in Senate debate. Yet as chairman he was determined to establish a dedicated professional staff—separate from an administrative staff responsible for scheduling the hearings and assembling the committee report and bill—that could study the executive requests in depth and analyze budgets. He wanted thorough research and detailed investigation of executive activities. "Bridges operated on the premise," said a veteran staff man, "that in a government this big there must be something wrong and the staff's task was to find out what it is." The chairman set out to build the requisite staff. In doing so, he followed the model already established by House Appropriations.

THE HOUSE APPROPRIATIONS MODEL. After consultation with FBI Director J. Edgar Hoover during the Second World War, House Appropriations arranged to borrow, on a rotating basis, one or two key FBI investigators to head its investigations staff. These men in turn were to borrow additional executive personnel as needed for specific inquiries. Employees from one part of the executive branch were to be on loan to investigate another part of the executive branch. In 1946, Robert E. Lee, a veteran of ten years of service with the FBI, was brought in to serve as chief of the investigative staff.

When Republican John Taber of New York became chairman of House Appropriations in the Eightieth Congress, Lee received authorization to "research" government programs "from top to bottom" rather than merely to investigate isolated abuses (although the Republicans were not above hoping for a few of the latter during the Truman administration). Suspicious of personnel recruited from an executive establishment they had not controlled since early in 1933, the Republicans organized task forces made up of personnel from the General Accounting Office and accountants, analysts, and auditors on loan from industry. The American Institute of Accountants, for example, established a special ten-man group to work with the committee. Retired management experts from major corporations such as American Telephone and Telegraph and Standard Oil of California were brought in for brief periods. At times there were as many as thirty temporary consultants from private industry. Major studies were completed, including a nine-state review of the practices of the Public Housing Administration, an examination of the United States Employment Service, a detailed analysis of the methods and organization of the Bureau of Internal Revenue, plus studies of the Department of Agriculture, the Alaskan Government, Army procurement, the Department of the Interior, the Maritime Commission, the Departments of Navy, State, and Treasury, the Veterans Administration, the War Assets Administration, and other agencies.[21]

Before a team was sent downtown, Lee obtained authorization from the chairman and ranking minority member of both the full committee and the subcommittee and met with the agency head. Usually office space was provided by the agency. After from one to four months' work, the task force study was submitted to Lee, who would review it and forward it to his superiors. The team might then appear before the responsible subcommittee to respond to questions. Specific recommendations for cuts were made if the facts seemed to justify such action. Since Lee cooperated closely with Bridges and his staff, the report was also given to the appropriate Senate subcommittee and sometimes a joint meeting was held. Occasionally, the Senate staff also participated in the agency study.

Cannon, as ranking minority member on House Appropriations, was not pleased with the activism demonstrated by the majority's investigative staff and the influx of part-time industrial consultants. He accused the Republicans of displacing "the nonpartisan investigators used by the Committee on Appropriations up to the opening of the Eightieth Congress."[22] When Cannon became chairman again in 1949, he quickly changed the Taber-Lee procedures. Disbanding the permanent investigative staff, he returned to using specialist personnel as needed from the executive branch, with the staff director on rotation from the FBI. Republicans objected that such a system was likely to result in a whitewash of one part of the executive establishment by another. Cannon countered that his own system was economical, obtained those persons best qualified for a particular study, and provided "no opportunities to establish cordial relations" with the bureaus under investigation.

Before resigning as staff director, Lee had several meetings with Cannon. He opposed the rotating investigator system. Lee believed

21. In noting some of these studies in the House of Representatives on February 15, 1949, Republican Richard B. Wigglesworth of Massachusetts stated that "the over-all result was that the committee was able to effect savings or rescissions . . . of some $9,800,000,000 in 2 years. . . ." *Congressional Record*, Vol. 95, Pt. 1, 81 Cong. 1 sess. (Feb. 15, 1949), p. 1223.

22. *Ibid.*, Vol. 93, Pt. 6, 80 Cong. 1 sess. (June 27, 1947), p. 7831.

that constantly changing investigators would prevent the committee from building its own expertise and performing "real research" in various program areas. In addition, he was convinced that the agencies would not release their best investigators for the job and that the men who came over encountered hardships in securing promotions once they returned to their agencies. Cannon, who was fond of Lee, wanted him to stay on as chief of staff but without his regular investigative staff. Lee refused, becoming minority clerk instead.[23]

THE BRIDGES STAFF. On the Senate committee, Bridges followed Lee's approach. He recruited college graduates who had research or investigative experience in business, state, or local groups including taxpayers leagues and chambers of commerce. The staff was split into administrative and professional components. Under Chief Clerk Everard Smith, a small group handled the traditional administrative details related to appropriation bills. This group personified, as one participant at the time expressed it, "the old school which did the clerical work at the edge of the table and which had been taught that the decisions were to be made by the members themselves."

The "new school" was represented by Dr. Leslie M. Gravlin, whom Bridges made "Chief, Professional Staff" in the first session of the Eightieth Congress, and Dr. Thomas J. Graves, Gravlin's successor in the second session. Gravlin was recruited from the Hartford, Connecticut, Chamber of Commerce. After a year with the committee, he returned to his former employment. Graves, with a Princeton doctorate, had been slated to be director of the research bureau for the Pennsylvania State Chamber of Commerce in Harrisburg. But after serving briefly on loan to Lee's House Appropriations staff, he was recommended to Bridges, who hired him without asking his politics.

The two directors wanted staff members with government experience who could examine the numerous executive programs. But they had

23. In 1953, with the Republicans in control, Lee again headed the investigative staff as director of surveys and investigations. Besides five regular investigators, he used thirty-four part-time consultants (including two future directors of the budget, Rowland R. Hughes and Maurice H. Stans). He also borrowed twenty-four investigators from fourteen executive agencies that were now under Republican control. On Oct. 6, 1953, President Eisenhower appointed Lee to the Federal Communications Commission, where he continued to serve under both Presidents Kennedy and Johnson. For the affiliations of some of the private consultants Lee used in 1953, see *Congressional Record*, Vol. 99, Pt. 8, 83 Cong. 1 sess. (July 29, 1953), p. 10341.

difficulty finding such personnel because they were uncertain of the sympathies of those employed by the New Deal–Fair Deal agencies. Eventually ten to twelve men were added to the professional staff, mostly from the business community. Another dozen part-time consultants were brought in for short periods from national and state taxpayer-research organizations. Most of those hired were "determined to cut costs," as one put it. Staff studies and recommendations based on an evaluation of administration programs and proposals were offered. For some of the veteran senators and staff members, these recommendations appeared to be a substitution for committee judgment and decision. Although the new professionals denied that this was their intent, they defended their recommendations when called upon to do so in an executive session. "Their goal," a staff member at the time recalled, "was simply to gather information on a given situation and to provide it in an intelligible form."

Friction existed between the traditional staff under the chief clerk and the new professional staff. This was not unique to Appropriations, however, since it existed in varying degrees on most congressional committee staffs as part of the growing pains connected with implementation of the Legislative Reorganization Act.

DEMOCRATIC CONTROL—A MERGER OF TRADITIONALISM AND PROFESSIONALISM. The Senate and the committee returned to Democratic control in 1949. Neither McKellar, who again was chairman, nor Carl Hayden, the ranking Democrat behind McKellar, cared for investigations—especially of a Democratic administration—and the professional staff as a separate entity was abolished. Both administrative and substantive functions were combined in a single professional staff member, the subcommittee clerk, who was assigned to, and held responsible for, a particular appropriation bill. That pattern has continued, although when Bridges was chairman again in the Eighty-third Congress (1953–54), he brought in another staff director and once more expanded the investigations group. But the combined administrative and substantive functions remained with the subcommittee clerks.

In 1966, the staff was headed by a chief clerk and an assistant chief clerk. There was also an assistant clerk, a special counsel, and sixteen professional staff members for the majority, as well as a special staff for the minority that included a minority counsel and three professional staff members. The minority staff was set up by Leverett Saltonstall in 1961, when he became ranking Republican upon Bridges' death. While Bridges might have favored professionalism for the regular committee staff, he regarded the minority staff as his private fiefdom with several members working in his office rather than serving the committee. Saltonstall sought a minority staff that would be helpful to all Republican senators.

The committee staff, whether appointed by Democrats or Republicans, has always prided itself on being nonpartisan and professional. As one able staff member noted in 1966, "Most of us don't think of ourselves as members of the 'majority' staff. In fact I do far more work for the ranking Republican on my subcommittee than I do for the chairman and the Democratic members." Said another, "A Republican gets information just as fast as a Democratic senator—and I keep track of his interests just as much as I do those of a Democrat." This nonpartisanship is epitomized in the close working relations that exist between the regular committee staff and the minority staff.

The committee has had only seven chief clerks since its establishment in 1867. The seventh and current chief clerk, Thomas J. Scott, was officially appointed on January 1, 1966, although he had been managing the staff informally for more than a decade. Three of the seven chief clerks served for periods of thirty-seven years, twenty-seven years, and twenty-six years.[24] The tenure of these men, and their continuity regardless of the party in power, symbolize the professionalism and nonpartisanship that has been a tradition for the staff as a whole. It is a professionalism of stable tenure and acquired expertise rather than a professionalism one can be taught before joining the committee.[25]

STAFF BACKGROUND. Capitol Hill, unlike the executive branch and much of American industry, uses no achievement or personality tests, no personnel counselors or career advisers to bring the prospective

24. House Appropriations has had a similar record of continuity for its chief clerk. Between 1865 and 1941, it had twenty-one chairmen but only three chief clerks. Edward T. Taylor, *A History of the Committee on Appropriations, House of Representatives* (Government Printing Office, 1941), p. 15.

25. Writing during the Second World War, political scientist Arthur W. Macmahon noted that the Senate and House Appropriations Committees and the Joint Committee on Internal Revenue Taxation had "for many years provided an expert, stable personnel for committee work." With regard to Appropriations, "the smallness of the staff," continued Macmahon, "was offset by its continuity and experience." Macmahon, "Congressional Oversight of Administration: The Power of the Purse," *Political Science Quarterly*, Vol. 58 (June 1943), pp. 181–82.

office or committee staff recruit together with his potential employer. Access to a particular senator or representative and availability when a job opportunity beckons are the initial means.

Of the twenty-two professional staff members in 1966 (including the four on the minority staff) who had substantive, as opposed to editorial, responsibilities on particular appropriation bills, eleven had worked in some part of the legislative branch prior to their appointment. Two of them had been borrowed from the General Accounting Office during the Second World War and had stayed. Five had been with other Senate committees, including such nonlegislative groups as the Republican Policy Committee and the Democratic Senatorial Campaign Committee. And four had first worked in the office of the senator who was responsible for their placement on the committee.

Four others of the twenty-two had had extensive prior experience in various departments of the executive branch. The remaining seven staff members had come directly from private life, having had either direct or indirect contact with the senator responsible for their appointment. Their positions prior to joining the staff ranged from fledgling lawyer to director for nineteen years of the annual federal budget study prepared by the National Association of Manufacturers.

Although a few of the twenty-two professional staff members had received their training in "the school of hard knocks," most had completed their undergraduate education. Half of them had undertaken some graduate work; five were lawyers and two were Ph.D. candidates who had long since given up writing a doctoral dissertation while working in Washington (the city of unwritten dissertations). One was both a lawyer and a certified public accountant. Staff members differed over the preparation they thought was most helpful. Several who were neither lawyers nor accountants felt that both specialties would have been useful to them. A few others, however, argued that the fundamentals of accounting could be acquired on the job and that most important were investigative experience and work in the executive branch, preferably in the department whose budget was supervised. Particularly valuable, they explained, was an understanding of budget preparation and the program-planning processes in a department. Regardless of their background, their senators almost without exception held their work in high regard. Democratic and Republican committee members alike described the staff as "excellent," "very competent," and "well equipped."

The Work of the Staff

The degree to which a particular budget is scrutinized is directly dependent on the quality of staff work and, eventually, the willingness of the chairman and other members of the subcommittee to use what the staff has done. Different subcommittee chairmen seek various things from their professional staff. Some rely extensively on them to prepare hundreds of specific questions for use in examining executive witnesses. Others merely ask for background memoranda and formulate the questions themselves as they "feel their way along" during a hearing. Subcommittee chairmen such as Richard B. Russell do not need endless briefings on the agencies for which they are responsible. Over the years they have picked up the relevant information. Staff-prepared background material may trigger their memory, but the questions are usually their own. Generally the questions and memoranda prepared by the staff are for the subcommittee chairman or, if prepared by the minority staff, for the ranking Republican. When other subcommittee members request it, the staff also assists them, although the junior members in both parties are largely left to fend for themselves. Most subcommittee chairmen have excellent working relations with their minority counterparts and share staff work with them.

The staff member looks to a variety of sources in meeting his chairman's needs. Each day federal agencies put out press releases favorably noting their own activities. (A staff member can compare what is said in these releases with what should have been said to accord with agency testimony and committee action: "We appropriated for six nuclear subs; yet here Defense announces that it is contracting only for five. Why?") Agency task forces, advisory committees, and study groups submit reports to cabinet officers and the President. Reporters cover the Washington bureaucracy daily. Technical journals and specialty magazines publish feature stories. Career civil servants write and give speeches to lay groups throughout the country. Papers are read at professional and scientific meetings. The comptroller general submits reports to Congress prepared by the expert staff of the General Accounting Office on particular aspects of executive maladministration. Background briefings are given by departmental personnel—trips to the field, slides, movies. The staff members of the Senate Committee on Appropriations rely on all these and many other sources of information in their attempt to discern how an executive program has been carried out and the alternatives that are involved.

In this information gathering process, scholarly works have little effect since they are usually written after the fact and the staff and committee members are concerned about the future more than they are about the past. Similarly of little value are the numerous annual reports prepared by the departments and agencies; they lack currency and deal in generalities. Also seldom used are the more general and speculative committee studies such as those prepared by the Joint Economic Committee.

Basic to staff analysis, however, are the annual "subcommittee prints" for each appropriation bill prepared by the House Committee on Appropriations, and the justifications submitted by the individual departments and agencies to back up their requests for funds. The *Subcommittee Print on the Department of Defense Appropriation Bill for 1967*, for example, totaled 243 pages and contained numerous tables comparing, title by title, the appropriations for fiscal year 1966, including supplementals, and the budget estimate for fiscal year 1967. Following the language of each section of the proposed appropriation bill were supporting tables and narrative statements. The departmental justifications are in even greater detail. The Department of Defense justifications for fiscal 1966 came to over 3700 pages and included analysis, narrative description, and supporting tables for each program, as well as a breakdown of appropriations by activities (pay and allowances of officers, pay and allowances of enlisted personnel, permanent change of station travel, and so on), by financing (receipts and reimbursements from administrative budget accounts, trust fund accounts, nonfederal sources, and so on; the new obligational authority sought; and the relation of obligations to expenditures), and by object (personnel compensation, personnel benefits, travel and transportation, supplies and materials, and so on).

A review of the hearings of the House Appropriations Committee also is basic to a Senate staff member's preparation. So are the relevant authorization hearings of the various legislative committees. Occasionally the staff of a legislative committee is consulted but not as much mutual exchange takes place as perhaps should. Except for the Defense and Military Construction appropriation bills, for which there is a close liaison between the Senate Committee on Armed Services and the two Appropriations subcommittees because of joint authorization hearings, few professional staff members from legislative committees regularly attend appropriations sessions.

Of considerable importance to the staff is the prepared statement of the principal executive witness at a hearing. This statement usually opens the hearing and therefore provides the witness with the opportunity to guide the direction of the committee's attention. Staff members attempt to secure these statements at least three days in advance so they will have time to analyze them and to brief the chairman and other interested members with supplementary background material.

In addition to all the written sources, each staff member has official and unofficial personal contacts throughout the department or agency for which he is responsible. The official contact is usually the budget director, comptroller, or an assistant or deputy assistant secretary for administration. This official is backed up by a budget liaison staff whose aim is to respond rapidly to an inquiry from those on the Appropriations Committees of either house. Most of these officials are at the top of the career civil service. Some have held their positions for a decade or more, and they are experienced and shrewd in the ways of Capitol Hill. They have seen administrations and cabinet officers come and go while they and many of the bureau chiefs remain.

The unofficial contacts range from the cabinet-level appointee who is an old friend to the summer intern from the home town. Primarily they consist of the program managers and specialists who year in and year out fulfill the agency's mission. Sometimes in a situation in which a political appointee is saying one thing while the agency—in the career bureaucracy sense—is doing or wants to do another, these career men may tip off their friends on the committee staff. On other occasions, when a middle management official is involved in an internecine bureaucratic war, he often provides inside information "to get the other side." The availability of inside information varies from agency to agency depending on the leadership skills of the top management, employee morale, and the differences that exist between the ideological commitments of the career personnel, outside pressure groups, and the political appointees.

Operating Problems

To review even summarily much of the available information would be an endless task. Staff members, like their senators, pick their way among the relevant and the irrelevant and the high priority and the low priority. Sensitive antennae are required to discern their chairman's needs and what is likely to arouse subcommittee interest. The staff members need access to the subcommittee chairmen—and not merely in a crisis period or immediately before the hearings.

But time is a most precious commodity. A senator's day includes a seemingly endless schedule that mixes the social, political, legislative, and administrative in one grand potpourri. After surmounting the hurdle of this hectic schedule, the professional staff member still has to get past the senator's own barriers. As one put it, "I have to figure out what the senator's absorption rate is and weigh, in the time allowed, what I consider the most important thing to say to him which will be helpful."

Not all professional staff members deal directly with their subcommittee chairman or the senators on their subcommittees throughout the year. Over time an attempt is usually made to establish a working relationship with the appropriate people in the senatorial office who have the member's ear on a day-to-day basis. There are several difficulties in establishing such a relationship, however. A senator is surrounded by office assistants eager to learn the latest baronial whim and to filter the calls on his time and attention. As one professional staff member noted:

> The biggest problem you have is in dealing with the member to whom you bear the responsibility. You can't go through his administrative or legislative assistant. You have got to get the member's ear. Invariably you incur the ill will of the administrative assistant or legislative assistant because of this. Some are real ornery in maintaining the strength of their position around the senator.

Frequently the office assistant is convinced that there is no real need for a committee professional to bring a report to the senator: "He is just doing it to curry the senator's favor and let him know he is around." The traditional office-committee rivalry reflected in this attitude has another source, too. The harassed office assistant, often working late into the evenings and on weekends, is well aware that his committee counterpart usually has a normal eight-hour day except during crisis periods.

Another cause of strain between the office and committee staffs is the rule denying senators' legislative assistants access to the markup sessions held on the Defense appropriation bill and, beginning in 1965, on the foreign aid bill, even though they have been cleared for top secret information. The committee's regular and minority staff members, however, do attend. The subcommittee member's legislative assistant may have spent months going to hearings, meeting with agency officials, and reviewing bundles of material only to be denied access to his member in the crucial markup session when he is most needed. The argument of those who have imposed the rule is "the fewer people present, the fewer opportunities for a leak." But, as the committee staff recalls, the information leaks that have occurred have been made by senators. "We can't do anything about the members, but if someone on the Appropriations staff gives out information, he can be fired. On the other hand, we can't fire a man from a senator's office who gives out information." Some legislative assistants, however, are convinced that the rule has been imposed partly to maintain the subcommittee chairman's control and his monopoly of knowledge in markup sessions.

Probably the principal source of the difficulties in office-committee staff communication is the small number of legislative assistants who actually devote as much as a fourth of their time to appropriations matters. Most committee members—like most senators—assign the appropriations work in their office to a case worker or a press secretary who, as time allows, keeps track of bills, answers constituent letters, and occasionally issues a press release when an appropriation is made to fund some project in the home state.

In attempting to meet subcommittee needs the staff is affected by other organizational situations as well. Just as there is no coordination of the committee members by the chairman, there is no coordination of the staff by the chief clerk. "Each staff member," remarked one, "is expected to run his own show." Most professional staff members in 1966 were pleased that the staff was run in a loose manner. One who had witnessed what excessive centralized control could do within the executive branch said with pride: "There is a lot of autonomy when you're on this staff. In the executive branch I always had a superior. Here you operate on your own responsibility and you operate on the basis of feeling what is acceptable. Downtown you have the manual to refer to and guide you. Here it is osmosis, tradition, and precedent." A few staff members, however, and several of the senior senators on the committee objected to the looseness of the staff organization and the failure to hold any staff meetings to examine the budget as a whole.[26]

26. In no other area is the lack of chairman-chief clerk coordination more evident

The situation that perhaps most affects the nature and performance of the staff's work is the simple lack of manpower. This is most evident, of course, for the minority staff. During the 1965–66 period, for example, one minority staff member was responsible for the $46.7 billion Defense bill, the $1.7 billion military construction bill, over $10 billion in supplementals, and the $190 million legislative bill. Another minority professional was assigned to the $3.9 billion foreign aid bill, the $14.2 billion independent offices bill, and the $7.6 billion Treasury–Post Office bill. Many of the hearings occurred at the same time. With such minimal staffing, housekeeping tasks were performed but not much else. Intensive program review and field investigation seldom occurred except on a haphazard basis.

Despite the much larger size of the regular staff, most committee members believe that it, too, is understaffed and overworked. As one subcommittee chairman observed in 1966:

> The staff is fine as far as the work they do—but it is primarily housekeeping. Each subcommittee has one professional staff member but they cannot really do the checking that needs to be done. None of the staff ever seem to go down into an agency. I don't think it is the failure of the chairman or the subcommittee chairmen. I think it is the failure of the whole Congress for not providing the staff that it needs to do the job which must be done.

* * *

The aspirations that a member of Appropriations brings to his assignment must be tempered by the realities of the organizational

than in the haphazard and infrequent foreign and domestic travel undertaken by both members and staff. Domestic travel information is unavailable, but foreign travel is illustrative. In calendar year 1965 only eight of the twenty-seven senators on Senate Appropriations traveled abroad at government expense. Only two of the eight—Hayden and Cotton—specifically traveled under Appropriations auspices. The comparable figures for House Appropriations during 1965 show that twenty-five of the fifty committee members traveled abroad at government expense, nineteen of them under Appropriations auspices. *Congressional Quarterly Weekly Report*, Vol. 24 (March 4, 1966), pp. 505–20. As revealed in the *Congressional Quarterly* survey, the travel pattern of House Appropriations was slightly above the 43.7 percent overall House average, while that of Senate Appropriations was substantially below the 53.5 percent Senate average. Four of the regular staff (three professionals and one clerical assistant) traveled abroad, as did three of the four-man minority professional staff. *Congressional Record*, Vol. 112, Pt. 5, 89 Cong. 2 sess. (March 17, 1966), pp. 6084–86. In comparison, fourteen members of the House Appropriations professional staff traveled abroad. *Ibid.*, pp. 6222–26. Some in the press have applied the term "junket" to practically all congressional travel. Sometimes the term has been correctly used. But the opportunity such visits provide for enhancing an individual's perspective is vital if Congress is to understand and evaluate executive needs.

structure. Regardless of a senator's desires, seniority largely determines subcommittee assignments, although the committee chairman can at times have a significant effect by creating new subcommittees and expanding the membership of existing ones. It is likely that a newcomer will be placed on the subcommittees considered least important by his party's committee members.

Under the laissez-faire approach of committee chairmen, and particularly of Carl Hayden, Appropriations has developed a structure of strong, independent subcommittees, each going its own way in the handling of bills and the use of staff, without overall committee coordination. Often a subcommittee is the exclusive domain of its powerful chairman and ranking minority member, with ex officio members from the relevant legislative committee only occasionally—if at all—taking an active part, and other members mostly pursuing parochial interests.

Because of this subcommittee pattern and the time limitations that multiple committee and subcommittee assignments impose on members, the professional staff occupies a key role in subcommittee operations. Indeed, some have observed that "the staff *is* the Senate Committee on Appropriations." To a limited extent this is true. Depending on his initiative and his relations with the subcommittee leaders, a staff member can largely determine the degree of scrutiny given to an agency's budget request. His work during the annual hearing is only part of his role, although it is the most obvious. Equally important is the staff member's year-round relations with the agencies under his subcommittee's jurisdiction. What information he forwards to senators and agencies and how he determines to handle it can have a marked effect on the implementation of government programs. On Appropriations, the staff serves not only as eyes and ears but as strong arm as well.

CHAPTER THREE

Committee Life: Attitudes and Practices

Court of Appeals vs. de Novo Tribunal

A common but increasingly outdated thesis of most literature on Congress is that the Senate Committee on Appropriations "has become a quasi-judicial 'court of appeals' to which the agencies and the Budget Bureau resort after undergoing the knife or meat-axe of the House Committee."[1] One scholar has written that "the Senate Committee puts a high value on having agencies carry appeals to it," because "Senators are rather painfully aware of the House Committee's pre-eminence in the field of appropriations and they know that they cannot hope to match the time and thoroughness that the House body devotes to screening requests."[2]

No topic is likely to arouse more controversy among the members and staff of the committee than whether Appropriations does, in fact, limit itself primarily to agency appeals, and whether it ought to. In 1966 half of the senators believed that Appropriations did function as a court of appeals for the decisions of the House, but half of these

1. John S. Saloma III, *The Responsible Use of Power: A Critical Analysis of the Congressional Budget Process* (American Enterprise Institute for Public Policy Research, 1964), pp. 20, 92.
2. Aaron Wildavsky, *The Politics of the Budgetary Process* (Little, Brown, 1964), p. 52.

argued that it should not.[3] Most senators thought it was "in the nature of things to act as an appellate body when you were second to get the appropriation bill," but they hastily added that they did not feel they were limited to this function. They pointed out that as senators they view an agency from a different perspective than does a member of the House: they represent a larger and more diverse constituency; their membership on various committees means that they are not limited solely to the problems or way of life of the Appropriations Committee, as House members are; they are less likely to become isolated from the concerns of fellow senators or to develop strict budget-cutting attitudes.

A senior Republican held that having "a last shot at the bill" actually gives senators a better opportunity than representatives to affect appropriations if they want to take advantage of it. Often new facts and requirements develop as the year progresses. In addition, the individual senator, since he is on more subcommittees than his House counterpart, can—if he is willing to work—get involved in more areas and potentially have a greater personal impact. An equally senior Democrat commented: "The House writes the bill behind closed doors and then under the rules it comes up in the House and before you know it, it's passed on a take it or leave it basis. Then the House members refer their constituents over here and we get the reaction. It's really a second look more than a court of appeals for the Senate committee."

Senators were conscious that on some subcommittees they do not do a thorough job of scrutinizing many agency budgets. They pleaded a lack of time and manpower. They knew House members worked hard and they respected them for it. But, as implied in the above comment, there was also a strong feeling among committee members—especially those who had served previously as representatives—that consideration by the House was also less than thorough, that many cuts were made for show only. Such practices were described as "political skulduggery," "the cheapest game in the world," "phony," and "not genuine"—to mention a few of the printable epithets. Senators recalled voting for cuts in their younger days on the other side of the Capitol and then going hat in hand to the senators from their state to beg for a restoration.

The question is not really how the full Senate Committee on Appro-

3. The response did not depend on whether the senator was a Democrat or a Republican, a member of the committee for many years or a newcomer; nor did the answer depend on the actual practice of the subcommittee to which the member devoted most of his time. Many subcommittee chairmen and ranking minority members on the same subcommittees disagreed.

priations approaches its examination of the budget. In the Senate, as in the House, independently operated subcommittees review an agency budget. Therefore the practices of each subcommittee must be examined to judge properly the merits of the "court of appeals" label. To what degree do the individual subcommittees of Senate Appropriations limit their review to the framework set by the House? The result is mixed. A few subcommittees are clearly appeal bodies in attitude and end result; most are not.

Following the Second World War, Styles Bridges, as chairman of the committee during the Republican Eightieth Congress, wanted Senate Appropriations to examine President Truman's budget de novo. There was resistance among some senior staff members, however, and despite Bridges' attempt, until the Korean war the various subcommittees did not begin their hearings until the House had passed an appropriation bill. Then, beginning with the Agriculture Subcommittee under Richard Russell's chairmanship, this practice changed substantially. Russell, like many subcommittee chairmen, was increasingly irritated by the House accusations leveled in conference that the Senate had not thoroughly reviewed an agency budget and thus could not possibly know the real financial needs involved. If hearings were scheduled ahead of House passage, however, Senate subcommittees could no longer be limited to testimony regarding the differences between the House bill and the President's budget.

Table 3-1 shows for three postwar periods the average number of days before or after House passage that the first hearing on the bill was held by the responsible Senate Appropriations subcommittee. The first two periods include the only two Republican congresses since 1945, the Eightieth in 1947-48 and the Eighty-third in 1953-54. It made little difference which party or chairman was in control of a subcommittee during any of the three periods; the scheduling of hearings before or after House passage remained essentially the same. In the four years immediately following the Second World War, no subcommittee of Senate Appropriations functioned on other than an appeals basis. Every subcommittee from 1946 through 1949 began all of its hearings after the House had acted, with a single exception in 1948, the first year of the Marshall Plan appropriation for European recovery, when Senate Appropriations began its foreign aid hearings twenty-two days prior to House passage of the bill. By the 1952-55 period, the picture had changed substantially, with a number of the subcommittees almost

Table 3-1. Court of Appeals or de Novo Tribunal: Average Number of Days before (−) or after (+) House Passage of an Appropriation Bill That the First Hearing Was Held on It by a Senate Appropriations Subcommittee during 1946–49, 1952–55, and 1962–65

Subcommittee[a]	1946–49	1952–55	1962–65	Category in 1965
Agriculture	+26.2	−32.5	−90.8	De novo
Defense	+25.3	−48.0	−80.8	De novo
Deficiencies—Supplementals	+3.5	−42.0	−13.2	De novo
District of Columbia	+16.0	+14.3	+28.3	Appeals
Foreign Operations	−4.5[b]	−5.5	−9.3	Variable
Independent Offices	+16.2	+2.3	−36.5	Variable
Interior	+12.3	−3.0	−31.5	De novo
Labor-HEW	+11.8	−44.8	−50.0	De novo
Legislative	+7.8	+19.0	+5.3	Appeals
Military Construction	—	+1.0[c]	−37.8	De novo
Public Works—Civil Functions	+11.0	−57.8	−125.0	De novo
Public Works—Reclamation–Interior Power Marketing Agencies	—	−16.0[d]	−89.3	De novo
Public Works—AEC-TVA	—	−5.0[d]	+11.5	Appeals
State-Justice	+16.8	−30.8	+4.0	Appeals
Treasury–Post Office	+20.5	−9.8[e]	+20.0	Appeals

a. Subcommittee names are those used in 1965.
b. This figure represents an average for only two of four years in the period since the first hearing on the European Recovery Program began in 1948.
c. The Senate did hold special hearings on military construction problems 120 days before House passage in 1954 and 92 days before House passage in 1955 but without reference to an appropriation bill. At that time military construction appropriations were made in the supplemental appropriation bill.
d. The year 1955 was the first in which either Reclamation–Interior Power Marketing Agencies or AEC-TVA panels were in existence as part of Public Works.
e. During the twelve years included in the table, Treasury–Post Office began hearings prior to House passage only in 1952 (−31) and 1953 (−37).

always beginning their formal hearings ahead of House passage. During the 1962–65 period, six subcommittees and two of the three Public Works panels regularly began their hearings prior to House action on their appropriation bill. Only the AEC-TVA panel of Public Works and the Treasury–Post Office Subcommittee always delayed their hearings until after House action.

Of course, the timing of a subcommittee's hearing was not always an indication of its approach. While the District of Columbia and Legislative Subcommittees usually began hearings after House passage of their bills, they were often as thorough in their examination as the House subcommittees. Although Independent Offices and State-Justice frequently held long hearings and did intensive work on some of the budgets that were before them, the members essentially limited themselves to the differences between the House bill and the President's budget estimates. Treasury–Post Office was strictly an appeals body. Its hearings were cursory at best, usually taking no more than three days. The Foreign Operations Subcommittee, then made up of all members of the full committee, occasionally undertook an extensive examination of the foreign aid program. In 1963, Senator McGee chaired a long series of hearings on the staffing and operations of the Agency for International Development (AID) and submitted a special report to the full committee.[4] But in 1965 the subcommittee functioned solely as an appeals body under the guidance of Democrat John O. Pastore of Rhode Island, acting for Chairman Hayden.

One longtime staff member, when asked his opinion of the de novo approach, replied: "If we call in the same witnesses right after the House has called them in, their testimony won't be any different from what they told the House. They don't have another story to tell the Senate." Most of the more recently appointed staff members would not agree. They pride themselves on as thorough an examination of agency budgets as the House and feel that while the more aggressive subcommittees do receive essentially the same testimony as that given the House, the opportunity is provided for senators to make independent judgments on an agency's total program.

Agency heads generally view the various Senate Appropriations subcommittees as more interested in appeals from House actions than in a thorough review—at least they hope so. They seek, if possible, to direct their testimony at the discrepancies between the President's budget and the cuts made in their program by the House, and since their statements often provide the basis for questions, senatorial attention is drawn to these differences. As a matter of course, dating from a request of Republican Senator Wesley L. Jones of Washington, chairman of Appropriations from 1930 to 1932, agencies automatically file a formal letter of appeal following House action. Most departments and agencies attempt to absorb some of the House cuts and try to concentrate their Senate plea on the highest priority items, knowing that even if the Senate agrees with them, the difference might well be split in conference. Executive witnesses are often prodded to furnish new information not given to House Appropriations if they hope to arm the Senate with the weapons it needs to be successful in a conference

4. Senator Gale W. McGee, *Personnel Administration and Operations of the Agency for International Development.* Report to the Senate Committee on Appropriations, 88 Cong. 1 sess. (Nov. 29, 1963).

with the usually adamant House members. Actually, if there is a court of appeals for an agency, it is the conference committee meeting behind closed doors to resolve the differences between the two houses, rather than the Senate Appropriations subcommittee.

The court of appeals versus de novo argument is unlikely ever to be completely and consistently resolved for all subcommittees. Although for most of them there has been a substantial change in the extent of budget review since the Second World War, it is noteworthy that the habits of the District of Columbia and Treasury–Post Office Subcommittees—two low prestige groups—have undergone little change during the period. Much, of course, depends on the desires of each chairman. But also involved is the scope of a subcommittee's work. Given the complexities of modern agricultural and defense programs, for example, it is not difficult to see why the subcommittees appropriating money for them would lengthen the time given to taking and considering testimony. Certainly the overlapping chairmanships between some of the legislative committees and Appropriations subcommittees have led to a more thorough review, as in the case of Senator Russell, who has held joint Armed Services-Defense appropriations hearings early in the year. In other instances, the institutional pride of the Senate has become the impetus to work that will answer the taunts of House members in conference that senators have not sufficiently studied particular programs.

Economy or Policy Formulation?

Another important factor affecting how the subcommittees approach an appropriation bill is whether Appropriations senators see the saving of money or the consideration of policy as their primary task. Like members of the House Committee on Appropriations, members of Senate Appropriations view themselves as the most important committee in their body. However, unlike the House committee, those on Senate Appropriations are not united in the belief that their committee is *"the* most important, most responsible unit in the whole appropriations process," and that their "one, single, paramount task" is *"to guard the Federal Treasury."*[5] Although practically all senators on Appro-

5. The quotations represent a summary of the attitudes held by members of House Appropriations and are taken from Richard F. Fenno, Jr., "The House Appropriations Committee as a Political System: The Problem of Integration," in

priations claim they want to save the taxpayers' money, most know that over the years they have not really saved very much. For this they blame the system, the House, and, not least, themselves. Their active participation in the work of various legislative committees keeps them from being committed economizers like their House counterparts and gives them a strong interest in policy goals and ongoing programs.

If an "Appropriations type" exists in the House, it does not exist in the Senate.[6] Even those Republican and Democratic members who declare that their principal role is indeed to save the taxpayers' money reveal a greater interest in policy formulation than in economizing as an end in itself. For example, in 1966 a western Democrat, classifying himself with the conservative wing of his party, described his motive as seeing "that the money which is appropriated is necessary and justified." He believed "in saving where possible"; then he added, but "I think it is more important to meet the educational, recreation, and other needs and demands in every field, especially our military needs." A senior Democrat acknowledged:

> while Appropriations is not a policy-formulating committee, what we do can drastically affect policy even if we don't formulate it. I haven't been able to save too much money lately by being a member of the committee since it is really the trend in Congress not to save money. I'm still old-fashioned and conservative and would like to save some.

The dominance of policy considerations in the committee behavior of Appropriations members is typified by Senator Ellender. In terms of Senate voting behavior he has basically been an economizer. At the beginning of a session, Ellender has vigorously opposed expansion of the various committee payrolls. At the end of a session, he has prided himself on returning to the Senate the unused funds that have not been spent by his office or the Committee on Agriculture and Forestry. In the Appropriations subcommittees on which he actively participates,

---

American Political Science Review, Vol. 56 (June 1962), p. 311. This article is based on interviews Fenno held with forty-five of the fifty members of House Appropriations during the Eighty-sixth Congress.

6. A review of the 1965 roll calls shows no significantly higher level of policy disagreement between a senator on Appropriations and the colleague from his state who is not on the committee, than between two senators from the same state, neither of whom is on the committee. This was true whether the pairs of senators were Democratic, Republican, or from both parties. *Congressional Quarterly Weekly Report*, Vol. 23 (Dec. 10, 1965), p. 2448.

Ellender asks probing questions and is always on the prowl for hidden extravagance. Yet as chairman of the Public Works Subcommittee he justifies vast expenditures for rivers and harbors and flood control because he is deeply committed to the belief that such an outlay is a wise investment in the future of the United States.

Even on foreign aid, senators who consistently seek to trim the program usually act not to save money as such but because they disagree with the manner in which policies are being carried out. When they urge colleagues to vote for a lower level of expenditure, it is a change in direction and emphasis, not economy, that they seek.

It has been common for senators who hold deep policy commitments to use their Appropriations subcommittees to further them. Lister Hill probably did as much to catalyze and develop federal activity in the field of health as any other American. As chairman of the Committee on Labor and Public Welfare and its Subcommittee on Health, he passed authorizing legislation; later, in Appropriations, he doled out the money. Few of the former senator's colleagues objected since none wished to be accused of favoring cancer, heart disease, or any of the other maladies on which extensive testimony was regularly heard before Hill's committees.

Nevertheless, Appropriations hearings are sprinkled with reverent bows to the omnipotent deity of economy, especially when the hearings are directed at matters that do not affect one's state. As a staff member recalled when reflecting on the committee as a whole, the expression "I am for economy, but . . ." is age-old among politicians. He noted that Senator Robertson of Virginia would fight reclamation projects on grounds of economy since there were none in his state, but when it came to help for fish and wildlife, another function of the Department of the Interior, "Robertson would give the federal treasury away on that subject." The mixed goals held by committee members are clearly expressed in the remarks made in 1966 by an active committee Republican:

> You wear two hats. I am concerned with the maximum amount of efficiency and effectiveness and economy I can get. I want to squeeze out waste and keep the budget in balance. Having fought the good fight over the size of the pie, I want the biggest slice I can get for my state. I have a mixed personality on this. If I am opposed to a program such as foreign aid, I feel I have an obligation to provide funds to keep the program going and that we should cut the funds to the smallest amount that will permit the program to function effectively.

Most senators on Appropriations—and the staff members who have observed them over the years—believe that a senator's values are fairly well set prior to his joining the committee. On occasion, however, changes in perspective occur as legislators become more familiar with executive programs. Usually the change is from a more "liberal" view of spending to a more "conservative" one. A leading Democrat admitted a change in his own attitudes as a result of committee work: "I supported foreign aid until I got on the Appropriations Committee and found out how they were spending it. While I would not eliminate foreign aid altogether now, I would certainly cut it back. I think all federal agencies spend too much money." An active Republican explained his new perspective: "When I say the executive branch is filled with wastrels, now, after service on the committee, I know what I am talking about." A few who are rigid economizers before assignment to the committee sometimes undergo a change when they have an opportunity to examine an agency budget in detail. "They discover," remarked a member, "that funds are needed to carry out a program and in many cases they find that the money is being wisely and efficiently utilized." But the usual experience seems to be that described by a careful committee observer: "I have seen more liberals sour than I have seen conservatives enlightened."

Whether the committee emphasizes policy formulation or economy depends not only on the members' individual perspectives, but also on whether the administration and the committee are controlled by the same party. When there is a strong President of the same party as the Senate majority, committee members are convinced that his partisans will usually follow his recommendations. If the White House is controlled by one party and the committee by the other, review is apt to be more searching, as it was during the Republican Eightieth Congress when Truman was President and during the last six years of the Eisenhower administration when Congress was Democratic. But even when President and committee are of the same party, economy does occur. In 1965, for instance, Senator Stennis took pride in recommending a military construction appropriation bill for fiscal year 1966 that was $292,396,000 below President Johnson's budget requests.

Most members of the committee and the staff believe there is a great deal of "fat"—more funds requested by an agency than are needed to accomplish its mission effectively—in the federal budget. Democratic and Republican members alike are convinced that every agency has too many people, that federal personnel travel more than they should, and that too much is spent on promotional programs which the agencies describe as "public information." Complaining that "every time a department gets a new program or has a crisis, they want more people," a subcommittee chairman concluded: "If you can keep the people down, then you will keep the programs down."

There are almost as many opinions about where the fat in government is as there are programs. Frequently mentioned are defense, antipoverty, foreign aid, public works, reclamation, housing, area redevelopment, civil defense, agriculture, and, as one senator expressed it, "research, research, research . . . always research." Military and medical research draws the most fire—even from some of those who have consistently supported expenditures in both fields. Committee members feel at a loss to evaluate accomplishments in these areas and fret about duplication and the lack of communication among the subsidized scientists located around the world in government agencies, private firms, universities, and research institutions. Various subcommittees listen hour after hour to deans of agricultural research, administrators of experiment stations, generals, and civilian scientists. Senators are told in glowing terms of "accomplishment" and "progress" with the current year's expenditures, and encouraged to believe that a "solution" or the "next step" is just around the corner—if only sufficient funds are made available. Republican Gordon Allott of Colorado expressed in 1966 the frustrations of the conscientious legislator who has attempted to grapple with research and development requests and scientific terminology over the years:

> . . . I have never found any scientist that did not come in here and say that we could use $50 or $100 or $200 million, and if we put it in the budget you would grab it like that. There seems to be no limitation in the minds of scientists upon the amount that the Government should spend for this, and without respect to duplication.[7]

Many senators, rightly or wrongly, are convinced that agency administrators frequently practice retribution in the name of economy when cuts are made by Congress in their budget. To encourage restoration of the cut project or program, weather stations or other federal facilities are closed in a member's district. Then the community leaders —labor, business, and the mayor—descend on Washington to protest

---

7. *Independent Offices Appropriations, 1966,* Hearings before the Senate Appropriations Subcommittee, 89 Cong. 1 sess. (May 24, 1965), pp. 611–12.

the closing of the "needed" weather station or the "vital" army camp, arsenal, or navy yard.[8] "How do you prevent waste?" a senior staff member asked himself. "I don't know. I am a fatalist. The best thing you can do is to hold hearings and have a shotgun behind the door." Some members and staff believe that increased stringency by the Bureau of the Budget has taken much of the padding out of agency budgets, but they are convinced that some remains as a result of agency attempts to anticipate cuts by Congress. The question is how to pick those programs that can be reduced. Most senators and staff members recognize that across-the-board cuts are of little value, although a senior subcommittee chairman thought "any agency by making selective cuts could reduce its employees 10 percent without really affecting its efficiency." But senators also know that simply cutting personnel does not solve all their problems. In the $113 billion administrative budget submitted by President Johnson for fiscal year 1967, the total civilian personnel costs were only $21.2 billion.[9]

To reduce the padding, specific programs have to be cut, and that is

8. When Senator Bartlett of Alaska was on Armed Services, he began a campaign to modernize the Coast Guard. As a newcomer to Appropriations, he was assigned to the Treasury–Post Office Subcommittee, which reviews Coast Guard budget requests. In 1965, the House—concerned with the large amount of carryovers in the Coast Guard budget—cut $8,250,000 from the $109,250,000 requested for acquisition, construction, and improvements. Admiral E. J. Roland, the Coast Guard commandant, urged the Senate to restore the cut. He itemized the program elements selected to "absorb the proposed cut." Among them was a $3.75 million medium-endurance cutter for patrol of Alaskan fisheries and treaty enforcement. Senator Bartlett was obviously sensitive to such a cut. He extensively cross-examined the admiral as to the need for the vessel. Senator Allott cooperated by pressing Roland: ". . . We find, I might say, that when cuts are made in the Appropriations Committees, either the House or the Senate, that the cut is often applied by the departments of the Government in the areas where they tend to hurt most, or strike the most sensitive nerves. I am sure you are fully acquainted with this technique. Now, where would you apply the $3.75 million cut, in the event we decide to direct you to proceed with the medium-endurance cutter in any event?"

The admiral immediately "absorbed" a structure planned for the New York coast and some barracks to be located in North Carolina and Hawaii. Senators from New York, North Carolina, and Hawaii were not on Appropriations. Eventually no senator suffered since all the funds were restored—no doubt because of Senator Bartlett's activism at the subcommittee markup. *Treasury and Post Office Appropriations, 1966,* Hearings before the Senate Appropriations Subcommittee, 89 Cong. 1 sess. (April 13, 1965), pp. 285, 317–18; and *Report To Accompany H.R. 7060,* S. Rept. 275, 89 Cong. 1 sess. (June 3, 1965), p. 7.

9. *The Budget of the United States Government for the Fiscal Year Ending June 30, 1967* (1966), pp. 69, 402.

where the argument really starts and some economizers soon become spenders. The knowledge that some of the fat might be his own, and what is not his is probably coveted by someone else on the committee, usually restrains a member from pursuing economy too far—and further encourages the disposition toward policy formulation rather than money-saving in the committee's approach.

The Unwritten Rules of Behavior

Observers of Congress—and the participants themselves—have long been fascinated by the mores that guide legislative behavior in both the parent body and in its committees, which have come to be seen as miniature legislatures or microcosms of the parent body. In recent years political scientists have sought, using techniques from psychology and sociology, to determine how legislators actually behave.[10] Political scientist Donald R. Matthews has noted a number of unwritten rules and standards of conduct that apply in the Senate. Among them are *apprenticeship*—observing a period of listening, learning, and deferring to one's elders before attempting to participate actively; *legislative work*—performing the detailed drudgery of committee work rather than merely grandstanding on the floor; *specialization*—not trying to know everything but devoting attention to a limited area of legislation; *courtesy*—not letting political disagreements affect personal feelings; *institutional patriotism*—putting the dignity, power, and prestige of the Senate ahead of oneself and especially ahead of the President and the bureaucracy should they come into conflict with the institution; and *reciprocity*—"If you help me, I'll help you"—perhaps the key norm underlying a senator's own behavior and his evaluation of the requests of his colleagues. Such folkways, though never universally followed, have been helpful in preserving the institution, enabling men of diverse beliefs and experience to work together with a degree of effectiveness. But as Matthews himself suggests, more vigorous two-party competi-

10. The most frequent sources of inspiration from psychology and sociology are skillfully summarized by Theodore R. Sarbin (Chap. 6: "Role Theory") in Gardner Lindzey (ed.), *Handbook of Social Psychology*, Vol. 1: *Theory and Method* (Addison-Wesley, 1954), pp. 223–58. See especially the list of references on pp. 255–58. For a perceptive article on the need for an analysis of what actually occurs in legislative committees and the roles assumed by legislators under differing circumstances, see Ralph K. Huitt, "The Congressional Committee: A Case Study," *American Political Science Review*, Vol. 68 (June 1954), pp. 340–65.

tion, the increased demands of mass media such as television, and larger, more urban, constituencies tend to produce increasing departures from these norms of behavior.[11]

To what degree do the Senate's unwritten rules of behavior apply to the Appropriations Committee?

Reciprocity

The practice of reciprocity ("logrolling" or "backscratching" or "trading votes") has been called by some "a way of life in the Senate."[12]

---

11. Donald R. Matthews, *U.S. Senators and Their World* (University of North Carolina Press, 1960), Chap. 5, "The Folkways of the Senate," pp. 92–117. Matthews constructed, among other analytical devices, an Index of Legislative Effectiveness. He divided the number of bills and resolutions that a senator introduced and secured passage of during the Eighty-third and Eighty-fourth Congresses by the total number of measures the senator introduced. Matthews excluded from his computations private bills and cosponsorships (unless the bills and resolutions were introduced jointly by two senators). He then compared a senator's "effectiveness" with his amount of speaking on the floor (a folkway of the Senate being that new members are seen but not heard) and the degree to which the senator specialized (another folkway). Matthews concluded: "The less a senator talks on the Senate floor, and the narrower a senator's area of legislative interest and activity, the greater is his effectiveness. Conformity to the Senate folkways does, therefore, seem to pay off in concrete legislative results" (p. 115). Matthews has devised some intriguing and provocative indexes—regardless of whether you agree with his conclusions. This approach does have its pitfalls, however, as is reflected in the observation of one Senate staff member, a liberal Democrat, who wondered aloud: "How can you write a book on the United States Senate in the postwar period and never mention Richard B. Russell?" And, of course, the efforts and effectiveness of a senator who works on one major bill cannot be equated with the efforts of a senator who secures passage of several minor bills of little consequence. Nor can such indexes reveal the efforts of a minority senator who spends months successfully improving and rewriting a major administration bill, as Jacob K. Javits did on the Kennedy-Johnson administration's medicare bill.

12. *Ibid.*, p. 100. Fenno, "House Appropriations Committee as a Political System," is more concerned with reciprocity as a means of promoting integration and stabilization within a committee. For an excellent discussion of the cultural meaning of reciprocity, see Alvin W. Gouldner, "The Norm of Reciprocity: A Preliminary Statement," *American Sociological Review*, Vol. 25 (April 1960), p. 171. Gouldner has concluded from an analysis of the various concepts of reciprocity in different cultures that "a norm of reciprocity is, I suspect, no less universal and important an element of culture than the incest taboo, although, similarly, its concrete formulations may vary with time and place." This norm "makes two interrelated, minimal demands: (1) people should help those who have helped them, and (2) people should not injure those who have helped them." He notes that in the first decade of this century, Edward Westermarck observed: "To require a benefit, or to be grateful to him who bestows it, is probably everywhere, at least under certain circumstances, regarded as

If being helpful to other people in the expectation that someday they might return the favor is the indictment, then the Senate stands convicted—as do most groups and individuals. Votes have been won because some participants did not have deep feelings on an issue one way or the other and gave their support to the first person who asked. Votes have been lost because the believer in a cause was too busy to see his colleagues individually and ask for their support, preferring instead to lecture them in an empty chamber through the pages of the *Congressional Record*. Eager legislative assistants have helped their senators win committee battles by carefully counting noses and gathering proxies. Nobody says: "I'll support you, but I've got something I need your assurance on right now if I do." They do not have to. And this understanding does not imply that the support must be reciprocated on the next go-around. If the senator who has been helped has a deep commitment on an issue, he is not expected to sacrifice it. But chits have been stored away for the future. Ingrates in the Senate, as elsewhere, do not accomplish much.

The Committee on Appropriations is the focal point for many projects: agricultural experiment stations, airport control towers, dams, federal office buildings, military and veterans installations, and weather stations, to name only a few. Clearly, the practice of reciprocity often affects how Appropriations members treat the various budget requests before them. A committee member who was widely recognized as a "floor economizer" before joining Appropriations because of the budget-cutting amendments he offered, made the point explicitly in 1966: "If you were for saving money you might be less for saving money once you are on the committee since there is a tendency to go along with others in order to have them go along with you. Thus you support their projects."

Although "slicing up the pork" may seem to be the order of the day on the committee, the rule—if a member wants to be respected by his colleagues—is not to be greedy. A widely respected committee leader commented: "If the idea gets around that a senator is one who asks for too much for his state, then he gets marked for that." A senior Republican looked at it this way: "A member shouldn't overdo—that is a major unwritten rule. If he has six things he wants, he should forget three." Some senators ask for more than they can receive in the hope

---

a duty." Gouldner argues that the norm serves as a group *stabilizing* function. It is also a "starting mechanism" because it "helps to initiate social interaction . . ." (p. 176).

of getting something. A few, however, work diligently over several years for one major project.

How free are senators to object to another's pet project? One Republican explained: "There is no reason why you can't object to another's project except that he might object to yours, and that is a natural human consideration." A senator might raise a question about a particular project in a session, sometimes with the intent of with-drawing the objection and thus gaining the gratitude of the project's sponsor. But a senator, if he wants to be effective in the long run on the committee, does not press objections to another's pet project unless that project adversely affects vital interests in his own state. To do otherwise would violate the norm of reciprocity.

There is a recognized committee way of objecting to pet projects, however. Frequently a subcommittee chairman and ranking minority member simply refuse to recommend a project to their colleagues on the subcommittee or full committee. The project sponsor may try to ingratiate himself with the subcommittee chairman by diligently attending the hearings. Although the chairman may appreciate his presence and interest, rejections may still occur. Unless the senator advocating the project fails to get the message, he usually does not protest too much. He is often assured that he may try again when project planning is further advanced and the budget less tight.

Some senators, however, may continue to plead for help because they are up for reelection and their whole campaign seems to depend on whether or not that field office in Oshkosh remains open or a fish hatchery is located on Trout River. Then, with bipartisan camaraderie, the committee will add the project to the bill and the senator will be able to issue his press release for the home folks. But something often seems to happen to project items on the way to the White House. When the Senate and House conferees meet behind closed doors in search of agreement on a bill, they start to examine benefit-cost ratios. Projects disappear—even some of those sponsored by very senior members. But by that time the press release has gone out and the constituents know that their senator has made the old college try. "The committee will try and help a fellow out by putting a project in the bill," one senator explained, "as long as he understands it will not be pushed in conference." He added significantly: "When you get the real money—the big money—you have to have merit." Sometimes the "small" money or project does get by and those who are in a strategic position by virtue of subcommittee or conference membership can help themselves or their colleagues along, but the informal mores of committee life work against even a ranking member's taking undue advantage of the system.

Sometimes reciprocity—or the lack of it where its practice is expected —imposes its restraints on Appropriations members from the floor of the Senate. In March 1963, for example, a few months before William Proxmire became a member of Senate Appropriations, he successfully implored the Interior Appropriations Subcommittee to add $3.8 million to the Interior bill for fiscal 1964 for a wood chemistry and pulp and paper laboratory at Madison, Wisconsin. When the bill was before the Senate, Republican leader Dirksen sought to illustrate what he regarded as the spending proclivities of the Kennedy administration. The Interior bill exceeded the previous year's appropriations by over $43 million and Dirksen moved to recommit it with instructions not to exceed the total for fiscal 1963. The primarily partisan motion was defeated by a vote of 56 to 22. But among the twenty-two economy-minded senators there were five Democrats, including Senator Proxmire.

The next economy vote was on an amendment by Democratic Senator Frank J. Lausche of Ohio to strike $310,000 in funds for a National Fisheries Center and Aquarium. This was merely seed money to finance the preliminary plans of what was estimated to be a $10 million project. It was dear to Democratic Congressman Mike Kirwan of Ohio, a long-time member of the House Committee on Appropriations, who was chairman of its Interior Subcommittee and second-ranking member of its Public Works Subcommittee. The Lausche amendment was rejected 58 to 22. Five Democrats also supported that motion, among them Senator Proxmire.

The Interior bill passed the same day and eventually a conference was held with the House to resolve differences between the House and Senate versions. The conferees had hardly sat down when Congressman Kirwan indicated that since Senator Proxmire wanted to save money on the Interior appropriation bill, a good way to start would be to eliminate the $3.8 million forest products laboratory at Madison, Wisconsin. Out went the project with the concurrence of the Senate conferees.

Courtesy and Deference

Courtesy and deference, at least as formalities, are deeply rooted in Senate—and committee—practice. In a chamber of one hundred barons, each believing himself supreme in his fiefdom, each with skin toughened by the abuse of primary and general election opponents, each confident he is right, and each a big man in his state even though he is only one of a hundred in the Senate, the forms of courtesy aid in reducing the chance of permanent damage to human relationships. Even if one senator dislikes another, he smiles and extends his hand when they meet on the floor: senatorial canons emphasize that dislike applies to a colleague's ideas but not to the colleague himself. After all, he might need the other's vote someday. And the "friend" might be in a position to stall a favorite bill of his and thus cause him trouble. Senators are politicians who have educated themselves to appear to like the most difficult people—even their colleagues.

Courtesy and deference take many forms. Partly, of course, they are a manner of speaking. Illustrative are the remarks Senator Ralph Yarborough of Texas made to the Agricultural Appropriations Sub-committee in 1965, when he was last in seniority on the subcommittee and on the Democratic side of the full committee. He beseeched the subcommittee chairman, Spessard Holland of Florida, to appropriate more federal funds to prevent screw worm infestation of cattle in Texas and the Southwest. Holland had urged the states and industries affected to contribute more of their own funds to the program. Yarborough began as follows:

> Mr. Chairman, I want to express my great esteem for the chairman of this subcommittee. I have heard his days and days of meticulous hearings on the closing of various agricultural experiment stations. I have seen his careful work on the floor of the Senate on many bills and on behalf of the meat industry of the Southwest. I want to ask him to carefully reconsider this, not asking him today, but ask him to consider it in connection with many facts that we don't have time to present now.

Yarborough proceeded to plead his case in several hundred words, liberally sprinkled with references to "the able and distinguished chairman" and praise for "the chairman's great knowledge in agriculture and his great demonstrated ability in the Senate." Holland thanked Yarborough for "his friendly comment" but was unmoved and later sustained his point in the Senate. However, with senatorial deference, it is not whether you win or lose but how you play the game that counts, and Yarborough had played correctly.[13]

Senate watchers have long held that new senators are expected to remain silent, observe their elders, and then speak only when they have

13. *Agricultural Appropriations, 1966,* Hearings before the Senate Appropriations Subcommittee, 89 Cong. 1 sess. (April 28, 1965), Pt. 2, pp. 132–34.

something to say—preferably not for many months after they are sworn in. There is no strict unwritten rule that enforces this apprenticeship period for new members of Appropriations. Newcomers are usually not new to the Senate, often having served from two to ten years prior to their selection. Consequently, senior members do not feel that newcomers have to remain silent. A Democratic leader, when interviewed in 1966, observed:

> I've never noticed too much silence on the part of a new member, but a new man obviously doesn't try to take over because he does not want to look foolish. However, a man can be here twenty years and still make a nuisance out of himself. I never had any hesitancy when I was a new member of the committee to speak up when I knew something about the subject that was before us.

Another senator, a Republican, suggested:

> This is an individual matter; I think whether or not you're in the committee or in the Senate you do well to feel your way along. I don't think you should be dumb, but on the other hand, I don't think you should talk on everything.

Younger members in both parties agreed. They sensed, as one put it, that "a new member should not be silent, but he should be less vocal until he attains seniority and experience." Another relative newcomer who had spoken up in committee offered:

> I think if a member spoke on defense matters without previously checking with Senator Russell he would be in a pretty tough spot. It's a matter of competence. If you're going to persuade the committee to change its views on something, you should go to the subcommittee chairman first and build your support in the subcommittee.

Many on the committee's professional staff, however, believed that new members should remain silent. "New members should be seen and not heard" was repeatedly stated in staff interviews. One staff member reflected: "I never cease to be amazed that the effective ones in committee are the ones who listen." He added, "It is one thing to do something on the floor, it is another to do it in committee. Senators are reluctant to look bad in their colleagues' eyes."

Committee members recalled a newcomer to Appropriations who once spoke out of order in a committee session. An agency witness had finished his presentation. Chairman Hayden asked Senator Russell if he had any questions. Russell had none, so Hayden called on Senator Saltonstall, who was next in order as ranking Republican. Before

Senator Saltonstall could answer, the newcomer announced: "If you'll excuse me, I've got a lot of questions to ask and I have a very important engagement to keep." Then he began his interrogation. One of the senior Democrats spoke up calmly and firmly: "I think the senator should understand that others have many things to do also." Then he added pointedly: "Did you have anything to say, Senator Saltonstall?" At this, the newcomer left the room and did not return; presumably, he had learned a lesson.

A practice demonstrating committee respect both for specialization and for a norm of courtesy and deference is that a senator does not attend a markup session of a subcommittee unless he is a member. As one staff member observed: "To attend without being a member would be regarded as shrill." The subcommittee chairman might not deny a request to attend, but if a senator did participate, he would be regarded as an interloper. Neither his case nor his colleagues' respect for him would be enhanced by a violation of this unwritten rule.

In view of the pressure to conform to the norms of courtesy and deference, can a member fight subcommittee and committee decisions? Those who want to be effective soon discover that it is better to confer with the subcommittee chairman in advance, to ascertain his feelings and to avoid forcing colleagues to vote against him in committee. Senators do not like to be put on the spot. They prefer to operate by consensus. Much committee time is spent in an attempt to accommodate divergent views and convince obstinate members so that the committee can stand together in the Senate. If a determined senator makes a case for his point of view and has participated in all the hearings, the committee might go along. But if a senator is adamant and appears to lack a grasp of the facts, then the chairman will let him go his own way. Generally the chairman has sufficient votes to deal with the wayward member. To avoid the impression of any personal feelings, senators often defer to "objective" standards such as benefit-cost ratios or priority lists determined by the responsible executive agency.

Senators and staff generally believe that there is no resentment by other Appropriations senators if a member feels he has to fight a committee decision on the Senate floor. But most agree that as a matter of courtesy the senator should give notice to his committee colleagues and "reserve his right" to disagree later. If a senator sits through the committee discussion without informing his associates that he intends to fight the bill, he has committed a breach of trust. But if he notifies

them, senators respect a colleague who fights for what he believes in—
"as long as he does not overdo it."

Homework and Specialization

As in the Senate as a whole, the degree to which an Appropriations
member's views are respected and sought by his colleagues is directly
related to their estimate of his knowledge and the amount of attention
he has given a subject. As a senior Republican expressed it: "Does he
know his stuff? If he does and is well informed, then it doesn't matter
whether he is a Democrat or a Republican; they will listen." That is
why the chairman and ranking minority member on each subcommittee
are in so strategic a position: if they have done their job, they hold a
monopoly of knowledge. Repeatedly, senators refer to "doing your
homework." Homework is equated with respect.

Each senator is recognized as an expert on the problems of his own
geographic area, but as one subcommittee chairman advised: "You
can't know everything, so it's better to specialize and then the other
members of the committee will listen to you and value your opinion in
a particular area just as you will consult them on matters on which they
have specialized." One of the hardest working senators on the committee stated: "I try to get to the bottom of any question. I am simply
inquisitive. The trouble is that a lot of senators come without properly
trying to find out what the functions are of the departments whose
budget is before them. It's useless unless you do because you simply
can't ask intelligent questions." A colleague and subcommittee chairman agreed: "The first rule of getting ahead is to attend the hearings
and participate in them if you want to be respected."

Respect does not depend on seniority as much as on knowledge. Of
the eighteen Democrats on the committee in 1965–66, Mike Monroney
ranked eleventh in seniority. An accomplished private pilot, Monroney
was also chairman of the Commerce Committee's Subcommittee on
Aviation. When aviation matters came up in an Appropriations executive session, the senior members in both parties deferred to Monroney.
They knew that he had done his homework as a specialist.

Nonpartisanship

What a senator promises on the campaign trail and what he argues
in the Senate during partisan debate are not necessarily what he recommends in the Committee on Appropriations. Senators of both parties,

from the ideological left to the ideological right, from rural southerner to urban northeasterner, are in agreement that nonpartisanship is the rule within the committee. That does not mean there are no differences of opinion. But these are differences between conservatives and liberals about support for domestic programs, or between farm and city, or public power and private power, among others. In this regard the committee's norm for behavior among its members is far stricter than the parent body's: there are seldom differences between Republicans and Democrats per se.

At least, this was the case during the 1960s. Certainly in a body controlled more than two-to-one by the majority party, a policy of active partisanship would not have paid off for the minority. But nonpartisanship has not always been the way of life on Appropriations. During periods when there was a more equal division between the two parties in the Senate, or the Senate was controlled by one party and the administration by another, partisanship came into play more freely. Many on the committee still recall the working over given Dr. Arthur Larson, director of the United States Information Agency in the Eisenhower administration, by the Democratic majority on the committee in 1957. Larson had claimed in a Lincoln Day speech in Hawaii that "throughout the New and Fair Deal, this country was in the grip of a somewhat alien philosophy imported from Europe." Lyndon B. Johnson, as chairman of the Appropriations subcommittee reviewing the USIA budget, reduced Larson's budget request $16 million below the House of Representatives, which had already cut USIA funds almost $38 million.[14]

The advent of a Republican administration under Richard M. Nixon in 1969 raises the question whether the nonpartisanship of the 1960s will be followed, as it was preceded during the Eisenhower administration, by a more partisan attitude on the part of the committee's Democratic majority. At the time of this writing, staff members see no increase in partisanship—though some observe that the Republican members have had to moderate some of their criticism of executive programs now that their own party has responsibility for the executive branch.

14. *State, Justice, the Judiciary, and Related Agencies Appropriations, 1958,* Hearings before the Senate Appropriations Subcommittee, 85 Cong. 1 sess. (May 2, 1957), pp. 503–05; and *Conference Report on H.R. 6871,* H. Rept. 492, 85 Cong. 1 sess. (May 23, 1957), p. 6.

The Domination of the Inner Club

Perhaps the clearest indication of the importance the Senate's code of behavior has for life on the Appropriations Committee is the close relationship between the committee and the Senate's "Inner Club." In the mid-1950s William S. White popularized this term to describe "the minority-within-a-minority" that commands the inner life of the Senate. For White the Inner Club was "an organism without name or charter, without officers, without a list of membership, without a wholly conscious being at all." While the southerners stood at the core and "with rare exceptions automatically assume membership almost with the taking of the oath of office," participation was not limited to Democrats from the South or to conservatives. Members could be from differing regions and of differing parties, beliefs, and socioeconomic status. But each exemplified a "Senate type . . . a man for whom the Institution is a career in itself, a life in itself, and an end in itself." A member viewed the Senate as his home "in a deeply emotional sense." He was concerned with tradition and the lore of the institution. He was "nearly always a truly compassionate man, very slow to condemn his brothers." Some senators spoke to the country and to the world; the man in the Inner Club spoke to the Senate. He was judged by his fellow members not for loyalty to his party or to his administration but for his loyalty to the Senate. He had what White described as "character in the sense that the special integrity of the person must be in harmony with, and not lesser in its way than, the special integrity of the Institution— the integrity of its oneness."[15]

Senator Joseph Clark failed to share White's enchantment with the Inner Club. For the reform-minded senator from Pennsylvania, White was the poet laureate of an establishment that hindered reform within the Senate and, as a result, stifled the progress Clark believed was

---

15. William S. White, *Citadel: The Story of the U.S. Senate* (Harper & Brothers, 1956), p. 84, and "The 'Club' that is the U.S. Senate," *New York Times Magazine* (Nov. 7, 1954), pp. 9, 30, 32–34. For a critical view of Inner Club fanciers and folkway articulators, such as White and Matthews, see the section entitled "The Distribution of Power: Is There an Inner Club?" in Nelson W. Polsby, *Congress and the Presidency* (Prentice-Hall, 1964), pp. 32–41. The question is not which analyst is correct as to the existence of an Inner Club; the question is, do junior members of the Senate believe there is an Inner Club? The answer is yes. Being a member of the Inner Club, of course, does not mean that a senator can accomplish anything he wants, just as being an outsider or maverick does not mean that a senator will never accomplish anything. The point is that some accomplish more than others because they understand how things are done.

sought by the American constituency. He looked on this Inner Club as "the Senate establishment" where the "procedures, customs, traditions, manners, and mores" were based "too much on unwritten, unspoken, and largely unnoticed informal agreements among men."[16]

If the Senate has had an Inner Club, its board of directors has largely been on the Committee on Appropriations. White wrote that Carl Hayden "could very nearly be the president of the Club, if only it had officers." If Hayden were president, Richard B. Russell—whom White eulogized as "incomparably the truest current Senate type, and incomparably the most influential man on the inner life of the Senate"— would be chairman of its executive and membership committees. White also listed Senators Hill, Holland, McClellan, Mansfield, Pastore, Stennis, and Young in the Inner Club category.[17] Over a decade later, in 1967, columnist Clayton Fritchey compiled a roster of those he believed were in or out of the Inner Club. He described Russell as its president. Fritchey noted that in his search for members of the Club, one senator advised him: "Go look up the Appropriations Committee. They're all there." Among the twenty-seven he identified as full-fledged members, Fritchey listed fourteen from Appropriations: Bible, Byrd, Ellender, Hayden, Hill, Holland, Republican Roman L. Hruska of Nebraska, Magnuson, Mansfield, McClellan, Mundt, Pastore, Russell, and Stennis. (Robertson and Saltonstall, who were on the committee through 1966, were also described as charter members.) There were fourteen senators almost inside—or "half or three-quarters fledged," as Fritchey put it—of whom five were on Appropriations: Allott, Republican Norris Cotton of New Hampshire, Kuchel, Monroney, and Young. Twelve others were thought to be on the way to membership; two of them, Bartlett and McGee, were on Appropriations. In the non-Club group were five members of Appropriations: Proxmire, Yarborough, Republican Margaret Chase Smith of Maine, Republican Clifford P. Case of New Jersey, and Javits. Excluding Senator Smith, a woman, the other four were last in committee seniority.[18]

How do the committee's senators and staff view the Club within the Club? When asked in 1966, those considered Inner Club members generally denied that there was such a group. The staff and those

16. Joseph S. Clark, *The Senate Establishment* (Hill & Wang, 1963), p. 15.
17. White, *Citadel*, pp. 69, 73, 88, 90, 92, and 131.
18. Clayton Fritchey, "Who Belongs to the Senate's Inner Club?" *Harper's*, Vol. 234 (May 1967), pp. 104, 106, 108, and 110.

senators who were not included—and who were looking up from below on the seniority ladder—were convinced that such a phenomenon did exist. In their opinion Hayden and Russell were at the very center of it.[19] One junior senator described the committee's Inner Club as

> an interlocking directorate of southerners who are on every subcommittee in depth. If you get rid of one, you still have another southerner. But these boys are coming to the end of the line. It is an old generation of southerners. Their days are numbered. Then there will be a complete revolution.

The qualities that mark the Inner Club senator were made clear by one careful observer who commented:

> Senator ——— is not in the Inner Club even though he is very effective because he is so articulate and he carries the administration's ball. Just by watching other members when he makes his comments I get the feeling that he really isn't in the Inner Club since he gets too vehement and he annoys some of the senior members by getting so vehement. Whereas when Russell speaks, the feeling of the members is that he knows whereof he speaks and that he doesn't go off half-cocked. The members know that Russell will not just be a zealot for the administration. They know that he's watching out for the Senate Committee on Appropriations first and then the Senate.

Hard work is a basic criterion for Inner Club membership. One of the most active members of the committee, Allen J. Ellender, was chairman of the powerful Public Works Appropriations Subcommittee. He

19. Senators in both parties on the committee in 1966 almost universally volunteered that Russell was their most "influential," "respected," and "effective" colleague. His leadership was felt even more than Hayden's. At eighty-nine, Hayden had slowed down, but he continued to amaze many on the committee and its staff. As one put it: "Hayden has built up an expertise and knowledge which is astonishing." He maintained a strong focus of power both because he was chairman and because of his close working relationship with the committee's chief clerk, Thomas J. Scott, who was Hayden's "eyes and ears."

Also considered a key part of the Inner Club were ranking Republican Leverett Saltonstall and his heir apparent through seniority, Milton Young of North Dakota. Saltonstall and Young were both regarded as true committee men. Saltonstall, referred to by his colleagues as "the great compromiser," sought more actively than Young to resolve the differences between contending parties on an issue and thus risked the displeasure of those who did not get all they wanted. Young was more likely to use his influence only on issues that were of deep concern to him and to his state. For years Saltonstall—a vigorous supporter of foreign aid under both Republican and Democratic administrations—had been allied with Hayden and John O. Pastore, who presided for Hayden when foreign aid was under consideration. The three formed a united front to support the mutual security program. One staff man remarked: "If that combination agrees, nobody can tip it over."

In the judgment of senators and staff, other members of the Inner Club included Stennis, Magnuson, and Hill, followed by Ellender, Holland, Monroney, and possibly Pastore for the Democrats; and Mundt, with Allott and Hruska as initiates in the lodge, for the Republicans.

sat for months, mostly alone, listening to an endless parade of witnesses discuss public works projects in every state. When he came to the subcommittee and later to the full committee with his recommendations, they were seldom revised because of the respect his colleagues had for his diligence and judgment.

Senators also knew that Ellender's recommendations would be nonpartisan—another important characteristic of the Club. As one said:

> I have seen some Democrats ask for something year after year and they still don't get it; yet a Republican will get it if it's a good project and he's a member of the Club. Nothing is ever said about this, but it is understood. We approved one project in terms of both authorization and funding. As such, it was subject to a point of order since you are prohibited from legislating in an appropriation bill. Yet no question was raised in the Senate or the House. Since the Democrats were also in control of the House, if they had wanted to play politics they could have cut this item out in conference, but they did not.

A senator on Appropriations may still accomplish his purposes even though he is not fully accepted in the Inner Club. He can secure support for programs of benefit to his state. He can be the acknowledged expert in a specialized area. He can be effective especially if he observes certain unwritten rules of conduct that largely guide the way of life within the committee.

* * *

In the Appropriations Committee, as in most institutions, the informal attitudes and practices of the members significantly affect the nature and outcome of the work. The breadth and depth of subcommittee review of budget requests are determined to a large extent by whether the members view their subcommittee as a court of appeals or a de novo tribunal. Spending decisions are influenced by whether the members prefer to focus on policy considerations or on saving money.

Committee members quickly become aware of the restraints imposed on them by the unwritten rules of legislative life. Reciprocity between members is expected, as it is between subcommittees. Senators are considered expert on matters affecting the vital interests of their states. A subcommittee's recommendations are regarded in a similar manner because of the expertise it has developed through the hearing process. Thus a few individuals and subgroups are expected to have more to say than the others at any particular time. Yet the result is not complete laissez faire for the few and silence for the many. Senators also weigh the merit in the advice given by a member or a subcommittee and make their judgments accordingly.

CHAPTER FOUR

The Information-Gathering Process

A member of the Committee on Appropriations is surrounded by many sources of information. The formal public hearing is only one —although an essential one, for there the public record is made to which both supporters and opponents can retreat as they cite with praise or quote with alarm. Each day senators receive a flood of information from colleagues, personal staff, committee staff, lobbyists, constituents, and agency officials. Careful assistants cull newspapers, news tickers, reports from federal agencies, newsletters, and trade journals for fresh insights to bring to their senator's attention. To all of this information a senator applies his professional experience, his sensitivity to the various forces at work in his state and in society, his personal values and goals, in an effort to sift the relevant from the irrelevant and to distinguish high priority matters from low.

External Sources of Information

The Executive Branch and the Bureau of the Budget

Senators look to the executive branch for guidance and for the setting of priorities among programs. They know that within the vast bureaucracy are practitioners of almost every occupation from the manufacture of ice cream to the designing of missiles and manned space vehicles. The executive branch has a near monopoly of program knowledge.

The legislative branch has a variety of opinions as to goals, with a smattering of program knowledge based on the degree to which each legislator has followed his particular interests. In an attempt to satisfy itself that it has an adequate basis on which to make judgments, Congress probes and pries as the mood directs. Congress wants to know what the agencies think: whether the agencies are for or against a proposal or an appropriation, and how they would modify it to make it acceptable.

Coordinating the official communications to Congress that provide the administration's position on legislation and appropriations is the Bureau of the Budget.[1] A creation of the Budget and Accounting Act of 1921, the Bureau of the Budget was designed to assure that the President's interests were pursued by the diverse agencies of the executive establishment.

President Harding's first budget director, Charles G. Dawes, a Chicago banker who had served on General Pershing's staff and organized the supply system for the American Expeditionary Force, was a vigorous advocate of budget reform and sought to bring the various executive departments together under the President's direction. With the cooperation of the chairmen of the House and Senate Appropriations Committees, who had long objected to the system whereby major departments secured appropriations directly from the legislative committees that had authorized their programs, Dawes set about to bring

---

1. Under Reorganization Plan No. 2 of 1970, transmitted to Congress on March 12, 1970, President Nixon reorganized the Bureau of the Budget into an Office of Management and Budget, effective July 1, 1970. The literature on the Bureau of the Budget and its role in the budgetary process is growing. Some of the more useful items include Fritz Morstein Marx, "The Bureau of the Budget: Its Evolution and Present Role," *American Political Science Review*, Vol. 39, Pt. 1 (August 1945), pp. 653–84, and Pt. 2 (October 1945), pp. 869–98; Arthur Maass, "In Accord With the Program of the President?" *Public Policy*, Vol. 4 (1953), pp. 77–93; Arthur Smithies, *The Budgetary Process in the United States* (McGraw-Hill, 1955); and Aaron Wildavsky, *The Politics of the Budgetary Process* (Little, Brown, 1964). For a masterful summary of the evolution of the Budget Bureau's central clearance function between 1921 and 1954, see Richard E. Neustadt, "Presidency and Legislation: The Growth of Central Clearance," *American Political Science Review*, Vol. 48 (September 1954), pp. 641–71. For the thoughts of two recent budget directors, see Kermit Gordon, "Reflections on Spending," *Public Policy*, Vol. 15 (1966; Brookings Reprint 125), pp. 3–22; and Charles L. Schultze, *The Politics and Economics of Public Spending* (Brookings Institution, 1968), pp. 1–17. For the views of a longtime senior career official in the bureau, see William D. Carey, "Roles of the Bureau of the Budget," *Science*, Vol. 156 (April 14, 1967), pp. 206–08, 213.

financial coordination to the executive branch.[2] He issued Budget Circular 49, which provided in essence that no request for appropriations or for legislation that would result in appropriations should be submitted by an agency or department to Congress—to either house or to any of their committees—without having first been approved by the President. The circular also provided that when a committee requested an agency or department to comment on legislation, the department head should ascertain through the director of the budget whether such legislation was in accord with the financial program of the President.

The resistance of the departments to presidential disruption of their long-established relations with "friendly" legislative committees was strong and clear. But the principles outlined by Dawes prevailed, though their application sometimes varied according to the willingness of a budget director to do battle with members of the cabinet. In the 1920s the emphasis was primarily on spreading efficient business methods throughout, and securing economies within, the federal establishment. Dawes made clear in 1922 that the director of the budget bureau,

> unlike a Cabinet officer, is not concerned with policy, except as to economy and efficiency in routine business, and in connection with the transmittal of statements of the President's policy to Congress furnishes simply convenient machinery. The present Director of the Bureau of the Budget and his successors, if they are to succeed, must always keep this principle firmly in mind, otherwise they will become involved not only in misunderstandings with the Cabinet officers but with Congress as well.[3]

Early in the New Deal, President Franklin D. Roosevelt—faced with an ever-expanding group of agencies eager to push their particular

2. Neustadt noted in his 1954 article on "Presidency and Legislation: The Growth of Central Clearance" that the intent of the Budget and Accounting Act was that "one committee in each House of Congress was to receive and review appropriation requests," and concluded: "Here, prescribed in law, was a new restrictive way of handling the life-and-death concerns of every agency—and most congressmen. And here were new organizations with a tremendous institutional stake in the successful assertion of that new way: the presidential Bureau of the Budget and the congressional Committees on Appropriations. Furthermore, these organizations had a clear mutuality of interest in closing off, as nearly as might be, all avenues to action on appropriations save their own." (P. 643.)

3. Charles G. Dawes, *The First Year of the Budget of the United States* (Harper & Brothers, 1923), pp. 161–63.

legislative proposals—stressed policy clearance of legislation rather than simply financial clearance. For a year, administration policy clearance was handled by a New Deal coordinating mechanism known as the National Emergency Council. Then, in December 1935, the Bureau of the Budget issued Circular 336, which required that agency legislative proposals and reports on pending legislation, with the exception of private relief bills, be submitted to the Budget Bureau "for consideration by the President" before they were forwarded to Congress.[4]

In 1939, as a result of the report of the President's Committee on Administrative Management (the so-called Brownlow Committee), and under the authority of the Reorganization Act of 1939, President Roosevelt transferred the Bureau of the Budget from the Treasury Department to the newly created Executive Office of the President. Greater emphasis was placed on policy coordination. Since then, as a matter of course when legislation is introduced, congressional committees ask the interested departments for their views. The views are coordinated through the Budget Bureau's Office of Legislative Reference. Once cleared, the individual departments and agencies forward their comments to the appropriate congressional committees with a notation stating whether the views are in accord with the program of the President.[5]

Departments and agencies conformed with the clearance of formal communications—but no system could prevent the continuation of long-

4. Neustadt, "Presidency and Legislation: The Growth of Central Clearance," pp. 649–50. Neustadt cites an undated memorandum written during this period by F. J. Bailey, who was to become the first assistant director of the budget for legislative reference, pointing out that "there is no authority whatever in the Budget and Accounting Act for our procedure with respect to reports on legislation." Bailey argued that Budget's authority over executive reports came from executive authority rather than congressional act.

5. Departmental interests may be served by the mere absence of an objection from the Budget Bureau. In that case a department can attempt to gain approval for its program on its own initiative and avoid restrictive administrative prescriptions. Arthur Maass, in an essay on the staffing needs of the presidency, argues that "the Budget Bureau is to a considerable degree institutionally incapable of positive policy formulation." He believes that the Budget Bureau, with its institutional interest in budget paring and its "permanent and career nature," is "overly cautious and thus not well-suited for making or proposing political decisions on important matters of policy." Arthur Maass, "In Accord with the Program of the President?" pp. 77–93.

established informal relationships behind the scenes between the career civil servant and the sympathetic legislator. Testimony in congressional hearings eluded control as well. With only the printed transcript available afterward, it was difficult to discern the degree of earnestness with which an agency witness had defended the President's budget—and especially any cuts the President had made. It was also impossible to prevent the agency witness from replying to a direct congressional inquiry in a hearing. While the implications of Dawes's original directives in Budget Circular 49 encompassed oral testimony before Congress, it was not until Budget Circular 336 that a specific attempt was made to include it. Since that time, other circulars have been issued in a continuing effort by the President and the Bureau of the Budget to exert some discipline over the views expressed by members of the executive branch—even though cries of "gag rule" have occasionally been hurled at the Bureau of the Budget by a legislative advocate who sensed that executive control was being applied from above to squelch what he believed was enthusiastic agency support for a pet project.

In 1966, Budget directives provided that "frank and complete answers will be given to all questions of fact." Agency officials were admonished not to volunteer personal opinions "which reflect positions inconsistent with the program and appropriation requests the President has transmitted to the Congress." If they did express personal opinions, they were to refer "to the extent, if any, to which these opinions differ from the President's recommendations, and should make clear that the expression of the opinions is not a request for additional funds." Witnesses were also directed to clear any written responses with their agency heads.[6]

With varying degrees of success, cabinet officers have prevailed upon subordinates to follow this presidential policy. The armed services have been the most recalcitrant. Legislators are more concerned to know what the professional military want than what the civilian "whiz kids" think. Nevertheless, under both Republican and Democratic administrations, secretaries of defense have sought to remind the civilian and military officials who annually testify before Congress that their responsibility is to support the President's program, that is, the cuts made by

6. See section 6, "Agency testimony and communications on budgetary matters," Bureau of the Budget Circular No. A–10, Revised (Jan. 18, 1964). Reprinted in *Congressional Record*, Vol. 112, Pt. 12, 89 Cong. 2 sess. (July 20, 1966), pp. 16286–88.

the secretary and the President in the original service requests. During consideration of the defense appropriation bill for 1967, this guidance came under attack by House Republicans. In defending a memorandum that had been issued by the deputy secretary detailing the conduct expected of departmental witnesses, the House Appropriations chairman, Democrat George H. Mahon of Texas, noted: "There must be some discipline, some orderliness, in any organization. The alternative is chaos."[7]

The Budget Bureau is a convenient scapegoat for all legislators whose bills have not received the presidential imprimatur that they are "in accord with the program of the President." Appropriations hearings are scattered with references to the evils committed by the seemingly anonymous group of career men in the bureau. Typical is the attitude expressed by Democratic Senator Abraham Ribicoff of Connecticut, a former cabinet officer, during the hearings on the supplemental appropriation bill for 1966. Upset because he thought the Budget Bureau had deleted $500,000 for a commission he had proposed to study the care and treatment of emotionally disturbed children, Ribicoff recalled that the authorizing legislation had been approved by the Committee on Finance, had gone through the Senate without a dissenting vote, and had been accepted by the conferees. "Now the Budget Bureau in its wisdom believes it isn't necessary. My feeling is, Mr. Chairman," he declared, "if a proposal goes through the Finance Committee, it goes through the Senate, and then the conferees agree, I don't think it is up to the Bureau of the Budget to tell the Congress whether it thinks it wise, after Congress in its wisdom has come to a decision."[8]

A senator has difficulty determining whether a cabinet officer has cut his favorite item, or whether it was reduced by Budget Bureau careerists, or personally by the President. When asked at 1965 hearings how much the Post Office Department had originally requested for a particular function and how much was allowed by the Bureau of the Budget, Postmaster General John A. Gronouski replied:

> Actually, it was an interchange of discussions and you never end up with a specific cutback by the Bureau of the Budget, per se. It is a matter of reexamining both on the part of the Bureau of the Budget and on the part

7. *Ibid.*, p. 16286.
8. *Supplemental Appropriations, 1966*, Hearings before the Senate Appropriations Subcommittee, 89 Cong. 1 sess. (Oct. 12, 1965), p. 65.

of the Department, certain items, but from what we started out with there was a very substantial reduction ultimately in what the President actually requested.[9]

Pity the poor budget director when Congress gets its hands on him. The director has long been a favorite congressional whipping boy. He heads a dedicated career staff that is regarded as "the President's own" and that largely continues from administration to administration, regardless of party, even if he does not. Appointed to his $42,500-a-year post without Senate confirmation, he is strictly the President's to hire or fire.

Informal contacts between various legislators and the director and Budget Bureau staff are many and daily. Occasionally the director meets privately on the Hill with a legislator or a small group. They importune him as to why the administration ought to take this or that factor into account in formulating its position on a particular bill or appropriation. Legislators and their staff repeatedly call the bureau to check on the status of a project proposal or a legislative report. Once a program has been authorized, senators are well aware that if they can get it into the budget a good part of their battle for the appropriations has been won. In the annual economy charade, the presidential sanction of budget approval is usually essential.

But despite the range of informal contacts, the director's formal appearances before congressional committees generally are few. At the beginning of a session he travels to Capitol Hill to testify on the budget outlook before the Joint Economic Committee and before the House Committee on Appropriations. Otherwise, except for testifying on raising the debt limit or on his own appropriations, he usually remains downtown.[10] It is when the director comes to the Hill to defend several small budgets related to the Executive Office of the President, of which the Bureau of the Budget is a vital part, that a few members of Congress finally have an opportunity to corner him. The arena is the Treasury–

9. *Treasury and Post Office Appropriations, 1966,* Hearings before the Senate Appropriations Subcommittee, 89 Cong. 1 sess. (April 14, 1965), p. 562.

10. Budget directors have had different practices as to the number of formal appearances they make on the Hill. Some have preferred to let the cabinet carry the load; a few have waded into the legislative waters with delight. According to the Bureau of the Budget, in the eight years 1959–66, budget directors appeared before *all* congressional committees on 90 occasions: Maurice H. Stans (Eisenhower), 1959 (1) and 1960 (5); David E. Bell (Kennedy), 1961 (9), 1962 (17), and 1963 (13); Kermit Gordon (Johnson), 1964 (5) and 1965 (10); Charles L. Schultze (Johnson), 1965 (6) and 1966 (24).

Post Office Appropriations Subcommittee of either House. Not much time is spent on what he actually comes to advocate.

The appearance of Budget Director Kermit Gordon before Senator Robertson's Treasury–Post Office Subcommittee in 1965 was illustrative. Senator Yarborough, then on Appropriations for only four months, had long sponsored the so-called cold war GI bill, which would extend to men on active duty in the cold war period educational and veterans' benefits similar to those provided for veterans of the Second World War and Korea. After directing a few cursory questions at Gordon, Yarborough articulated what really bothered him:

> Mr. Gordon, in the last 6 years you and your predecessors in office . . . have uniformly and unanimously sent up letters to the Congress opposing the passage of a GI bill to educate these cold war veterans. . . . How many of that staff of yours did it take and what process of auditing did you use to come up with the solution that this was not a good thing for the Government to give these veterans an opportunity to go to school after they got out of the service? What process did you use?

Gordon replied that his bureau did not determine the position of the administration on legislation; rather, it had "a coordinating function." That did not satisfy the senator, who continued to lecture the director on the advantages of his proposal and scolded: "The Bureau of the Budget should not send up a letter like that if it is based on your independent judgment, because it is wrong." Yarborough admitted, however, that "if the administration, the President, tells you to take that position, that is a horse of a different color." After Gordon reaffirmed the bureau's role in soliciting the comments of interested federal agencies and reconciling any differences that appeared, Yarborough turned to veterans' programs in general, accusing the bureau of cutting back on funds for veterans and "whittling down at the farmers." The director was eventually able to explain the other appropriations requests he had come prepared to defend. There were no questions.[11]

Gordon's experience was not unique. Twenty-one years earlier, Budget Director Harold D. Smith commented in a Senate Appropriations subcommittee meeting:

> . . . the test of the situation comes when I come up here before the House Committee or this committee, and discuss the Bureau of the Budget. I get about 10 minutes on my budget and 2 hours on everybody else's budget, which indicates to me that you have in your minds questions which you

11. *Treasury and Post Office Appropriations, 1966* (April 15, 1965), pp. 573–87.

would like to have answered, and you feel that you only have a chance to get at the Director of the Budget when he appears before you.[12]

Smith urged that better communication be established between his office and the committees, and volunteered to come up for a special session any time questions arose. While the House Appropriations Committee now schedules a regular hearing with the director of the budget at the beginning of each session, the Senate committee seldom does.

The General Accounting Office

Thirteen blocks closer to Capitol Hill than the high-ceilinged, mid-Victorian Executive Office Building housing the Bureau of the Budget stands the massive modern headquarters of the General Accounting Office. The GAO, with over 4,300 employees, is a part of the legislative branch. But while close in location and statutory tie, it seems at times far removed from the congressional appropriations process.

Like the Bureau of the Budget, the GAO was established by the Budget and Accounting Act of 1921. Under that act the audit responsibility that had rested in the Department of the Treasury and the executive branch since the earliest days of the Republic was transferred to a General Accounting Office. The purpose was to assure an independent audit free from possible executive influence. For a quarter century, the GAO was regarded as an independent agency rather than a part of the legislative branch. In the Reorganization Act of 1939, Congress placed the GAO with various regulatory and independent agencies in a category beyond the President's power to reorganize by executive order. Finally, with the Reorganization Act of 1945, Congress added a sentence in section 7 that, in defining "agency," provided: "Such a term does not include the Comptroller General of the United States or the General Accounting Office, which are a part of the legislative branch of the Government."[13]

Like the Budget Bureau, the GAO is highly professional. Over 2,500 of the GAO personnel are professional, and more than 400 of these are certified public accountants. Where the Bureau of the Budget is the stronghold of the Ivy League graduate with his Ph.D. in economics or political science, the GAO attracts accountants and attorneys from

12. *Independent Offices Appropriations, 1946,* Hearings before the Senate Appropriations Subcommittee, 79 Cong. 1 sess. (Feb. 28, 1945), p. 309.

13. 42 Stat. 23, sec. 301; 53 Stat. 561; 59 Stat. 616.

colleges all over America. Headed by a $42,500-a-year comptroller general of the United States who is appointed by the President and confirmed by the Senate for a fifteen-year term, the GAO and its policies are not subject to the changes of executive whim.

The chairman of the House committee that reported the Budget and Accounting Act declared:

> It was the intention of the committee that the Comptroller General should be something more than a bookkeeper or accountant; that he should be a real critic; and at all times should come to Congress, no matter what the political complexion of Congress or the Executive might be, and point out inefficiency. . . .[14]

Over the years, the GAO has conscientiously observed this mandate. Some in the executive branch have decried its emphasis on exactitude, and every young management intern has heard the story of the career civil servant who received a check for one cent as a result of an audit conducted years after the fact. But no one doubts that the very presence of the GAO has saved the taxpayers many billions of dollars.[15]

Although the purpose of the 1921 act establishing the GAO was to provide Congress with a means to oversee the administration of government programs, little was done to bring the GAO and its legislative parent together until the selection of Lindsay C. Warren as comptroller general in late 1940. A North Carolina Democrat, Warren served sixteen years in Congress before his appointment. He realized that much of the excellent work of the GAO was not being used effectively by the legislative branch. He sought to bridge the gap. In a foreword to his final report in 1953, Comptroller General Warren noted:

> Since I have held the office of Comptroller General I have continuously sought to fulfill this need by maintaining a close liaison with the Congress, and by so gearing the operations of the General Accounting Office that we can be of real assistance to the legislative branch. I have considered the legislative reporting function and the related duty of furnishing assistance to the committees of Congress as two of the most important tasks of the General Accounting Office as the agent of the Congress.[16]

14. Cited in *Annual Report of the Comptroller General of the United States for the Fiscal Year Ended June 30, 1962*, p. 17.

15. In his annual report, the comptroller general notes the "refunds, collections, and other measurable financial benefits resulting from the work of the General Accounting Office." For fiscal year 1965, this totaled $186,780,000; for fiscal year 1964, $321,489,000; for fiscal year 1963, $247,547,000; and for fiscal year 1962, $162,875,000. *Annual Report of the Comptroller General of the United States,* appropriate fiscal year, p. 1.

16. *Ibid.,* fiscal year 1953, pp. iii, 5.

When Warren retired in 1954, President Eisenhower nominated as his replacement Joseph Campbell, who served until mid-1965. Campbell, a member of the Atomic Energy Commission for a year prior to his appointment, had become familiar with the advantages of effective legislative liaison. He continued Warren's emphasis in this area. Campbell's successor, Elmer B. Staats—a career official of the Bureau of the Budget long exposed to the congressional way of life—has been intensifying these efforts.

Under the rules of the Senate and the House of Representatives, all GAO reports are received by the Committees on Government Operations. Copies of these reports are also made available to the relevant legislative committees and Appropriations subcommittees. In fiscal year 1965, 411 audit reports were made to Congress. During that period, committees and members asked the GAO for 167 special reports. In addition, at the request of various committee chairmen, the comptroller general submitted 476 reports on pending bills.[17] Direct staff assistance is also made available to congressional committees. In fiscal year 1965 it amounted to 7,600 man-days. In most instances the GAO is not reimbursed for the cost of the personnel it makes available. The Senate Committee on Appropriations, however, follows a long-standing policy of reimbursing the GAO. Usually three or four GAO professionals are assigned, by request, to Senate Appropriations, and twelve or so to House Appropriations. Other committees make equal or greater use of GAO personnel. The GAO provides witnesses to testify in public and closed hearings on the results of their investigations. In hearings, GAO reports and decisions of the comptroller general are referred to by senators and agencies alike to question, support, and condemn various executive actions.

As the difference in the amount of GAO staff assistance indicates, Senate Appropriations has not used the resources of the General Accounting Office as extensively as has its House counterpart—although there are some exceptions, including the Agriculture, District of Columbia, Labor-HEW, and State-Justice Subcommittees. An analysis of both House and Senate Appropriations hearings shows a substantially greater use of GAO reports and material by the House Committee.[18]

17. *Ibid.*, fiscal year 1965, pp. 19, 21, 22, and 26.
18. *References to U.S. General Accounting Office in Hearings before House and Senate Committees on Appropriations, 1966, 89 Cong. 1 sess.*, Prepared by United States General Accounting Office Legislative Digest Section, Pt. 1 (Civilian Activities).

In recent years some House Appropriations subcommittees have also met with the GAO staff expert on a particular program prior to the agency hearings. Since 1955, at the request of the House Appropriations chairman, the GAO has prepared an annual report summarizing its significant audit findings on an agency by agency basis for convenient use by the members during the hearings.

Most senators and staff members who have taken the trouble to scrutinize GAO material and to avail themselves of its staff assistance label the quality of work "excellent," "invaluable," and "most helpful." A few on the staff, however, are not pleased. For example, one who believes that the GAO has done "tremendously good work in many areas," added:

> The General Accounting Office is so engrossed in the matter of reducing its findings to writing and trading letters back and forth with agency heads that by the time they are ready to publish their results, the agency head will have corrected the error and all of the air has gone out of the thing. They never really come to grips with the basic and underlying problems.

Another staff member objected that the GAO does not give Congress a report "until two years after the fact." Perhaps these critics fail to realize that in the long run Congress and the General Accounting Office need each other if either is to be successful in assuring the wise expenditure of public funds, since only by calling administrators to account during the appropriations process and imposing sanctions on repeated violators can a waste of public funds be curtailed.

President Johnson informed his cabinet on May 2, 1964:

> I want all reports made by the General Accounting Office and any Congressional committee to be given prompt and thorough and careful attention. Honest mistakes can be forgiven, but it is hard to forgive failures to examine and tighten agency procedures to guard against a recurrence of an error that is uncovered by the GAO or by a Congressional committee. Look into them promptly. If the criticisms are justified, I will expect you to take corrective action so that the error is not repeated.[19]

It would seem that the committees of Congress might give the GAO reports equal emphasis. But few Appropriations subcommittees have done as the Senate's Treasury–Post Office Appropriations Subcommittee recommended in its report submitted shortly after President Johnson gave his instructions. Noting that the committee shared the President's

19. *Congressional Quarterly Weekly Report*, Vol. 22 (May 8, 1964), p. 939.

views, the report urged departments "to give prompt and vigorous attention to deficiencies and recommendations contained in reports of the Comptroller General."[20] Granted that senators are busy men, pulled among numerous responsibilities, and lacking time for adequate briefing; still, it is this very situation that creates a great need for more imaginative use of Congress' willing aide, the General Accounting Office.

Advice on Science Policy

President Johnson's budget for fiscal year 1967 included requests for more than $15 billion in research and development funds. Although the bulk of such funds is expended by the Atomic Energy Commission, the Department of Defense, and the National Aeronautics and Space Administration, hardly a major department of government lacks an "R&D" program that affects the scientific and industrial community. Senators and their staffs, like most Americans, are not well schooled in the complexities of modern science and technology. They worry over needless duplication; they suspect that a large portion of the research programs contain padding; they feel inadequate as lay legislators to cope with and evaluate the jargon and the world of those they view— sometimes with awe—as technocrats.

Confronted with similar frustrations, President Eisenhower established the Office of Special Assistant to the President for Science and Technology in 1957. In 1962, President Kennedy secured congressional approval to institutionalize this function in an Office of Science and Technology that, like the Bureau of the Budget and the Council of Economic Advisers, now forms a vital part of the Executive Office.

In the early 1960s, various members of the House and Senate advocated the establishment of a congressional scientific advisory staff. In 1964, House Appropriations—over the opposition of the Senate Appropriations Legislative Subcommittee, then chaired by Senator Monroney—added funds for the Legislative Reference Service of the Library of Congress to set up a Science Policy Research Division. While excellent work has been done by this division in examining various scientific programs—especially those that cut across several agencies—the demand for its services has come primarily from individual legislators and a few legislative committees, not from Appropriations.

20. *Treasury, Post Office, and Executive Office Appropriation Bill, 1965*, Report to accompany H.R. 10532, S. Rept. 1095, 88 Cong. 2 sess. (June 17, 1964), p. 3.

In 1965, Senator Stennis established an ad hoc subcommittee within Defense Appropriations to consider and evaluate research and development requests. With that exception, little innovation in this area has occurred within the committee and no staff members have been recruited who are skilled in analyzing scientific programs. The lack of scientific advice remains one of the great unmet needs of the committee.

The Hearing

The Purposes of the Hearing Process

The congressional committee hearing has long been a battleground where contending forces seek to produce the public record needed to win the fight behind closed doors or, later, on the floor. A Democrat, who had substantial House-Senate experience as well as many years in the witness chair as the representative of a cause, expressed the sentiment of many colleagues when he remarked that "the hearing process is both essential and meaningless at the same time." This legislator was disturbed by how often he found himself "beguiled or repelled by the character and the quality of the witness" before him. He thought that before his colleagues listened to witnesses, they should scrutinize the agency budget and see if they could secure an "impartial feeling of the agency activity."

To the hearing legislators bring the many bits of information they have gathered informally. The hearing can be the formal crucible in which this information is tested. As another subcommittee chairman observed, "The hearing opens things up. That, plus a special inquiry, will usually do the job." He believed that the hearing process enabled the committee "to determine whether the agency administrator is merely parroting the written statements that his budget officer has given him or whether he really knows what is going on in the various programs for which he is responsible."

The formal hearing provides the opportunity for Congress to wheedle from administrators, who are under "guidance" to defend the President's budget, just what their "real" needs are. Senator Mundt, during an interchange with a witness at agricultural appropriations hearings in 1965, explicitly noted this tendency:

> The department people usually encourage us to ask, and view with open arms, a series of questions of that type. That is one way we can make

progress and elicit information from you which under the rules of the game we presume you would not want to volunteer. It is appropriate for us to say, on any project in Government at a given level recommended by the Budget or Department, "If you had had your own way, and you had a little more money, do you think it can be fruitfully used?"[21]

From the President's viewpoint, agency heads all too frequently "tell all" when they are questioned about what happened to the requests they originally submitted to the Bureau of the Budget.

Of course, a certain amount of protocol and charade must be observed. In 1965, Buford Ellington, then director of the Office of Emergency Planning, testified before the Independent Offices Subcommittee on a request for $35 million for disaster relief from floods in Colorado, Kansas, and New Mexico. Ranking Republican Allott naturally was interested in seeing that sufficient funds were appropriated, since he was also the senior senator from Colorado. The budget request had been submitted directly to the Senate because the appropriation bill had already passed the House. Allott sought to develop a clear Senate record as it would be the only one available on this item in conference.

> SENATOR ALLOTT: . . . I know that you cannot request funds above what the Budget Bureau has authorized you to request. But I think, also, that I can without embarrassing you and certainly without any embarrassment to myself ask you what funds you think you might reasonably need.
> MR. ELLINGTON: This would be, Senator——.
> SENATOR ALLOTT: In the next 2 months.
> MR. ELLINGTON: This would be purely a guess and speculation, but I would say $25 million additional.[22]

Allott made sure the "$25 million additional" was provided as far as the Senate was concerned.

Some agency heads are very circumspect in commenting on Budget Bureau decisions. They know that the bureau's examiner for their agency reads the hearings and that they will have to face him all too soon in preparing their budget for the next fiscal year, as well as for apportioning the expenditures to be made under current appropriations. Thus, in 1965, Senator Hill and the chairman of the National

21. *Agricultural Appropriations (Research), 1966,* Hearings before the Senate Appropriations Subcommittee, 89 Cong. 1 sess. (March 11, 1965), p. 492.

22. *Independent Offices Appropriations, 1966,* Hearings before the Senate Appropriations Subcommittee, 89 Cong. 1 sess. (June 22, 1965), p. 1340.

Labor Relations Board, Frank W. McCulloch, verbally danced about what the Budget Bureau had actually done with the NLRB requests:

SENATOR HILL: What is your general feeling about the budget allowance before us? Are you reasonably well satisfied with it?

MR. MCCULLOCH: Yes, the agency can work with it.

SENATOR HILL: It can?

MR. MCCULLOCH: Yes, sir. I think the Budget Bureau has entered into the consideration of our request very fully. We had a long discussion with them, a very full discussion, and we took down our hair about all of our problems, and they quizzed us very sharply. They asked us to make some reductions, and we did, and we have reached a figure that we think is a workable figure.

SENATOR HILL: You think it is workable?

MR. MCCULLOCH: Yes.[23]

Others are bashful only for a time. In the 1965 agricultural appropriations hearings, Chairman Holland attempted to pry from S. R. Smith, the administrator of the Consumer and Marketing Service in the Department of Agriculture, a statement of the need for an additional $500,000 requested in Smith's original budget and missing from the President's budget:

MR. SMITH: . . . I conclude by saying that the need is there, as we see it. But we, of course, are obliged, as you know, to support what is part of our budget request.

SENATOR HOLLAND: You are not obliged to refrain from expressing your own opinion when this committee asks you to express your opinion, which is what we are doing now.

MR. SMITH: You do not think I have expressed my opinion yet?

SENATOR HOLLAND: I have not really understood that you have. You have said a good many words, more than you generally use, but I have not yet understood what you mean.

MR. SMITH: We have been of the opinion that there is need for more funds than are currently available, and we still believe that to be the case, sir.

SENATOR HOLLAND: You still support in your own thinking the need for the additional $500,000 which you requested from the Budget Bureau?

MR. SMITH: And more than likely in making up the budget for the fiscal year following the one to which we are addressing ourselves, we will probably do the same thing.[24]

23. *Labor-Health, Education, Welfare Appropriations, 1966,* Hearings before the Senate Appropriations Subcommittee, 89 Cong. 1 sess. (March 26, 1965), Pt. 2, p. 1873.

24. *Agricultural Appropriations, 1966,* Hearings before the Senate Appropriations Subcommittee, 89 Cong. 1 sess. (June 4, 1965), Pt. 1, pp. 302–03.

Senators interested in public works development are especially concerned with the amount that the Corps of Engineers can use during the next fiscal year in planning or constructing a given project. Throughout the hearings of the Public Works Subcommittee, the Army Engineers, whose working relations with Congress generally transcend any direction secretaries of the army and even presidents have been able to exert, are repeatedly asked by the chairman and members: "What is your capability?" which means: "How much do you need?" Legislators do not come into the hearing room untouched by the desires, competitions, and bureaucratic fights of the Washington world outside. And agencies are only too willing to tip off a friendly legislator in advance of the hearings as to what to ask—if it means more funds and more people for them. The hearing simply provides formal recognition of these informal aspects of political life.

The Witness

Senators, hurrying from one meeting to another with little time to probe an agency's justifications, do not base their judgments merely on "facts." They recognize that spenders and economizers, advocates and objectors all have facts to support their cause. A legislator constantly seeks to sift the relevant from the irrelevant and the genuine from the false in terms of his own policy preferences. If he lacks deep convictions on a subject—and in dealing with the funding of particular programs it is easy to forget purposes and become immersed in details—then he is often willing to listen and to be convinced. A key factor is the ability of the witness supporting (and, in the case of outside witnesses, occasionally opposing) a program to convince the busy legislator in a limited amount of time.

THE SUCCESSFUL PRESENTATION. What are the characteristics of the successful agency witness? Universally, senators and committee staff members agree that knowledge of the subject, clarity, brevity, and candor are the essential ingredients. Sincerity is important: "He should show he is not just doing a job." Proper deference for the committee and its prerogatives is also very helpful.

The witness who presents his case in a manner that shows thorough knowledge evokes the confidence of committee members. A long-time Appropriations member noted in 1966:

> After you've served for a while on a subcommittee you learn which bureau heads really know their business. They come up year after year and you get

to know how qualified they are and how good they are and how reliable what they have told you has been. With Cabinet members you are usually dealing with them on high policy and you do not expect them to know everything—although when you deal with a person like [Secretary of Defense Robert S.] McNamara, he will tell you what is going on right down to the last horseshoe and he will know his facts.

Senator Ellender, an experienced prober of executive witnesses, concurred, as his remarks at the 1966 Defense appropriations hearings made clear:

> It is very refreshing, to say the least, for a witness to be able to stand before us without a bevy of advisers to inform him on subjects that are up for discussion.
>
> Mr. McNamara seems to know every part of his subject, and I am sure that it is due to the fact that he does his homework well. I wish more people would do that, we might save a lot of time.[25]

Focusing on the virtues of brevity and clarity, another senator commented: "The successful witness is one who has a complete statement which is put in the record, summarizes it for delivery very succinctly, and answers questions with ease and directness." A veteran staff member, urging graphic as well as oral presentation, stated: "Members are faced with a deluge of words which they need synthesized. The man who predigests it for them, puts a handle on it, and lets them know the priority of needs is the most successful." "Once he has sold his point of view to the committee, the successful witness will shut up," emphasized one senator. He recalled his days in the state legislature when he was chairman of the appropriations committee: "One fellow wanted $2,000 from us and all the members of the committee were ready to give it to him. It was late in the afternoon when the witness was called on to testify, but he decided that he wanted to make a speech. He made it and we gave him only half of what he wanted."

Another senator remembered meeting with an assistant secretary of state a few days before his budget was scheduled to be heard. The official proudly exhibited the many pages of testimony he would submit at the hearing. "I told him it was too cumbersome," said the senator, "and that he ought to take it back to his shop and spell out in simple terms what funds were needed for this aspect of our foreign policy and the contributions our government has made to these programs." The

---

25. *Defense Appropriations, 1966,* Hearings before the Senate Appropriations Subcommittee, 89 Cong. 1 sess. (Feb. 26, 1965), Pt. 1, pp. 298–99.

official was hesitant to take the advice and replied unenthusiastically: "Well, the staff has spent a lot of time preparing this statement and they are proud of the job that they have done." He reluctantly accepted the senator's counsel and recast the statement. The result was that the assistant secretary was before the committee for less than half an hour. In previous years, he had spent four hours or all day explaining his program. The assistant secretary became adept in presenting his material not the way his staff preferred, but the way it was most useful to Congress. He found that brevity is always appreciated.

Senators also want plain language. In requesting further explanation on a Department of Defense item, Senator Stennis advised an agency witness: "All right. Let's get a letter from Dr. Brown [the director of Defense research and engineering] in language that we can understand. We don't want scientific terminology."[26]

Nothing so disturbs senators as lack of candor. They want straight answers. After listening to Rex M. Whitton, the federal highway administrator, and Lawrence S. Casazza, director of the Office of Administration in the Bureau of Public Roads, at hearings on the 1966 Supplemental Appropriations bill, Senator Saltonstall was moved to comment: "I respect the frankness with which these gentlemen testify, which is a little, I won't say unusual, but is a little different from what we get sometimes . . . and it makes a good impression."[27] Senators easily recognize the slogan with little substance and the use of tricky statistics; they have probably resorted to such devices themselves and all are convinced that their opponents have.

Proper deference for the committee and its members is appreciated. In the judgment of several senators, some executive witnesses—"especially those from the State Department" and "some scientists"—appear with chips on their shoulders. They seem "to resent Congress questioning their activities and it shows in their attitude and response to questions." "When an agency witness has been asked a ridiculous question," suggested one member, "he would be well advised to follow the policy of praising a senator excessively as he seeks to correct him." And even if a senator is not wrong, it does not harm executive-legislative relations to praise him anyway. Deference should also continue after one's ap-

26. *Military Construction Appropriations, 1966,* Hearings before the Senate Appropriations Subcommittee, 89 Cong. 1 sess. (May 12, 1965), p. 687.

27. *Supplemental Appropriations, 1966,* Hearings before the Senate Appropriations Subcommittee, 89 Cong. 1 sess. (Oct. 15, 1965), p. 707.

pearance. On occasion, an executive witness has testified before an Appropriations subcommittee and then, after returning to his office, "shot his mouth off," as one senator put it. Often the word finds its way back to Capitol Hill and an executive career is jeopardized.

THE UNSUCCESSFUL WITNESS. "Doesn't understand his own program," "bluffs," "evasive," "lectures the committee," "mumbles," "lacks facts at his fingertips," "talks down to the committee," "dictatorial," "fuzzy," "long-winded," "argues"—these are some of the descriptions committee members have given of the unsuccessful witness.

Reflecting on the many agency witnesses who have failed in their presentation, one senator said: "When you appear before the committee, you are doing a selling job. Yet a lot from the executive branch don't look at it that way. They act like they are in a court under oath where the attitude is 'I'm not going to tell you anything unless you ask me specifically.' " Particularly bothersome are "the number of agency people who come before the committee and simply cannot explain their program without rummaging through the huge briefing book that is in front of them—and then usually they cannot find the right answer when they do rummage through it." Equally annoying is the argumentative witness: "It is O.K. to stand up for your agency and try to be objective, but there is no point in going to the floor and rolling around and tangling with a senator. The witness should say, 'Well, we can't agree on that, Senator, but perhaps if I could come by and provide you with further information, it might be helpful.' " Committee members are also irritated by an official's failure to admit that his budget can be tightened. "After all," a Democratic senator noted, "everyone can save a little more money in any program and the successful witness will admit it." Equally irritating are witnesses who do not admit error. Said a subcommittee chairman: "I've seen some administrative officers get into tremendous difficulty with the committee because they were afraid to admit an error. When they try to cover up they get into real trouble. After all, we are human and we can understand that errors can be made and it would be better for them to come out and make a frank admission that an error was made but that they were trying to correct it."

Judged even more inept were many public witnesses. Indeed, committee members and staff personnel have found that the public—or outside—witnesses are usually the worst prepared. Some do not fully understand the content of the programs they espouse. Others erroneously believe that the longer they talk the more impressed senators will be. Senators repeatedly urge witnesses to summarize briefly their prepared testimony and then simply file their formal statement in the record. Some, however, never learn.

In 1965, one public witness before the Labor-HEW Subcommittee was a last-minute substitute for the person originally scheduled to testify:

> SENATOR HILL: . . . I have no disposition to cut you off in any way, but we have a number of witnesses waiting yet to be heard. Would you put your statement in full in the record and then summarize it for us? Would that be satisfactory?
>
> WITNESS: The statement, Mr. Chairman, is the statement of. . . . I have not read the statement that carefully, that I could properly summarize it.
>
> SENATOR HILL: I see. You are not too familiar with it yourself?
>
> WITNESS: Not with the statement in its total length; no.
>
> SENATOR HILL: All right you may go ahead, then.[28]

So the witness who had not read the statement went ahead. There were no questions when he finished. Then there was the witness who did not really know what had happened to the item in which he was interested.

> SENATOR HILL: The House increased the budget estimate, did it not?
>
> WITNESS: I haven't heard of that.
>
> SENATOR HILL: It did, by a sum of over $3 million, almost $4 million.
>
> WITNESS: That is very encouraging.[29]

Most senators wonder why some agency and public witnesses—who obviously go to a great deal of trouble to testify—do not stop to analyze the effect their manner of presentation will have on their ability to persuade the committee.

The Questions—or, Who Does the Work?

At the heart of the hearing and essential to the information-gathering process are the questions posed by the senator as he seeks facts, opinions, reassurance, or even—on occasion—"executive blood." The ques-

---

28. *Labor-Health, Education, Welfare Appropriations, 1966,* Hearings before the Senate Appropriations Subcommittee, 89 Cong. 1 sess. (June 18, 1965), Pt. 2, pp. 2336–40.

29. *Ibid.* (June 11, 1965), Pt. 2, p. 2254.

tions reflect the values, experience, and knowledge of the legislator. They reveal his concerns and frequently those of the diverse constituency that will confront him at the ballot box.

Many members feel that some questions asked by the subcommittee chairmen are too routine or easy. Cabinet officers have been known to remark that the "dry runs" conducted by their own subordinates in advance of a hearing are much more difficult than committee questions. "A lot depends on how well you do your homework and how well you are acquainted with the subject," said a senior subcommittee chairman.

It is difficult to judge the motive for and intent of each question asked in a hearing. The questioner's view of the hearing process, his intonation, habits of speaking, and mannerisms are all involved. So is the personality of the witness. The written record (especially since it is edited before publication) can never fully reveal the interrelations between a witness and the various subcommittee members.[30] A self-satisfied senator may snap out a belligerent query to the harassed administrator whose soft answer neutralizes the intended barb. One legislative assistant, noting that his senator "views the hearings as an adversary proceeding," mused: "I can see the old district attorney come out in him as he closes in on an agency witness." A senator may stumble and grope, yet unearth significant data.

It is possible, of course, to analyze the more objective aspects of the questions posed in appropriations hearings. Is the role of the questioner policy formulation, or saving money, or adding money; and is this role related to the questioner's authorization committee assignment? Is the purpose of the question to seek new information the witness has not previously referred to; to seek clarification of a witness's statement; to praise a witness; to admonish a witness for not doing enough; or to admonish a witness for doing too much? Is the question related to background, or program administration, or program cost, or to the value of the program? Is it concerned with a new or an old pro-

---

30. For an interesting attempt to analyze agency presentations and the interaction between subcommittee members and agency representatives, including the tendency of an agency to respond to subcommittee questions in an evasive manner, see Ira Sharkansky, "Four Agencies and an Appropriations Subcommittee: A Comparative Study of Budget Strategies," *Midwest Journal of Political Science*, Vol. 9 (August 1965), pp. 254–81. See also Robert F. Bales, *Interaction Process Analysis* (Addison-Wesley Press, 1950), pp. 9, 177–95.

gram? Is the geographic focus international, national, state, or local? Is the questioner seeking to elicit a fact or a value judgment? Is he asking for himself, another senator, the committee staff, an outside party from his own state, or an outside party from elsewhere? These questions are only suggestive of the many that could be asked about the hearing questions.

Who asks the questions at the hearings—who does the work—is significant because participation in the committee's hearing process usually correlates with, or can lead to, a role in its decision making. The number of public hearings a senator attends is one way to judge his involvement in the committee's work. But attendance alone is not a satisfactory criterion. In 1965, for example, each senator on Appropriations was assigned to at least five of the fifteen subcommittees or panels into which the work of the full committee was then divided. Often several subcommittees would meet at the same time. Thus it was very difficult, if not impossible, for a senator to participate in many of the formal subcommittee hearings. On the other hand, a senator may drop in on a public hearing and then wander out as silently as he arrived, never having asked a question and perhaps having glanced only hastily at the testimony of the witness. He may receive credit for appearing, but he will not have affected the work. While lengthy questioning by a senator may occasionally reflect only garrulousness, usually it is a clear indicator of involvement in the committee's work.

Table 4–1 ranks the 1965 members according to their hearing attendance and juxtaposes this to their party seniority. Table 4–2 ranks each senator according to the number of questions he asked as compared to the total number of questions asked in all of the subcommittees of which he was a member during 1965, again in juxtaposition to party seniority. Table 4–2 gives junior senators more just recognition for their efforts than would a comparison of their questions to total questions in a single subcommittee.

Ten of the fourteen senators who were in the upper half of Table 4–1, ranking their attendance, were also in the upper half of Table 4–2 as those most actively involved in the questioning process. Of these ten, only Senator Allott was not a subcommittee chairman. The predominance of the subcommittee chairmen is explained partly by the intense questioning they conducted in the subcommittees over which they presided. But that effort also meant that sometimes they did not

Table 4–1. Percentage of Total Public Hearings on Appropriations (Full Committee and Assigned Subcommittees) Attended by Each Member of Senate Appropriations in 1965, in Juxtaposition to Party Seniority

Name	Party seniority	Per-centage	Name	Party seniority	Per-centage
Saltonstall (R–Mass.)	1	53.1	Magnuson (D–Wash.)	7	22.1
Ellender (D–La.)	3	48.7	Mundt (R–S. Dak.)	3	20.1
Allott (R–Colo.)	7	48.4	Pastore (D–R.I.)	10	18.5
Yarborough (D–Tex.)	18	43.0	Hill (D–Ala.)	4	18.4
Byrd (D–W. Va.)	13	41.7	Case (R–N.J.)	9	14.3
Young (R–N. Dak.)	2	40.4	Hruska (R–Nebr.)	6	13.6
Hayden (D–Ariz.)	1	37.7	Robertson (D–Va.)	6	12.0
Monroney (D–Okla.)	11	31.1	Bible (D–Nev.)	12	10.5
Bartlett (D–Alaska)	16	30.9	McGee (D–Wyo.)	14	9.9
Smith (R–Maine)	4	30.5	Cotton (R–N.H.)	8	8.4
Stennis (D–Miss.)	9	28.8	Kuchel (R–Calif.)	5	7.3
Holland (D–Fla.)	8	27.5	Mansfield (D–Mont.)	15	3.8
McClellan (D–Ark.)	5	23.3	Russell (D–Ga.)[a]	2	2.4
Proxmire (D–Wis.)	17	22.3			

a. Senator Russell was absent from the Senate during most of the 1965 session recovering from an operation; ordinarily, he is one of the most active members of the committee as chairman of the Defense Subcommittee.

have much time to participate in the other subcommittees to which they were assigned. Consequently, in terms of aggregate subcommittee opportunities for participation, the subcommittee chairmen's high percentages were well deserved.

As Table 4–1 shows, among the fourteen members of Senate Appropriations leading in total attendance during the 1965 hearings, there were as many junior Democrats (in the lower half of their party in terms of committee seniority) as there were senior Democrats. The junior Democrats were not assigned to as many of the major subcommittees as their seniors. Participation by the junior Republicans was quite spotty. Table 4–2 shows differences between the parties but no differences because of seniority. Among the fourteen senators most active in the questioning process were twelve Democrats and only two Republicans. Among the thirteen less active senators were six Democrats and seven Republicans. In both categories, the parties had an equal number of senior and junior members. The greater activity of Democrats reflects the dominance of the subcommittee chairmen, but

Table 4-2. Amount of Questioning by Each Committee Member during 1965 Public Hearings on Appropriations as a Percentage of Total Questions Asked in Each Member's Assigned Subcommittees

Name	Party seniority	Percentage of total questions asked in assigned subcommittees	Number of questions asked by senator in assigned subcommittees
Ellender (D–La.)	3	25.6	5,954
Holland (D–Fla.)	8	14.8	3,204
Byrd (D–W. Va.)	13	12.3	2,052
Magnuson (D–Wash.)	7	11.6	2,630
Stennis (D–Miss.)	9	11.4	3,042
McClellan (D–Ark.)	5	9.2	1,744
Allott (R–Colo.)	7	8.7	1,561
Hill (D–Ala.)	4	7.8	1,863
Monroney (D–Okla.)	11	7.7	1,439
Pastore (D–R.I.)	10	6.0	1,349
Saltonstall (R–Mass.)	1	5.6	1,100
Bartlett (D–Alaska)	16	5.1	467
Bible (D–Nev.)	12	4.1	671
Proxmire (D–Wis.)	17	3.7	503
Mundt (R–S. Dak.)	3	3.2	738
Hayden (D–Ariz.)	1	3.2	690
Young (R–N. Dak.)	2	3.0	775
Smith (R–Maine)	4	2.6	569
Yarborough (D–Tex.)	18	2.5	286
Robertson (D–Va.)	6	2.0	430
Hruska (R–Nebr.)	6	1.6	363
Cotton (R–N.H.)	8	1.6	251
Case (R–N.J.)	9	0.7	88
McGee (D–Wyo.)	14	0.6	99
Russell (D–Ga.)[a]	2	0.3	78
Mansfield (D–Mont.)	15	0.2	36
Kuchel (R–Calif.)	5	0.06	13

a. Senator Russell was away from the Senate during most of the 1965 session recovering from an operation; ordinarily, he is one of the most active members of the committee as chairman of the Defense Subcommittee.

the figures also show that the ranking minority members, although a part of the bipartisan subcommittee leadership, were generally much less active than other members of the majority party.

Figure 4–1 shows who does the work in each subgroup of Senate Appropriations. It gives the percentage of total questions that each category of members asked in each subcommittee's public hearings in 1965. In more than half of the Appropriations groups, the chairman clearly dominated the questioning process. Where the chairman was not the principal participant, other Democrats were the most active. This was especially true of the full committee, the Subcommittee on Foreign Operations, the Subcommittee on Interior, and the Public Works panel on Reclamation—Interior Power Marketing Agencies. Although in each of these instances Senator Hayden was the nominal chairman, because of his age he limited his activity to the Interior Subcommittee, the Public Works panel, and one hearing of the full committee. Consequently, greater opportunity was provided for other Democratic members to participate and to develop the hearing record than would ordinarily be the case.

Equally as evident as the dominance of the chairmen is the low level of participation by many of the ranking Republicans. The participation of the other Republican members on the subcommittees surpassed that of the ranking Republicans approximately half the time. But in some cases the participation of all the Republicans was almost non-existent. This was especially noticeable in the subcommittees on the District of Columbia and Public Works—AEC-TVA. There was even less participation, however, by many ex officio members. Of the twenty-seven ex officio members only thirteen questioned a witness at a hearing during 1965.[31]

In these circumstances it is understandable that subcommittee decisions are largely shaped by the chairman and his professional staff member, with only occasional assistance from the ranking minority member. With few exceptions, it is the subcommittee chairman alone who is thoroughly conversant with program requests and who does the work. Of course, the dominance of the chairman over decision making is a cause as well as an effect of his dominance in the questioning process at hearings. Because they feel that the chairman will make the basic decisions anyway, some members make no attempt to participate in the hearings.

The Investigative Function

The regular annual appropriation hearing, however intensive the questioning, is insufficient if the committee is to scrutinize executive operations effectively throughout the year. Equally important are some means to analyze those programs and functions that cut across the work

31. See Chap. 2, pp. 60–62.

Figure 4-1. Who Does the Work: Percentage of the Total Questions Asked at the 1965 Public Hearings of Each Senate Appropriations Subcommittee by Each Category of Members

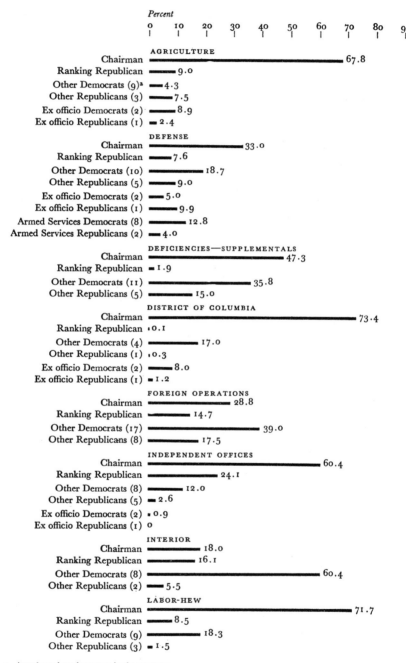

Percent

AGRICULTURE	
Chairman	67.8
Ranking Republican	9.0
Other Democrats (9)[a]	4.3
Other Republicans (3)	7.5
Ex officio Democrats (2)	8.9
Ex officio Republicans (1)	2.4
DEFENSE	
Chairman	33.0
Ranking Republican	7.6
Other Democrats (10)	18.7
Other Republicans (5)	9.0
Ex officio Democrats (2)	5.0
Ex officio Republicans (1)	9.9
Armed Services Democrats (8)	12.8
Armed Services Republicans (2)	4.0
DEFICIENCIES—SUPPLEMENTALS	
Chairman	47.3
Ranking Republican	1.9
Other Democrats (11)	35.8
Other Republicans (5)	15.0
DISTRICT OF COLUMBIA	
Chairman	73.4
Ranking Republican	0.1
Other Democrats (4)	17.0
Other Republicans (1)	0.3
Ex officio Democrats (2)	8.0
Ex officio Republicans (1)	1.2
FOREIGN OPERATIONS	
Chairman	28.8
Ranking Republican	14.7
Other Democrats (17)	39.0
Other Republicans (8)	17.5
INDEPENDENT OFFICES	
Chairman	60.4
Ranking Republican	24.1
Other Democrats (8)	12.0
Other Republicans (5)	2.6
Ex officio Democrats (2)	0.9
Ex officio Republicans (1)	0
INTERIOR	
Chairman	18.0
Ranking Republican	16.1
Other Democrats (8)	60.4
Other Republicans (2)	5.5
LABOR-HEW	
Chairman	71.7
Ranking Republican	8.5
Other Democrats (9)	18.3
Other Republicans (3)	1.5

a. Actual number of senators in the category.

Figure 4–1 *(Continued)*

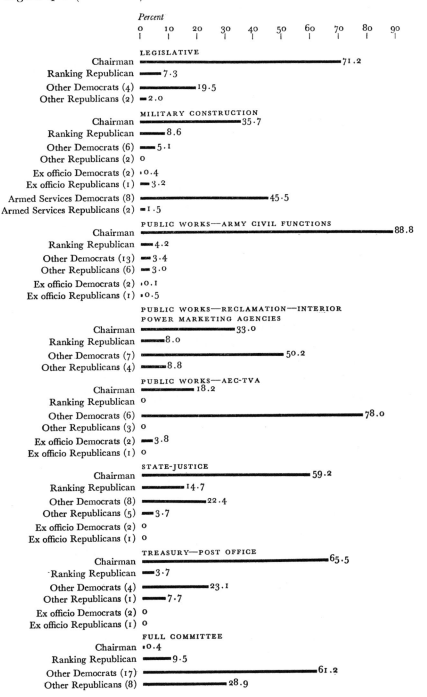

of various departments and subcommittees. Also necessary is the capacity to undertake long-term investigations in particular areas without shortchanging day-to-day work on agency appropriations.

When, in 1947, Chairman Bridges began building the modern professional staff of the committee, great emphasis was placed on the investigative function. Bridges saw to it that the thrust of the investigative work was directed to the foreign aid program. With the return of the committee to Democratic control in 1949, interest in investigations dwindled, especially during a Democratic administration. The exception was Nevada Democrat Patrick A. McCarran, an active member of Appropriations with a penchant for investigations, who was also chairman of the Joint Committee on Foreign Economic Cooperation, a watchdog committee of House and Senate Foreign Relations and Appropriations members authorized by the Foreign Assistance Act of 1948 (the Marshall Plan). When this joint committee was dissolved in September 1950 because of flagging interest on the part of the House, the remaining staff of thirteen was reassigned under the Legislative Branch Appropriations Act of 1951 to a new subcommittee of Senate Appropriations, the Special Subcommittee on Foreign Economic Cooperation, where it continued its watchdog functions over the growing foreign aid program.

In 1952, McCarran appointed Paul E. Kamerick, a former FBI agent who had been lent to Congress at various times to conduct investigations, as the staff director of this group. When Bridges again assumed the chairmanship during the Republican Eighty-third Congress (1953), he took McCarran's foreign aid investigation staff and established a separate office of investigations within the Committee on Appropriations. Besides Kamerick and a clerical staff, the office included ten accountants, investigators, and lawyers. Under Kamerick's leadership, reports were made to the full committee on numerous subjects, such as aid to India, the mutual security program in the Middle East, the "giveaway" of machine tools to Great Britain, the subsidization of Britain's civilian aircraft industry, aid to France, and paperwork management in the federal government. Most of these reports were initiated by the staff and developed without special hearings. Once completed, they were submitted to the full committee for use in the regular budget hearings. Many, such as the one on paperwork management, resulted in basic changes in executive procedures.

Carl Hayden, taking over the chairmanship in 1955, did not think that investigations, even of a Republican administration, were an appropriate function for the committee. Believing that the Committee on Government Operations (especially its Permanent Subcommittee on Investigations) was the proper investigative arm of the Senate, he made an informal arrangement with Senator McClellan, who was chairman of Government Operations and a member of Appropriations, to transfer the investigating function. In February 1956, Kamerick moved to the Permanent Subcommittee on Investigations as assistant counsel. A year earlier, the rest of the investigative staff had drifted off to other jobs.

In theory, Appropriations was to refer matters found worthy of further inquiry to Government Operations. In practice, however, with the exception of a few informal staff tips regarding the TFX airplane procurement contract in 1963, no requests for investigations have come from the Committee on Appropriations. Since 1955, except for special counsel Paul J. Cotter, who began conducting investigations for Chairman Hayden in 1956, the investigative function has fallen on the professional staff members assigned to each subcommittee.[32]

Bridges was dissatisfied with the new arrangement, but with Congress controlled by the opposition there was little he could do. He felt, as one close associate recalled, that "an investigation by Government Operations was like locking the barn door after the horse was gone. He believed that if a defect showed up before the Appropriations Committee then you could shut off an agency's water [that is, its money]." Several senators in both parties were also concerned that the Committee on Government Operations seemed more attracted to the headline-making investigation, such as the inquiry into labor racketeering, than to the thorough (and perhaps plodding) review of how effectively departments and agencies were using their funds. On the other

32. Cotter is highly regarded by most senators and staff members. The only complaint is that his studies often have not been brought to the attention of many committee members either before or after they are undertaken. A particularly glaring failure to give notice to concerned senators occurred when he undertook his controversial investigation of the Head Start program in Mississippi in 1965. The assignment was given to Cotter by Chairman Hayden at the request of Senator Stennis, but the chairman and ranking minority member of the Subcommittee on Deficiencies and Supplementals, which had jurisdiction over the relevant appropriations, did not learn of Cotter's investigation or his findings until Stennis used them in the subcommittee's public hearings. The ill feelings this investigation aroused among colleagues confirmed some senators in the view that investigations by the committee should be avoided.

hand, a Democrat known for his detailed digging thought Bridges' approach had been too partisan: "[His staff was] more interested in finding fault than in broadly reviewing agency programs." This senator, agreeing with Hayden, preferred "getting the facts and letting the departments know that we are watching them." Still a third view, a middle ground between Hayden and Bridges, was held by a Republican senator who argued that "the authorizing committees, not Appropriations, should investigate program matters. Appropriations should limit its investigation to how well the money is being spent." In recent years, both Democratic and Republican members have increasingly favored a stronger investigative role for the committee. One senior Republican has argued that a lack of thorough investigations "is the biggest weakness in the whole Senate appropriations process."

A thorough investigation—one beyond a simple query to an agency—usually depends on staff initiative and a willingness by the subcommittee chairman to pursue a line of inquiry even if executive obstinancy is encountered. Such full-scale studies by professional staff members are rare. The usual practice is for the staff members, as their instincts or a senator's inquiry dictates, to frame questions and submit them to the departments for an official response.

Some staff members make great use of the General Accounting Office. Others do not. Some of the professional staff prefer to contact the GAO informally rather than write a formal letter requesting an investigation. "If you write them a letter, they will give a copy to the department and then it gets to be a federal case," said a staff member who made frequent use of the GAO.

Between sessions, the staff has been encouraged to visit the agencies for which they are responsible. Given the length of congressional sessions, this has become increasingly difficult. Some make the visits; others prefer to stay in Washington. There is no overall schedule of assignments to provide a coordinated look at the implementation of government programs. Some of the subcommittee clerks do not believe they should be conducting investigations. They claim that they lack the time to undertake such an effort since it requires concentration in one area and they are besieged with requests covering all aspects of an agency's programs.

Some subcommittees have found alternatives to long-term studies of particular programs by their own staff in the investigative staff work of their members' legislative committees and in the information senators gather as ranking members on legislative committees. For example, in the 1965 hearings before the Defense Appropriations Subcommittee, extensive use was made of material that the staff of the Armed Services Preparedness Investigation Subcommittee had developed on inadequacies in the Defense budget for fiscal year 1966. The joint authorization-appropriations hearings by Armed Services and Defense and Military Construction Appropriations that Senators Russell and Stennis held in 1965 epitomize the opportunity many members have had to become thoroughly grounded in the diverse aspects of major programs. Still, the investigative function within the Appropriations Committee has not received the emphasis it should have. Most senators readily concede that the breadth of knowledge available to the committee through the members' wide range of legislative responsibilities cannot itself substitute for thorough analysis by a competent investigative staff.

* * *

If the Senate Committee on Appropriations is to meet its responsibilities as an active participant in the appropriations process, then it needs to be fully informed about the programs whose budgets it must judge. Although the committee makes use of a wide variety of information resources, both formal and informal, internal and external, in general it does not take sufficient advantage of the very pertinent work of the General Accounting Office, nor does it give its own staff an adequate investigative role. Nonetheless, the subcommittee chairmen usually become well versed in the business of the agencies under their jurisdiction. And despite the inadequacies of the hearing process, a public record is developed that the committee can turn to when it makes its decisions in markup.

CHAPTER FIVE

The Decision-Making Process

The phrase "the executive proposes and the Congress disposes" is probably of as doubtful validity as the cliché that it replaced: "Congress initiates the laws and the President administers them." The complexities of twentieth century society and the concentration of expertise in the executive branch have indeed given the President a major role as legislator. He submits the basic agenda and legislative program upon which the attention of Congress and the country is focused. But the opportunity for legislative decision making does not simply come at the end of an executive assembly line. Before a presidential proposal is made public, a great deal of advice, frequently including draft bills, has been provided to the executive branch by the legislative. A President and his staff, just as a legislator and his staff, respond to many forces, and a proposal is seldom framed to satisfy presidential demands alone. If it is possible to please a member of Congress, so much the better. No words need be exchanged; the expected reciprocity is well understood. As this is true of the legislative process generally, it is true of the budget process that is one specialized aspect of it.

At Committee Level

The informal legislative decision making that is thus begun before a budget measure ever reaches the House and Senate is continued throughout the congressional appropriations process. A telephone call from the President convinces a chairman or ranking minority member that his subcommittee must provide the funds for a certain program. A colleague with reelection troubles corners a subcommittee chairman in a Senate cloakroom and secures a commitment about a favorite project. A subcommittee chairman and ranking minority member, sitting side by side while a witness testifies, nod, grunt, and whisper a tentative decision to each other as program after program is reviewed. A member of the committee's professional staff writes a persuasive memorandum, which is readily accepted. These are but a few of the informal occasions when decisions, consciously or unconsciously, are made.

The formal stages in the decision-making process of Senate Appropriations are more easily recognized: the pre-markup session between the subcommittee chairman and ranking minority member, the subcommittee markup, the full committee markup, floor consideration, and the conference with the House. Colleagues, President, cabinet officers, White House staff, departmental liaison, bureau chiefs, lobbyists, and other interested parties attempt to influence outcomes along the way, but the key participants in these formal stages are the Appropriations Committee members themselves, and in particular the subcommittee chairmen.

The Markup Sessions

"Of course the real markup takes place prior to the meeting of the subcommittee. You're too late when you go into the subcommittee markup and ask for something. It's already been decided." This observation by a senior member of Appropriations' professional staff accurately suggests that the most crucial decision-making point is the informal session that a subcommittee chairman quietly holds with his ranking minority member prior to the subcommittee markup. The pre-markup session can take place in the subcommittee chairman's office or on the neutral ground of a committee room. The meeting might last only an hour or, if larger bills are involved, the sessions might be held over several days. The two men with their staff go over each item, line by line, just as the discussion will be conducted at the subcommittee meeting still a few days away.

Even before this informal conference, there is often a "pre" pre-markup meeting of the subcommittee's regular and minority staff—the only men thoroughly familiar with the justifications and with what has occurred in the hearings. To narrow the possible differences, they may trade some figures informally, each consulting his principal in the process. Sometimes the two senators—not wanting to admit that the staff has played a prominent role—will then go off alone to reach tentative agreement. However, staff members are usually invited to participate in the pre-markup sessions. Sometimes, when scheduling difficulties arise, the regular professional staff member is the only link between the principals. He will clear items with his chairman and the ranking minority member by holding several long sessions with each of them.

Besides the staff "pre" pre-markup that often occurs, during Senator Saltonstall's tenure as ranking Republican the GOP members of the committee also met before the two principals got together. Thus, all minority senators on Appropriations had an opportunity to hear an explanation of a bill by the ranking Republican who had sat through most of the hearings. The various GOP members "could get anything bothering them off their chests," as one participant noted. The ranking Republican then went into the pre-markup meeting knowing where his colleagues stood should an issue come to a show-down in subcommittee or full committee. In the mid-1960s, although Republicans were outnumbered two to one on the subcommittees and full committee, the differences among Democrats enabled the Republicans to hold the balance of power on many issues.

As the two principals go over an agency's program in the pre-markup session, they usually try to reach an understanding and form a coalition. Sometimes the chairman will accept the view of his minority colleague in the hope of preventing a later challenge to a critical portion of the bill. On other occasions, the subcommittee chairman may say, "I really can't do that. Why don't you bring it up when the subcommittee meets and we'll have a vote on it?" When the chairman takes that position, he undoubtedly has the votes he needs, and his colleague knows it. Or the chairman might want to give the agency its full request but the ranking minority member objects. Then the chairman—aware of the divisions in his own party—rapidly calculates the unity of the minority on this issue and whether or not their votes would be decisive. If they would be, he is likely to accommodate the minority rather than risk losing in either the subcommittee or the full committee. Sometimes both the chairman and the ranking minority member see the wisdom of funding a particular program, but know that they will have difficulty getting the consent of their subcommittee colleagues. At this point, both agree on their final line of retreat. Occasionally, disagreement will occur over the actual intent of executive testimony and the real needs of an agency. Then the subcommittee chairman might telephone the responsible cabinet officer and ask his minority colleague to join him in the conversation. The two principals usually have served with each other for many years and have become warm personal friends. They have sat together through days or weeks of hearings when their colleagues were elsewhere. If the minority party became the majority, their positions would be reversed. Each acts in the pre-markup meeting with respect for the knowledge, prerogatives, and views of the other.

In 1965, on nine of the thirteen subcommittees, the chairman and ranking minority member met in such pre-markup sessions. In other instances such cooperation did not occur—for example in the District of Columbia Subcommittee, where a deep ideological gulf separated Chairman Byrd from ranking Republican Case. With respect to the army civil functions aspects of the Public Works Subcommittee, Senator Ellender provided a solo performance. After sitting through months of hearings—usually alone—he met with his professional staff member and submitted his recommendations to the subcommittee clearly labeled "Senator Ellender's recommendations."

Each subcommittee chairman is well aware that his colleagues at the subcommittee and full committee level look both to him and to the ranking minority member for guidance and recommendations. As one expressed it, "They are busy men. They want direction and look to us for it. We are seldom overruled." Subcommittee chairmen and ranking minority members estimate that they make between 80 and 99 percent of the decisions on their appropriation bill during the pre-markup session. One of the most powerful subcommittee chairmen observed in 1965:

> The subcommittee will approve 95 percent of what we agree to. Sometimes the ranking minority member and I will change our mind if a senator has some new information which we didn't have when we made the basic decisions. But we've never been defeated in subcommittee and I suspect we've only changed our mind two or three times in the last eight or ten years.

Nevertheless, the subcommittee serves as an important ratifying body. Since choice as well as seniority has determined the members' assignment, their presence is usually evidence of more than casual interest. They have some knowledge with which to evaluate the work of the principals, and a few, such as Senator Monroney on aviation matters or Senator Proxmire on dairy questions, are recognized experts in a particular field. When a senator speaks regarding an issue that affects his state, he is acknowledged to be the expert.

In a subcommittee markup, value judgments are freely expressed. Detailed budget comparisons and comprehensive field reports from both the staff and the agencies often become integrated in simple statements: "These enlisted men are stuck way out in the Pacific on this island; they need a movie theater." "Those bachelor officers' quarters can wait another year." "Well, I can't say, but the congressman from the district is a pretty decent fellow." "If Dick [Russell] wants it, I'm for it." "We can turn him down on this one since we gave him an earlier project." "Let him bring it up in the full committee."

As the subcommittee chairman proceeds through the bill, he knows that one or more of his colleagues are likely to press him to see if additional funds can be secured for a program or if a cut can be made in a specific budget. Anticipating constituency-oriented pleas, some chairmen attempt to head them off by evoking sympathy for their diligent efforts: "I worked rather long on this and didn't try to bother many senators." This elicits an immediate "You did a marvelous job" from the potential dissident before he probes to see how much the subcommittee chairman can be moved, if at all. Another chairman may inform his subcommittee: "I have been over every single item in this bill both on the authorization committee and in the hearings. I met with my colleague [the ranking minority member] and the committee clerks more than once and we went through the bill several times on an item by item basis." At this point the ranking minority member may make a strong plea for economy. He will praise the chairman for his "excellent job," which invariably causes the chairman modestly to admit: "Well, senator, you have done as much as I have." By now the committee members realize that the deck has been fairly well stacked against changes.

Regardless of the chairman's strategy, however, members are sure to raise various matters affecting their states or interests, even if it is only pro forma. Then, with a clear conscience, they can tell a constituent or a lobbyist that they waged the good fight. One or two on Appropriations regularly offer three or more amendments to a bill when it is in markup, hoping that the chairman and ranking minority member will settle for one of them. Some senators try to bring the subcommittee chairman around with a gingerly reminder of reciprocity: "Now, Mr. Chairman, we all want to give you full support when you go to the floor, so perhaps you could give a little here." Only rarely does a committee member try the most risky ploy of all: to object to what the chairman and ranking minority member want in hope of getting something from them in return for withdrawing the objection.

To reject a member's plea, the chairman might urge economy and the need to protect the bill from unreasonable assault on the floor; or ask the senator to postpone his request for a year because of a tight budget; or advise him that if he came back next year he would have a better chance in conference with the House; or agree to ask in the report for the development of additional information on the feasibility of the project prior to the next annual hearing. Or the subcommittee chairman might tell a member, "Well, if you will knock out one of the projects we have given you, we will consider it." Usually the member agrees to leave things as they are rather than risk letting the home folks find out that he chose one project in his state over another. If a member persists, the subcommittee chairman can always accept the amendment and then fail to fight for it in conference (where, unless it is the amendment of the ranking minority member or a senior colleague who is also in the conference, it is usually dropped without a murmur).

One subcommittee chairman noted that "the chairman can be overruled on policy—on such a matter as private versus public power—but usually you are not going to overrule him on money." Another active participant observed: "One rule the wise member follows is not to put other senators on the spot in deciding between him and the subcommittee chairman. After all, the subcommittee chairman is lord and master." In light of these maxims, it is clear that for the member (or nonmember) who wants an amendment for some project or for more program money, the most effective approach is likely to be a personal visit with the subcommittee chairman before the markup process begins.

Many senators and staff members believe there is a direct relationship between seniority and success in getting one's proposals adopted. In 1965–66, a few subcommittee chairmen claimed that in their subcommittees senior members had no advantage when decisions were made. "The merit of the program or project is what counts," said one. Another noted that "personality, attitude, aggressiveness, and the work a member does" were even more important than seniority. The reality was perhaps best expressed by a long-time staff member when he noted, "Seniority will not always win, but it will mean you are listened to."

The gambits for additional funds employed at the subcommittee level are used again with the full committee. But at that stage it is no longer only the subcommittee chairman and ranking minority member against the field; the allegiance of the other subcommittee members has usually been secured, and they form an interested phalanx against intrusion by outsiders—that is, by committee members not on the subcommittee.

Several differences distinguish the subcommittee from the full committee markup. First, a higher percentage of those on the subcommittee (including ex officio members) generally attend the subcommittee markup. They realize that if a decision is to be changed following the pre-markup session between the subcommittee chairman and the ranking minority member, the subcommittee is where it must be done. Second, while the two leaders tend to dominate the discussion during the subcommittee markup, other members who have not had access to the deliberations take up much of the time during the full committee markup. The subcommittee leaders, however, usually continue to maintain effective control of the proceedings. Third, the subcommittee is concerned with detail in all areas of the appropriation bill, while the full committee almost always accepts the recommendations of the subcommittee as a matter of form and then focuses discussion on a few controversial issues, which either have been deferred for full committee consideration or have been raised independently.

Practices in Committee Decision Making

THE AGENCY BASE AND INCREMENTALISM. It is no easy task to examine and judge the itemized requests in a budget of $200 billion. "We would spend five minutes approving billions of dollars for the Korean war and argue for a half hour whether or not we should give one of the cloak room attendants $300 more a year." This comment by a former subcommittee chairman illustrates a phenomenon noted by all participants in the appropriations process: the smaller the item, the more understandable it is; the more understandable it is, the more likely that a senator will have an opinion about it.

Appropriations members frequently arrive at their decisions by comparing what an agency was granted for the current fiscal year with what it has requested for the coming year. Of course, this "benchmark," "base," or "incremental" method of decision making is not of much assistance when legislators are confronted with buying new, expensive weapons systems and radically altering in a given year the balance among various types of forces in response to a changing world situation. One cannot compare the appropriation of funds for five submarines in the current year with three for the coming year when a strategic decision has been made that national security demands the procurement of additional land-based missiles. Nor is such an approach useful in evaluating public works or military construction appropriations for one-time projects. Relating the level of appropriations for the current or past fiscal year to an agency's request for the coming year is more appropriate to the traditional domestic functions of government. The expenses of the old-line departments and regulatory commissions yield readily to an incremental comparison.

Obviously such an approach is fallible in that it assumes that the previous appropriation for an agency was correct (although it, too, was probably the product of a comparison with a former base, and so on back into history). Most senators, admitting their dependence on changes from the prior year's level, feel that not enough is done to reexamine a previous year's appropriation. A junior Democrat remarked: "This is the great weakness. There is a general feeling that you only look at the changes. And of course the bureaucratic tendency is to keep the jobs that they've won in previous years. I don't think we reconsider and scrutinize agency budget levels like we should." Part of the problem is a lack of time, but there is also a lack of methods for analyzing the effectiveness of an agency's expenditures during the recent fiscal year. A staff member summarized the feelings of many senators and staff when he remarked, "Until Congress has an oversight function and performs it, the base will always be what the department says it is. We have no way of knowing whether that base is in turn reasonable. If the legislative or appropriations committees really did their job, maybe this wouldn't be so."

In the judgment of committee members and staff, agency heads believe that future appropriations depend on their spending the previous year's appropriations fully to maintain their base; hence they have little incentive for thrift. The general view is that most agencies feel "fairly safe to get what we have already given them; the argument is over the increases." A senior Democrat who had observed the system over several decades thought it was "unfortunate that if an agency administrator failed to spend all of his budget, the Congress cuts back his appropriations." He added:

> I think this is wrong. I think we ought to give him the same figure and see if he could cut it back even more. In fact, I'd be willing to relate the salary of the civil servant who is administering the program to the savings he makes in his agency budget. Instead, with Congress's present practice in this area, the agency administrator is encouraged to spend everything by the close of the fiscal year on June 30th in order to maintain his program base.

THE INFLUENCE OF HOUSE DELIBERATIONS. Senators are aware of the thoroughness of the House hearings and their emphasis on detail. Most believe, however, that the House hearings have little influence on their deliberations. To expect busy men to read, much less absorb, the voluminous House hearings is unreasonable: senators poke among the maze of material as their experience, instinct, and staff lead them. The Senate Appropriations staff, on the whole, does go over House hearings, especially prior to a conference with the House, so that, as one stated, "we are not caught by surprise." With the growing practice of holding the Senate hearings almost simultaneously with the House hearings, there is even less influence evident, except in those subcommittees that continue to operate primarily on an appeals basis.

During a markup session, the report that accompanies the House appropriation bill is carefully scrutinized since it contains the arguments Senate conferees are compelled to answer if they make additions or deletions. Frequently, the House reports fail to spell out the reasons why a program is slashed or a project eliminated. When that happens, both the Senate committee and the affected agencies are at a loss to argue substantively with the House decision.

Some of the more cynical observers of Congress have long been convinced that Senate committees approve a higher level of funding than is merited in order to assure that a program will survive a House-Senate conference. The assumption is that the conferees will often merely "split the difference." Such a practice was once fairly widespread, and some members of House Appropriations are convinced that the Senate still bases many of its decisions on this premise. But economizers and spenders alike on Senate Appropriations believe, as one member observed, that "this is more talk than actual practice. The Senate does increase the budget, but on the genuine feeling that here's a program that the House has cut because they wanted to make themselves look good." A respected subcommittee chairman agreed: "I won't say this is never done, but usually you try to set the figure at what the agency really needs. But when there's a doubt about what they need you raise it, figuring you will know more about it by the time you get to the conference and you can settle it there." If there was a turning point in the Senate attitude toward raising funding levels above the House figures, it was the open confrontation between House and Senate Appropriations during 1962. Keenly sensitive to House charges that the Senate was extravagant and added to appropriation bills without reason, members of Senate Appropriations began trying to undercut the House figures in some areas.

"GOING ALONG." When a member has not had an opportunity to weigh alternatives or to compare an agency request with its previous base, he often simply goes along with the subcommittee chairman and ranking minority member. If they stand together on an issue, this decision-making crutch is all the easier to use. If they are divided, or if other senior members are in disagreement, then a member will choose as a guide the colleague who in his judgment has the greatest competence in the given area. While senators prefer to look to senior members and especially to Inner Clubbers for a lead—they know that by going along with them they are not only aided in making a decision but may also enlist influential support for their own policies in the future—a member's knowledge and experience are the overriding considerations.

Party and even ideological lines are frequently crossed in the search for advice. For example, in 1965–66 the committee members—whether Democratic or Republican, liberal or conservative—repeatedly noted that they looked to Russell and Stennis on defense matters; Hill on health; Holland, Russell, and Ellender on agriculture; Ellender on public works; Pastore on atomic energy; and Monroney on aviation. The general views of Saltonstall, a Republican, and Magnuson, a Democrat, were also influential. One senator commented: "Nearly every senator has his own opinion of senators in a specialized field. You try to follow the best-informed man. Generally you have a fair idea of who knows what."

THE USE OF PROXIES. Some members attend markups, as one put it, "not to decide issues but to prevent their own ox from being gored." Even if a member does not attend, however, his interests are protected. Unlike the Senate floor, where a member must be present to vote, Appropriations and most legislative committees allow an absent senator to leave a proxy and have his vote counted. "You don't roll a colleague while he is gone," said one senator. A vehement ideological opponent will often make an extra effort to inform his colleague of his rights and his interest in a particular bill.

The proxy is usually left with one's senior party member on the subcommittee concerned. On some ideological issues where the senior member is likely to be in disagreement, the absentee leaves his proxy with the senator who most closely represents his views. Proxies are seldom given in writing, although they may be. Usually a senator merely tells a colleague or his own assistant that he will be absent—or, if he is already in the markup, that he has to leave—and he would like his proxy to be voted a certain way. One southern Democrat was well known for getting up in the middle of a markup and, as he headed for the door, saying in a stage whisper to the subcommittee chairman, "I will leave you my proxy to vote against any amendment to add money."

Many senators are reluctant to vote another's proxy unless they have specific instructions from either the senator or his staff—or unless past experience has indicated how he would vote if he were present. During markup, some senators have contacted an absentee half way across the country in order to receive specific instructions. Senators are unanimous in holding that they have never seen a proxy misused intentionally. When a senator states that he has a colleague's proxy, his word is accepted without question.

The practices of subcommittee chairmen differ in regard to soliciting proxies. Some avoid importuning their colleagues, assuming the majority members will leave their proxies with them on their own initiative. Other subcommittee chairmen are more aggressive and actively solicit proxies when they anticipate trouble in the markup session. Similarly, a senator planning to contest the subcommittee leadership during a markup usually canvasses his fellows to secure any proxy he can from among those who will be absent.

Proxies seldom change the outcome of a markup vote, although occasionally they do make a significant difference. A striking instance occurred during the full committee markup of the District of Columbia appropriation bill in 1965, when the proxies cast outnumbered the senators who were present. At issue was whether Washington, D.C. should be included in the federal program to aid dependent children of unemployed parents. Subcommittee Chairman Byrd opposed the program. However, his subcommittee, with the additional votes provided by the three ex officio members, had voted 2 to 1 against him. But in full committee, even with the ex officio members voting, Byrd's amendment to overrule the subcommittee action was approved by a vote of 16 to 12. Ten of the sixteen votes cast for the Byrd motion were proxies, eight of which were cast by Byrd. Six of the twelve votes in opposition were also proxies. In addition, Byrd had in reserve two proxies he did not use. If the voting had been limited to those present, Byrd's amendment would have failed on a 6 to 6 tie.[1]

The Floor

Some students of government delight in noting that "debate on the floor doesn't change a vote because senators have made up their minds beforehand." Nothing could be further from the truth. Some debate does not change a vote; but some debate does. Republican leader Everett McKinley Dirksen of Illinois, standing in the center aisle on June 7, 1962, spoke of attending a Polish parade in Chicago and the bonds of kinship existing between Poles in America and their loved ones left behind in Poland. Dirksen so changed the mood of the Senate that it voted to remove the foreign aid restrictions against Poland and Yugoslavia that it had approved only a day before. While occasionally a floor exchange merely solidifies votes that have been wooed individually beforehand, debate is crucial to many an amendment's adoption or rejection during swiftly moving floor action on a bill.

Senators are well aware that their specialization in the areas covered by the bills reported from their committee gives them a strategic advantage during floor consideration. Many senators simply accept the committee members' views on a bill on the ground that "they have looked into it." Senators also know that if they raise havoc with the work of a particular committee, its members might in turn retaliate against their own committee's work or their individual proposals sometime in the future. Reciprocity and accommodation necessarily become paramount in many instances.

In such an environment, the Committee on Appropriations has a

1. This proceeding was in question because less than a quorum had actually been present, but no one raised a point of order in the Senate. Section 133 (d) of the Legislative Reorganization Act of 1946 provides: "No measure or recommendation shall be reported from any such committee unless a majority of the committee were actually present." 60 Stat. 831.

special strategic advantage. It is the largest committee, with almost one-fourth of the Senate on it, and its membership represents a broad spectrum from both political parties. It is responsible for budgetary and program details that few senators have time to learn in depth. Yet members of Senate Appropriations also know that floor consideration is the last stop for their decisions before the final action of the House-Senate conference, and that senators with deep policy commitments are alert to at least the broad dimensions of the financial support for particular programs.

Anticipation of Floor Problems

Committee members are sensitive to the desires and whims of potential antagonists on the floor and seek to anticipate them during the hearing and the development of the bill in markup. For instance, Senator Pastore pressed the director of the Bureau of Land Management during his testimony on a 1965 supplemental appropriation bill:

> I would like you people to tell me just why you are only asking for the $8.5 million and why you are not asking for the full damage so that at the appropriate time I can pick up this book and say to Senator Wayne Morse on the floor, "This is what they said." This is fair enough, isn't it?[2]

The subcommittee chairmen become conscious of potential floor difficulties in many ways. Floor debate on the authorization bill, which is often approved only a short time before the appropriation bill, may have revealed a senator's concern about an item. Senators also write to the committee, or testify for or against an item during the hearings. Threats that a floor amendment might be offered are sometimes used to wheedle an additional sum from the committee.

Some politically popular programs, such as those concerned with health and medical research, rural electric cooperatives, and soil conservation, have strong floor support. The Bureau of the Budget annually attempts to restrain spending in these areas. A battle then occurs in subcommittee and full committee to increase the funding. In these instances, the implied threat from program supporters that the matter will be remedied on the floor unless most of their demands are met usually does aid in securing a favorable accommodation at the committee level. As one senator noted: "If you don't add it in committee, you know that you will get an amendment on the floor and that the funds

2. *Second Supplemental Appropriation Bill, 1965,* Hearings before the Senate Appropriations Subcommittee, 89 Cong. 1 sess. (April 9, 1965), p. 377.

will likely be added there, so in committee you will often go further than you really want to in order to forestall an even bigger increase on the floor."

While subcommittee chairmen will accommodate a colleague to a limited degree in order to avoid a full-scale fight on the floor, sometimes they also advise a senator to bring his amendment up on the floor and take his chances. Since the subcommittee leaders in both parties are the key conferees, floor amendments have little chance of retention—unless they change the committee version of the bill to conform with the exact House figure, which takes the item out of conference.

Committee members exhibit great consciousness of the floor when they consider the desirability of incorporating an item that would be subject to a point of order. Senate Rule 16 provides that "no amendment which proposes general legislation shall be received to any general appropriation bill. . . ." In anticipation of a point of order being raised, the subcommittee chairman or an interested senator will usually file notice one day in advance of the bill's consideration that the suspension of paragraph 4 of Rule 16 will be requested. Once a quorum is present, a two-thirds vote of the senators voting is required for actual suspension of the rules. Rule 16 may be suspended without notice, however, by unanimous consent.[3] These intricate procedures, requiring a high level of senatorial consent, assure that authorizations on an appropriation bill are seldom brought forward.

Scheduling

When any Senate committee, including Appropriations, has completed its markup of a bill and written its report, the report and the bill are filed with the Senate. Because the continued operation of the government depends on their prompt passage, appropriation bills are almost always given rapid consideration in the Senate. The Legislative Reorganization Act of 1946 provided that printed committee hearings and reports must be available for at least three Senate calendar days before a bill is considered. If no point of order is made by a senator,

3. Charles L. Watkins and Floyd M. Riddick, *Senate Procedure: Precedents and Practices* (Government Printing Office, 1958), pp. 75–76, 565–68. If the point of order against a general appropriation bill reported by the committee is sustained because an amendment in the bill constitutes new legislation, then the bill as a whole is recommitted to the Committee on Appropriations. However, a committee amendment proposing legislation can be offered from the floor during consideration of the bill and only it, not the bill as a whole, will be subject to recommittal.

the bills can be—and occasionally are—considered earlier. On occasion, however, as when Lyndon B. Johnson was majority leader, consideration of measures such as foreign aid appropriations has been delayed until the last minute as leverage to discourage extended debate.

The calendar committees of both parties have agreed that no major bill should be passed on a simple call of the legislative calendar. Most senators and their office staff review the calendar list each day to see if a measure contains anything of particular concern to them. If a senator desires to have a bill delayed, he merely files an objection with the staff of his party policy committee or one of his party's floor assistants. Such a "block" alerts the floor leaders. Every few days, the majority leader moves that the Senate proceed to a call of the calendar. Then the bills or resolutions to which no senator has objected are passed on a simple motion. Often, in a matter of minutes, dozens of bills are approved by the Senate with only a handful of senators on the floor. They have been cleared at least tacitly by all members. The interest then centers on the controversial measures on which blocks have been placed.

A measure is scheduled for consideration by the majority leader after consultation with his policy committee, the bill manager, and the minority leadership. After Johnson became majority leader in 1955, he vigorously pursued committee chairmen urging them to complete their hearings so that legislation might be brought before the Senate for action. When the report and bill were filed, the majority leader and the southern-dominated Democratic Policy Committee tried to schedule the measure so that its timing could enhance the posture of Senate Democrats and impede the Eisenhower legislative program. However, since Mansfield became majority leader in 1961, no senator on Appropriations has found that the Senate leadership exerts undue pressure.

Debate and Amendments

Although floor consideration offers the first real opportunity for senators not on the committee to participate in the decision-making process for appropriations, few take advantage of the occasion. Committee members participate more in the discussion of the bills than do nonmembers and, on the whole, they speak at greater length. Although the authorship of amendments is usually fairly evenly divided between members and nonmembers, success in getting an amendment accepted is with those who are on the committee. Clearly, the members retain their domination over the various appropriation bills once they have reported them to the Senate. Their exposure to the details of the legislation in committee, even if cursory, gives them an advantage over all but a few senators who regularly engage in debate when appropriation bills are before the Senate.

As Table 5–1 shows, on twenty bills and resolutions reported by thirteen Appropriations subcommittees in 1965, the nonmembers led the members in amount of participation in floor discussion on only three occasions: during action on the Defense, Interior, and supplementals—full committee bills; and in two of these three cases the nonmembers led by less than 2 percent. Of the seventy-three nonmembers, fewer than half participated in debate on even one bill, while twenty-three did not debate at all. More than half of the committee members took part in debate on from four to nine bills. The members of Appropriations, who then comprised slightly over a fourth of the Senate, used more than two-thirds of the floor time.[4]

An examination of the Senate seniority of those who participated in debate on the most bills and those who participated for the longest period indicates that, on average, and in both categories, senators with the highest seniority were the most active. Analysis of the different subgroups within Appropriations shows that the subcommittee chairman was the leading floor participant for nine of the thirteen subcommittees. On average, the chairmen dominated floor debate at least a third of the time, with the range extending from one-tenth to almost two-thirds. Except for Labor-HEW and Military Construction, the ranking Republicans participated much less, although usually more than the total of all other Republican committee members. The other Democrats on Appropriations used a fifth of the floor time, with the junior members being more active than the senior members.

During 1965, forty-five floor amendments were offered to the various appropriation bills while they were before the Senate. These amendments ranged in importance from one that merely changed the titles of two Senate officials to one that attempted to cut $292 million from the military aid portion of the annual foreign assistance appropriation bill. The amendments were almost equally divided between those that sought to increase a specific appropriation or make the language in the bill less restrictive, and those that sought to decrease the amount recommended by the committee or make the language more restrictive.

4. The method of measuring participation in floor debate is explained in note *a* to Table 5–1.

Table 5–1. Percentage of Total Floor Debate[a] on Appropriation Bills Participated in by Members and Nonmembers of the Senate Committee on Appropriations in 1965

Subcommittee reporting bill	Subcommittee chairman	Ranking Republican	Other Democrats Senior[b]	Other Democrats Junior[c]	Other Republicans Senior[d]	Other Republicans Junior[e]	Ex officio Democrats	Ex officio Republicans	Total	Nonmembers (73) Democrats	Nonmembers (73) Republicans	Nonmembers (73) Total
Agriculture	41.3	4.2	—	14.3	—	1.0	0.0	1.0	61.8	17.2	21.0	38.2
Defense	35.6	7.4	2.3	1.3	—	—	—	2.5	49.1	45.2	5.7	50.9
District of Columbia	63.4	2.1	—	4.8	—	—	8.6	—	78.9	20.4	0.7	21.1
Foreign Operations	20.4	3.9	27.2	3.1	4.9	7.5	—	—	67.0	30.8	2.2	33.0
Independent Offices	20.9	6.2	10.3	10.8	4.6	2.6	3.8	—	59.2	25.3	15.5	40.8
Interior	9.5	—	6.4	33.3	—	—	—	—	49.2	30.2	20.6	50.8
Labor-HEW	29.8	28.9	—	7.9	—	13.2	—	—	79.8	12.7	7.5	20.2
Legislative	22.8	7.5	20.2	12.7	—	4.2	—	—	67.4	5.0	27.6	32.6
Military Construction	64.3	15.0	20.7	—	—	9.1	0.3	1.8	100.0	—	—	—
Public Works	19.4	3.5	13.8	21.2	—	9.1	—	—	69.1	27.1	3.8	30.9
State-Justice	30.7	8.3	1.1	7.6	5.3	9.1	—	—	62.1	4.9	33.0	37.9
Treasury–Post Office	50.5	3.4	—	27.0	—	3.4	—	—	84.3	15.7	—	15.7
Supplementals and Full Committee	12.4	2.1	6.0	13.2	3.8	4.4	1.0	—	41.9	39.7	18.4	58.1
Average percent of floor participation	32.4	7.1	8.3	12.1	1.4	4.2	1.0	0.4	—	21.1	12.0	—

a. For the purpose of measuring floor participation, the comments of various senators were compiled, bill by bill, on a column-inch basis from the *Congressional Record*. Exhibits and other material that were clearly not read during floor discussion (but which do appear in the *Record* as part of a senator's remarks) were not included in the compilation. The compilations for all the subcommittees except the last are based on the regular annual appropriation bill initially marked up by each of these subcommittees. In the supplemental and full committee category, eight bills have been grouped together: supplementals for Agriculture, South Vietnam, and Labor-HEW, as well as the second supplemental for 1965, the supplemental for 1966, and three resolutions for continuing appropriations.

b. Senior Democrats are the four highest Democrats in committee seniority.

c. Junior Democrats are the nine lowest Democrats in committee seniority.

d. Senior Republicans are the four highest Republicans in committee seniority.

e. Junior Republicans are the five lowest Republicans in committee seniority.

Twenty-three of the amendments were sponsored by members, five of them by the subcommittee chairman responsible for the floor management of a given bill. The Senate accepted almost 70 percent of the member amendments, regardless of the member's party affiliation. Only 36 percent of those submitted by nonmembers were accepted. Victory here was with the liberalizing amendments in both money and language. (See Table 5–2.)

Table 5–2. **Floor Amendments, by Category and Sponsor, Offered to Appropriation Bills Considered in the Senate, 1965**

| | Amendment sponsor | | | | | |
| | Members | | | Nonmembers | | |
Amendment category	Total	Dem.	GOP	Total	Dem.	GOP
Amendments to increase appropriations (18)						
Accepted (14)	8	6	2	6	6	—
Rejected (4)	—	—	—	4	2	2
Amendments to decrease appropriations (13)						
Accepted (1)	1	—	1	—	—	—
Rejected (12)	7	5	2	5	5	—
Amendments to adopt less restrictive language (4)						
Accepted (4)	2	1	1	2	2	—
Rejected (0)	—	—	—	—	—	—
Amendments to adopt more restrictive language (9)						
Accepted (4)	4	2	2	—	—	—
Rejected (5)	—	—	—	5	2	3
Other amendments (1)						
Accepted (1)	1	—	1	—	—	—
Rejected (0)	—	—	—	—	—	—
Total amendments (45)	23	14	9	22	17	5
Accepted (24)	16	9	7	8	8	—
Rejected (21)	7	5	2	14	9	5

Although a senator is successful in the Senate when his amendment is adopted, and though he secures the tacit consent of the majority and minority subcommittee leaders—sometimes only because they want to avoid a roll call and move ahead with the bill—a more difficult course lies ahead in conference. Neither the nonmember nor the Appropriations senator not on the subcommittee can be present in conference to defend his position. Both are consequently at the subcommittee chairman's mercy regardless of the victory achieved in the Senate.

Opposition by Committee Members

The substantial number of floor amendments offered by committee members indicates the relative independence of senators on the committee. During 1965, there were twenty-nine record votes in the Senate on various aspects of the regular and supplemental appropriation bills. No member of Appropriations—not even the chairman—supported the committee position (as enunciated by each subcommittee chairman) on all twenty-nine roll calls. (See Table 5–3.) On twenty-two, the subcommittee's chairman and ranking Republican were in agreement. Yet over a third of the Democratic members defected from the committee position on seven, and over a third of the Republican members strayed on eight.[5] On five roll calls, the subcommittee chairman and the ranking Republican disagreed with each other and each was backed by his principal on the full committee—Hayden or Saltonstall. There were two roll calls where the Democratic subcommittee chairman and the ranking Republican agreed but were opposed by Chairman Hayden. While most members usually did not make extended speeches against the committee position, when an amendment was offered that appealed to them, they voted for it. With many of the ranking conservative southern Democrats, this was partly a vote for the home folks. They might miss the foreign aid markup in order to help the President and they might aid him further by missing a close "economy" roll call on a key floor amendment. But if the vote on the floor was not too close, they usually voted their ideological position against increased federal spending.

Compared with House Appropriations, Senate Appropriations is less integrated internally as a committee, but perhaps more integrated externally with its parent chamber.[6] Although reciprocity generally

5. All of the major Democratic defections, and all but one of the Republican defections, occurred during the nine record votes held on cuts in the foreign aid appropriation bill.

6. In his classic analysis of the House Committee on Appropriations, Richard Fenno observes that a structure of decision making in which the work is divided "among a number of subgroups and a number of individual positions with their associated roles" results in a problem of committee integration: "How shall these diverse elements be made to mesh or function in support of one another?" Fenno also defines "integration" as "the degree to which the Committee is able to minimize conflict among its subgroups and roles, either by heading off conflict or resolving it when it does arise." Richard F. Fenno, Jr., *The Power of the Purse: Appropriations Politics in Congress* (Little, Brown, 1966), p. 191. See Chap. 5, "The House Committee III: Structure for Integration," pp. 191–263.

Table 5–3. Opposition by Members of the Appropriations Committee to Positions Established by the Subcommittee Leaders on Twenty-nine Senate Roll Calls, 1965

	Opposition to subcommittee chairman		Opposition to ranking Republican	
Name	*Percentage*[a]	*Roll calls*	*Percentage*	*Roll calls*
Richard B. Russell[b]	52.2	12	—	—
A. Willis Robertson	50.0	13	—	—
Roman L. Hruska[c]	44.8	13	41.4	12
Norris Cotton	44.8	13	41.4	12
John L. McClellan	41.4	12	—	—
Allen J. Ellender	41.4	12	—	—
Alan Bible	40.7	11	—	—
Robert C. Byrd	39.3	11	—	—
Karl E. Mundt	38.5	10	42.3	11
William Proxmire	37.9	11	—	—
Milton R. Young	30.8	8	34.6	9
John Stennis	25.0	7	—	—
Margaret Chase Smith	24.1	7	20.7	6
Thomas H. Kuchel	24.1	7	6.9	2
E. L. Bartlett	20.7	6	—	—
Leverett Saltonstall	17.2	5	0.0	0
Lister Hill	13.8	4	—	—
Spessard L. Holland	13.8	4	—	—
Clifford P. Case	13.8	4	17.2	5
A. S. Mike Monroney	11.1	3	—	—
Gale W. McGee	10.3	3	—	—
Gordon Allott	10.3	3	6.9	2
Carl Hayden	7.7	2	—	—
Ralph Yarborough	6.9	2	—	—
Warren G. Magnuson	3.6	1	—	—
John O. Pastore	3.4	1	—	—
Mike Mansfield	3.4	1	—	—

a. The opposition percentage was determined by comparing the total votes, pairs, and positions an individual senator took against the committee view (the subcommittee chairman's position), and against the view of the ranking Republican for the minority members, with the total votes, pairs, and positions that senators took on all twenty-nine roll calls. Where more than one senator had the same percentage, the senior member was listed first unless the junior had a greater number of actual votes (as opposed to pairs or positions) in opposition.

b. In a sense it is unfair to categorize Senator Russell as registering the highest degree of opposition to the committee position. Because of illness, he did not make known his views on six roll calls. Had he been present he probably would have voted the committee position on all of them. Then his opposition score would have been 41.4 percent, similar to the scores of Ellender and McClellan. Senator Robertson did not make known his position on three roll calls. Even if he took the committee position on all three, however, he still would have been first or second in opposition in an absolute sense, depending on how Russell would have voted.

c. Names of Republican members appear in italics.

exists between the various Senate Appropriations subcommittees at the full committee stage, just as it does within the House committee, in the Senate there is no suffocating demand for floor unity. Individual subcommittee chairmen would, of course, welcome united support for the measures they report, but since they themselves occasionally vote against some committee recommendations, a little deviation does not bother them. A closer committee-parent relationship exists in the Senate because of the overlapping memberships between Appropriations and the various legislative committees. Moreover, hearings are conducted in open session and those not on Appropriations can quite easily acquire information about committee receptivity toward programs in which they have an interest. Then there is the matter of size. Senate Appropriations includes almost one-quarter of the Senate; it can afford to let a few members stray. With House Appropriations, on the other hand, almost all members are limited to service on that committee; they hold their hearings in secret; their membership includes less than one-ninth of the House of Representatives. These factors, and the House committee's emphasis on economy as opposed to program advocacy, make for much greater pressures toward conformity.

The Conference

Ground Rules

Once the Senate has revised and approved an appropriation bill, the floor manager (usually the subcommittee chairman) moves that the Senate insist upon its amendments and request a conference with the House, and that the chair appoint the conferees for the Senate. After the motion is agreed to, a group of conferees chosen by the subcommittee chairman is appointed by the presiding officer. The "papers" are returned to the House with a formal message containing notification of the Senate's action and requesting a conference. In the House a motion is usually made that the request of the Senate for a conference be agreed to. As in the Senate, the presiding officer appoints the House conferees from a list submitted to him by House Appropriations.

Since House Appropriations subcommittees are small, almost always ranging from seven to ten members, all members of the subcommittee are usually appointed as conferees. In the Senate, generally only the senior members of a subcommittee are appointed. While the Senate appoints larger conference delegations than the House, the number of Senate conferees who attend is usually less. "Conferences," as one long-time Senate staff observer noted, "are free, frank, and friendly and often sparsely attended as far as the Senate is concerned. The House members, however, usually will all be in their places." Some Senate conferees never do attend. Instead, they take a colleague's word that the report (as the final conference document is called) is good, and sign their names to it as "Managers on the Part of the Senate."

Once the Senate amendments are available, the House conferees gather at the request of their chairman and discuss their strategy. When the House conferees enter the old Supreme Court chamber they ordinarily have an agreed position on most Senate amendments. At the conference table, their chairman does most of the talking. Usually a schedule is in front of each House conferee with notations reflecting the chairman's view of the type of settlement that should be made.

While the subcommittee chairman and ranking minority member might discuss an item before the meeting, or there might be a casual huddle prior to the session by those Senate conferees who arrive early, there are no regularly scheduled preconference strategy meetings among Appropriations senators. With the occasional exception of Holland's Agriculture Subcommittee, there have been no such meetings as far back as anyone can remember. Some subcommittee chairmen claim that it is difficult to find a convenient time for such meetings. Others note that the Senate has usually just completed its work on the bill and the various items are still fresh in the members' minds. Nonetheless, most subcommittee chairmen, members, and staff regret that no preconference meetings are held on a regular basis.

In a few instances, the Senate and House subcommittee chairmen meet or lunch together before the conference. Although occasionally some tentative decisions are reached, their meeting is more exploratory than decisive. Each seeks to determine the depth of the other's feelings on specific controversies that might arise. These discussions are often backstopped by meetings between the subcommittee clerks who "spar"— as one expressed it—with each other. They, too, try to discover the depth of commitment the various conferees have for particular items, projects, or language. With that intelligence, they help their principals to determine where the hard and soft spots are.

The conferees are usually old colleagues. The subcommittee chairmen have been bargaining and trying to persuade one another sometimes for a decade or more. While a conference is ad hoc, it is also in a very real sense a continuing institution. In the short run the issues may change; the participants seldom do. If a group of conferees is unsuccessful this year, there is always next year.

The conference confrontation is ordinarily between the two chairmen, who carry the load for each side. Unlike the House chairman, a Senate subcommittee chairman almost always has the assistance of his ranking minority member. The Senate chairman also is likely to call more frequently on an expert colleague than is his House counterpart. When a complicated supplemental bill is under consideration, the chairman of an agency's regular subcommittee is usually encouraged to assume some of the responsibility for defending and explaining the items with which he is familiar. When individual projects are involved —such as those in the agricultural, Interior, or public works bills—the burden of carrying the argument for a project is passed to the Senate sponsor if he is a conferee. When the discussion becomes agitated and the pace begins to quicken, the circle of participation broadens as individual conferees offer their own ideas of an acceptable package that will break the deadlock.

Staff members probably play a less active role in conference than at any other stage of the appropriations process. They prepare detailed notes for their members, but in conference it is legislator confronting legislator; the participants seldom want to be embarrassed by unseemly reliance on the staff. As an issue arises, many Senate staff members give their principals a card summarizing the arguments made in the hearings and in committee. But, aware of the entrenched House belief that they are helpless without their staff, and confronting House conferees in whose minds financial detail seems indelibly inscribed, the senators are not likely to welcome whispering staff members. It is negotiation. It is rapid. And the conferees are largely on their own.

As the final arbiters before a bill becomes law (except, of course, for ratification of their work by each house and by the President), the conferees are wooed intensively by interested parties from inside and outside the government. But, while many people are concerned about the outcome of a conference, no outsiders are present to witness the maneuvering of the participants. The meeting takes place behind closed doors and no verbatim transcript is maintained. When the job is completed, whether in an hour or a month, only the results and the inner satisfaction of the participants remain. It is always difficult to discern who or what broke a deadlock at the crucial moment. In this sense, "a conference," as one member noted, "is like a subcommittee markup that is not cut and dried beforehand."

Each group of conferees has one vote in conference, and a majority of each decides how that single vote is cast. As a result, deference for one another is generally the practice among the members of each group. "Even if I can't attend his hearings," noted a senior Senate subcommittee chairman, referring to a colleague on whose subcommittee he also served, "he still needs me when we get to conference, so he is going to listen to what I have to say and what my problems are." In some conferences the conferees act as a brake on the desires of their own chairmen. If they had had their way, the two Labor-HEW chairmen in 1965, Senator Lister Hill and Democratic Representative John E. Fogarty of Rhode Island, would readily have agreed with the highest figure before them for the National Institutes of Health. But this did not happen because both sets of conferees were more interested in economy than their chairmen, and the vote was determined by the majority.

Without additional approval by each parent body, the conferees are limited by the upper and lower figure that each house has approved for a particular line item in an appropriation bill. But which projects go to make up the amount within the higher and lower figure is quite often another matter. Technically, the conferees are not to consider items not approved by at least one of the houses. If the dispute is on language, however, the area for revision of general appropriation bills is wide, provided only that additions are germane. On the whole, conferees limit their discussion to a reconciliation of the differences in each bill, but sometimes they add what they please. Occasionally, they have no choice if an agreement is to be reached. In 1965, in order to reach a settlement on the agricultural appropriation bill after more than two months in conference, the Senate agreed to add funds that had not been in either the House bill or the Senate amendments. The first addition was $100,000 to develop the plans and specifications for a $1,035,000 expansion of the National Sedimentation Laboratory in Oxford, Mississippi—in the congressional district of Jamie L. Whitten, the chairman of the House conferees.

It is possible for the final version approved by the conference to differ from the total figures of both the House bill and the bill as amended by the Senate. The outcome depends on the combination of high and low items taken from the two versions. If the conferees consistently choose the high figures from both, the total may be higher than either. Conversely, the result may be a lower figure than either bill. As one aggressive Senate conferee put it, "You can do anything you want if you can get the agreement of the people around the table."

That is correct, provided that no member of either parent chamber raises a point of order—a possible sanction that ordinarily maintains a semblance of purity in the conference room.

There is a moral obligation on the part of the conferees to defend in conference the positions taken in their chamber.[7] Obviously, however, there must be some flexibility or agreement would never be reached. The question is how fast the other side will recede. Sometimes amendments are added in the Senate in the knowledge that the House will recede, it being assumed that the House was only trying to make an economy record in the first place. On other occasions, an amendment is accepted by the floor manager during Senate consideration in the expectation that the House will stand firm and the amendment will speedily be eliminated in conference.

Such an expectation can go astray. When the agricultural bill was before the Senate in 1965, Philip Hart offered a floor amendment to include $2 million for special assistance in making school lunches available to needy children. The authorization had existed since 1962, but the President had not recommended funds until 1965, when a budget estimate of $2 million was finally submitted. However, House and Senate Appropriations both turned down the request and the only recourse was the Senate floor. Floor manager Holland and the subcommittee's ranking minority member, Milton Young, were willing to take the item to conference. The assumption was that the House would stand firm and the amendment would quietly be killed behind closed doors, where no one could be accused of denying food to poor children. However, a telephone call from Republican Senator John Sherman Cooper of Kentucky to the second-ranking House conferee, Democrat William H. Natcher of Kentucky, secured the latter's support for the Hart amendment. Cooper and Hart had both been members of the Senate Committee on Agriculture and Forestry when it passed the 1962 authorization. To the Senate conferees' surprise, the House quickly receded from its opposition to the $2 million addition and the Senate was stuck with the program.

Senators who are personally opposed to a bill—such as Ellender in

7. Conferences are usually "free" in that prior instructions to maintain a certain position are seldom given to the conferees. In the House, once the conference is agreed to, a preferential motion to instruct may be made. It must be made before the conferees are appointed. While the Senate practice also allows for a motion to instruct the conferees, it has rarely been made. On occasions when the House conferees have been instructed, the Senate has refused to participate.

the case of foreign aid—generally adhere scrupulously to the Senate position even though it does not represent their views. They feel honor bound to represent their chamber once they have lost the fight on the floor. But not all abide by such a moral commitment. A few undercut the Senate position in conference by giving in early in the discussion. Others just sit silently—waiting for an item where their convictions and those of their colleagues coincide.

Conferences bring out the bargaining ability of the participants, but sometimes the spirit of compromise disappears. When a conferee has made a commitment to one of his colleagues, he fights hard to keep it. At times conferees exhibit the tactics of little boys. "Like children," said one participant, "sometimes you have to fight to be friends." Conferences can be a time for dramatics, as when one of the chairmen picks up his papers and heads for the door. In the Cannon days, such a grand exit was a recurrent event. It is less so since that time. Still, the threat to return to the parent chamber in disagreement can be far from empty. After a roll call occurs on a specific item and another conference is held, the bargaining becomes more rigid and the final settlement harder for the loser to swallow. Even if the chairman of one set of conferees does not threaten a roll call, his determination not to give way is reinforced by the awareness that some member of his chamber might offer a motion to recommit, or he might be defeated on his motion to recede and agree with the position taken by the other body. Nonetheless, most members contend that the conference is a time for accommodation. Sometimes "hams are traded for elephants," as one senator expressed it, but a bargaining and trading atmosphere prevails —as it must if agreement is to be reached.

Who Wins or Loses?

When questioned in 1965–66, senators and staff were divided three ways on whether the House or the Senate "won" or "lost" in appropriations conferences. Half of them thought that both bodies came out "about even" or that victories and defeats were "balanced over time." The other half were divided almost equally between those who were convinced that the Senate usually won and those who were convinced that the House was more often victorious. Although the answer given was based partly on subcommittee and conference experience, the response also reflected the individual's interpretation of the question. For some senators who were not subcommittee chairmen, the conference was not an arena where one battled for the Senate position on the bill as a whole; rather, it was a place where one defended the items in which one had a special interest and left the rest for somebody else. The senator who had saved a navy yard or a veterans' facility in his state felt like a winner regardless of what happened to the rest of the bill.

It could be argued that it is neither the House nor the Senate, but rather the administration that ultimately wins or loses in conference. This view aside, however, an analysis of the issues in dispute between the Appropriations Committees of the two houses in 1965 supports the thesis that it is largely the Senate Committee on Appropriations that is victorious.[8] An examination of the provisions of thirteen major appropriation bills showed that the Senate had complete or partial victories 54.2 percent of the time. The House had complete or partial victories 31.8 percent of the time. The remaining 14 percent of the items were in the "split the difference" category, which many have regarded as a much more frequent phenomenon.

Among the various sets of subcommittee conferees, there was wide variation in the degree of victory. (See Figure 5–1.) The Senate De-

8. Depending on the methodology they have employed, students of the problem have reached different conclusions as to who wins and who loses. For example, Gilbert Y. Steiner reviewed conference actions on fifty-six bills from the period 1928–48. The bills were distributed over ten general policy areas, and included five appropriation measures. He concluded that "the influence of the House of Representatives has been found to outweigh that of the Senate to a considerable extent." The House influence was predominant in conference on all five appropriation bills. Gilbert Y. Steiner, *The Congressional Conference Committee: Seventieth to Eightieth Congresses* (University of Illinois Press, 1951), pp. 170–71. For a criticism of the Steiner approach, see Jeffrey L. Pressman, *House vs. Senate: Conflict in the Appropriations Process* (Yale University Press, 1966), pp. 59–63. Richard F. Fenno, Jr. examined the appropriations requests made between 1946 and 1962 by thirty-six bureau level agencies representing seven of the ten cabinet departments. Of 331 instances in which the same budget estimate was before both House and Senate Appropriations and on which they disagreed, the Senate conferees won 187 times (or 56.5 percent), the House conferees 101 times (or 30.5 percent), and the difference was split 43 times (or 13.0 percent). Disagreeing with Steiner, Fenno states "at the very most, the data establish presumptive evidence that Senate, not House, conferees are the more influential in appropriations conferences." Richard F. Fenno, Jr., *The Power of the Purse*, pp. 663–64. L. Dwaine Marvick examined the legislative intent of various appropriation bills enacted between 1945 and 1951. His impressionistic review of conference outcomes indicated to him "that the conference typically ended with the House version prevailing on most minor points at issue and with the Senate version winning out on a few relatively important points." L. Dwaine Marvick, "Congressional Appropriation Politics: A Study of Institutional Conditions for Expressing Supply Intent" (Ph.D. thesis, Columbia University, 1952). p. 396.

Figure 5-1. Extent of Agreement with Senate or House in the Decisions of Appropriations Conferences, 1965

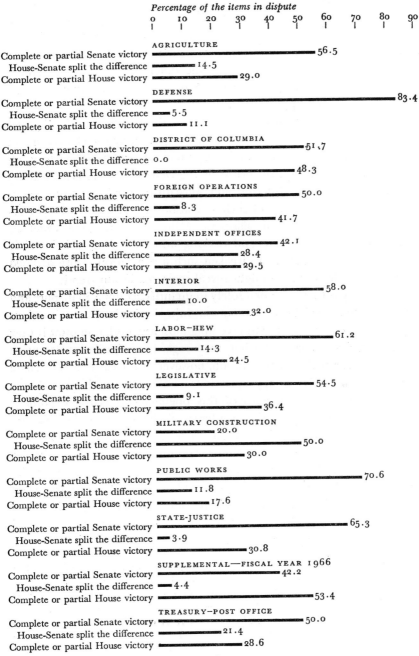

Percentage of the items in dispute

	0	10	20	30	40	50	60	70	80	90

AGRICULTURE
Complete or partial Senate victory — 56.5
House-Senate split the difference — 14.5
Complete or partial House victory — 29.0

DEFENSE
Complete or partial Senate victory — 83.4
House-Senate split the difference — 5.5
Complete or partial House victory — 11.1

DISTRICT OF COLUMBIA
Complete or partial Senate victory — 51.7
House-Senate split the difference 0.0
Complete or partial House victory — 48.3

FOREIGN OPERATIONS
Complete or partial Senate victory — 50.0
House-Senate split the difference — 8.3
Complete or partial House victory — 41.7

INDEPENDENT OFFICES
Complete or partial Senate victory — 42.1
House-Senate split the difference — 28.4
Complete or partial House victory — 29.5

INTERIOR
Complete or partial Senate victory — 58.0
House-Senate split the difference — 10.0
Complete or partial House victory — 32.0

LABOR—HEW
Complete or partial Senate victory — 61.2
House-Senate split the difference — 14.3
Complete or partial House victory — 24.5

LEGISLATIVE
Complete or partial Senate victory — 54.5
House-Senate split the difference — 9.1
Complete or partial House victory — 36.4

MILITARY CONSTRUCTION
Complete or partial Senate victory — 20.0
House-Senate split the difference — 50.0
Complete or partial House victory — 30.0

PUBLIC WORKS
Complete or partial Senate victory — 70.6
House-Senate split the difference — 11.8
Complete or partial House victory — 17.6

STATE-JUSTICE
Complete or partial Senate victory — 65.3
House-Senate split the difference — 3.9
Complete or partial House victory — 30.8

SUPPLEMENTAL—FISCAL YEAR 1966
Complete or partial Senate victory — 42.2
House-Senate split the difference — 4.4
Complete or partial House victory — 53.4

TREASURY—POST OFFICE
Complete or partial Senate victory — 50.0
House-Senate split the difference — 21.4
Complete or partial House victory — 28.6

fense Appropriations conferees, for example, won complete or partial victories in 83.4 percent of their disputes with the House. On the other hand, the Military Construction conferees won only 20 percent. In 1965, both of these sets of Senate conferees were headed by Senator Stennis. In the case of the military construction bill, half of the disputes were actually decided on a "split the difference" basis. The House conferees had a victory on a majority of the items in dispute on only one bill, the 1966 supplemental.

There is no clear correlation between the length of time devoted to public hearings or the degree of participation by the chairman and ranking minority member and the extent of conference victory, although the high degree of success by the Defense, Public Works, State-Justice, Labor-HEW, Interior, and Agriculture conferees would seem to suggest the possibility of such a relationship. However, the performance of the Independent Offices and Military Construction conferees, where both the chairman and ranking minority member held fairly extensive hearings, seems to weaken such a conclusion. More detailed study over a longer time might reveal some significant trends.

Any analysis that is limited solely to quantifying items in dispute and granting equal weight to each does an injustice in those rare situations where senators are willing to give up almost any dollar amount if they can secure approval for what they regard as significant language changes. Even with this reservation, however, it is clear that the Senate acquits itself well in appropriations conferences with the House. Among various explanations of this phenomenon is the hypothesis that the Senate Appropriations conferees win because their decisions are more firmly backed by their parent chamber. The comment of one of the most powerful leaders of House Appropriations suggests a simpler but equally valid reason: "We often cut below what we otherwise would, knowing that the Senate will add to the bill and we will yield to the Senate in conference." A cynic might conclude that if House members give in during a conference, it is frequently because they did not mean what they said in the first place.[9]

9. Richard Fenno, showing that Senate Appropriations wins in conference just as often (66.0 percent) when it supports the low figure as when it supports the high figure (64.6 percent), concludes that this is "because the Senate Committee and its conferees draw more directly and more completely upon the support of their parent chamber than do the House Committee and its conferees." He claims that the Senate has arrived at its figures with maximum participation and has achieved a more durable consensus than the House. The Senate bill "will be defended in conference by men who are the leaders not just of the Committee, but of the Senate." Fenno

Institutional Rivalry

The rivalry between the House and Senate Appropriations Committees that often becomes evident in conference grows out of many factors. One is that each committee suspects the motives underlying the other's approach to spending. Senators think the House members act irresponsibly in cutting essential appropriations, including contractual obligations of the government that must be met. They suspect that the cynical view of House motives is correct: the House members only want to look like good economizers to their constituents, and expect the Senate to restore the cuts. On the other hand, those on House Appropriations, having spent months in studying an appropriation bill, view their Senate counterparts as irresponsible when they add millions of dollars after a few days of testimony. They view members of Senate Appropriations as lackeys of the executive branch and look with disdain on their tendency to give administration officials much of what they ask for in the public hearings. As the House conferees enter the old Supreme Court chamber for a conference, all of their suspicions about a Senate-executive alliance against them seem justified as administration officials cluster in the hallway, some in last minute conversation with sympathetic senators.

In addition, House members are convinced that senators would be completely lost without their staff. House members tolerate the presence of the Senate committee staff in conference because their own committee staff is present, but on those rare occasions when a senator's legislative assistant attends, the word is quickly passed by the chairman of the House conferees that his further presence will not be welcomed. House members find other Senate practices annoying as well. They often arrive at a conference to find that senators have not yet appeared— and that when they do come, they wander in and out during the meeting. House subcommittee chairmen with decades of service are sometimes

---

notes that the high integration demonstrated by members of House Appropriations "acts as a deterrent to a higher degree of integration between it [the committee] and the House." He acknowledges, however, that various House members want increased expenditures and that the House conferees' awareness of this "may contribute to their willingness to yield in key situations. . . ." Fenno, *The Power of the Purse*, pp. 667–70. If senators are more successful in conference because of support by the parent chamber, perhaps this support is due to their assignment on several committees, rather than to any leadership position they hold in the Senate. The breadth of their interests, and their concern for policy as opposed to economy questions, prevent a strong anti-Appropriations feeling from taking root.

uneasy sitting opposite junior senators who have been given sub-committee responsibilities or are acting for an absent Senate chairman after only a few years of committee service.

Indeed, suspicion of the Senate is almost institutionalized in the House, where members view the Senate as a chamber with the pretensions of a House of Lords—but a House of Lords with power.[10] Particularly galling to the representatives are press references to the Senate as the "upper" house. The 100 senators have individual desks in the Senate chamber; lacquered snuffboxes rest on ledges near the rostrum and blotting sand is on each desk to help provide an atmosphere of leisure and prestige. In addition, as befits a gentlemen's club, senators can talk at length. The 435 House members, on the other hand, have no assigned seats except for the party leaders; they use microphones in order to be heard; total debate on nearly every bill is sharply limited by the powerful Committee on Rules, and individual speeches are usually held to a minute or five minutes.

Constantly irritating to those who inhabit the body presumably closest to the people are the innumerable appearances of senators on nationally televised public affairs programs. A senator seemingly bathes in the glare of publicity while the representative sits enviously at home. And the chic Georgetown dinner party requires the presence of a senator, no matter how incompetent, while the able House member eats sandwiches with his kids. In addition, many senators have large staffs with administrative, legislative, press, and research assistants. House members have an administrative assistant and several secretaries to help with the mail. They ordinarily do most of their own legislative

---

10. For example, when the conference report on the legislative appropriation bill was brought before the House on July 21, 1965, the following ensued:

Mr. H. R. Gross [R–Iowa]: Would the gentleman think that there would be enough money in the bill for the Senate to continue to purchase fragrant air bombs by the case and mountain spring water for drinking purposes instead of using tap water?

Mr. George W. Andrews [D–Ala., Chairman of House Appropriations' Legislative Subcommittee]: As the gentleman knows, we do not examine the budget for the expenses of the other body; they do not examine the budgets for expenses of the House. I am sure that the Members of the other body will see that their needs are met as they determine their needs to be.

Mr. Gross: I want to be sure that their free haircuts are continued, as well as manicures, the mountain spring water, or whatever it is, and fragrant air bombs. *Congressional Record,* Vol. 111, Pt. 13, 89 Cong. 1 sess. (1965), p. 17592.

work. Then there is that six-year term for senators and the two-year term for representatives. Senators have breathing space, and many a harassed representative who feels he is perpetually campaigning resents that also. And every administration seems to give the initial publicity to senators when it comes to announcing contracts and appointments. And so on, down a long series of institutional grievances—some real, some imagined, but all strongly held.

Senators have their own misgivings about the House, though a number of them served there and some enjoyed it. Almost to a man, senators are convinced that members of the House suffer from a collective and massive inferiority complex. A hard-working member of Senate Appropriations observed: "I would never go to the House to testify unless I was specifically requested. We think nothing of a Member of Congress coming over here to testify. He is treated very kindly and courteously. But if we go over there, we are viewed with jealousy and suspicion." Senators see their House colleagues as parochial in attitude and interest, and themselves as having the needs of their state, the nation, and—more and more—the world constantly before them.

The 1962 Confrontation

Most senators and staff agree that today the irritations in the relations between the two committees, while present, are subdued. Nonetheless they remain mindful of a long history of rivalry, and particularly of the open battle that raged between the House and Senate committees throughout the 1962 session. While it might have seemed petty to some, to the senior members on the Senate committee the 1962 struggle was critical. Some members of the press corps described the confrontation as a squabble between "two stubborn old patriarchs"—eighty-three-year-old House Chairman Clarence Cannon and eighty-four-year-old Senate Chairman Carl Hayden—but the more astute observers and participants knew better. At issue was an attempt to make a fundamental shift in American constitutional practice.

The founding fathers blurred the specific powers of the two houses as they pertained to the appropriation of revenue, which was clearly to be raised only by a bill originating in the House of Representatives. Although the House approved an occasional Senate-originated emergency appropriation, and an 1881 report by the House Committee on the Judiciary confirmed the Senate's coequal power to initiate appropriation bills, since 1789 the Senate had permitted the House to originate all regular annual appropriation bills.[11]

Also left unspecified by the Constitution was the exact procedure to reconcile the different versions of a bill passed by each house so that a single measure could be sent to the President for approval or disapproval. Following an English parliamentary practice dating from the fourteenth century, a form of conference procedure was established in the First Congress. Early Senate conferees were frequently selected without regard to committee assignment and seniority. In the decade prior to the Civil War, the presiding officer of each chamber began to appoint the majority and minority conferees primarily from the committee that considered the legislation, and these "managers"—as they are officially known—met to adjust the differences. Ada C. McCown, who has traced the origin and development of the conference committee, notes that by 1852, "the customs of presenting identical reports from the committees of conference in both Houses, of granting high privilege to these conference reports, of voting upon the conference report as a whole and permitting no amendment of it, of keeping secret the discussions carried on in the meetings of the conference committee, had become established in American parliamentary practice."[12] While the rules and practices relating to conferences are many and complex, and continue to evolve, prior to 1962 it seemed firmly established that conferences were held in the Senate wing of the Capitol and presided over by the chairman of the Senate conferees.

In 1962, Cannon, on behalf of House Appropriations, sought to change this procedure by demanding, first, that every other conference meeting on a bill be held on the House side and, second, that the chairmanship of the conference alternate between the two houses. His underlying goals were to shear the Senate Committee on Appropriations of some of its power, to cripple the Senate practice of raising the amounts in House-passed bills, and to slow down the Kennedy ad-

11. See Appendix B.

12. Ada C. McCown, *The Congressional Conference Committee* (Columbia University Press, 1927), pp. 23, 38, 63–64. For the precedents relating to the general principles of conferences, the appointment of conference managers, and the scope, privilege, form, and consideration of conference reports in the House, see Clarence Cannon, compiler, *Cannon's Precedents of the House of Representatives of the United States* (Government Printing Office, 1935), Vol. 8, pp. 709–97. For the earlier precedents, which Cannon's work updates to 1935, see Asher C. Hinds, compiler, *Hinds' Precedents of the House of Representatives of the United States* (Government Printing Office, 1907), Vol. 5, pp. 641–810.

ministration (and the House leaders, who had not paid him the heed he felt was his due). Especially disturbing to Cannon and other senior members of House Appropriations was the apparent inclination of the Kennedy administration and its Senate allies to use wherever possible so-called "backdoor spending"—that is, funding through public debt transactions authorized by legislative committees—rather than regular appropriations.[13]

The stresses and irritations that surfaced so dramatically in 1962 have existed since the First Congress. Aggression, however, seldom occurs without a leader, and Cannon—aided and sometimes prodded by Democrat Albert Thomas of Texas—was that leader. A member of the House from northeastern Missouri since 1923, Cannon had given the institution his whole life. In his view, the House was more than a coequal of the Senate; it was supreme—not only in the raising of revenue but also in the appropriation of public funds. Cannon ruled his committee with acid tongue and iron hand. He worked ceaselessly in what he regarded as a diligent attempt to save taxpayer dollars. In this effort he had the support of his ranking Republican, John Taber, and most of his economy-oriented committee. The first rule for those subcommittee chairmen and ranking minority members trained in the "Cannon school" was to give away as little as possible to the Senate. As an ex officio member on all of his conference committees, Cannon was known to burst in on a session that had been meeting for several days and scold the manager of the House conferees: "You gave away too much." Sometimes he would simply stay and take over—breaking up the meeting in the process.

Relations between the two committees had become increasingly strained in the hectic close of the 1961 session. Two examples will suffice. Seeking to continue the foreign aid appropriations conference in order to meet the adjournment deadline, Democrat Otto E. Passman of Louisiana, chairman of the House conferees, telephoned Hayden and asked to have an evening meeting scheduled on the House side. Hayden remembered that one of his predecessors, McKellar, had gone over to the House to hold a conference on public works in the 1940s. Although

---

13. Another motive for Cannon's adamant position in 1962 might have been related to his emphysema. He usually was driven the one block from his office to the Capitol because it was extremely difficult for him to walk. Conferences held in the center of the Capitol or on the House side would have been less painful for him to reach.

most senators had made no objection, Hayden knew that Richard B. Russell, who was as knowledgeable as Cannon about traditions and precedents, had been disturbed by that innovation. In light of Russell's reaction, Hayden turned down Passman's request. Then on the final night of the first session of the Eighty-seventh Congress, the House delivered the insult that was to rankle senators for a long time.

The House-Senate conferees on the $1.1 billion supplemental appropriation bill for 1962 had struck a bargain that contained some painful aspects for the Senate. The conferees reversed the Senate position that members of Congress should not be permitted to address unlimited quantities of franked mail to their constituencies simply by writing "Boxholder" or "Occupant" on the envelope. In addition, the House conferees, ignoring the comity of the two bodies, had succeeded in rejecting a housekeeping item increasing senatorial office funds. Finally, and particularly distressing to northern Democrats, conference action prohibited the use of administrative funds to implement backdoor spending programs pertaining to area redevelopment, urban mass transportation, and open spaces. The House conferees had successfully insisted that these programs be funded annually. After passing the conference report on the supplemental appropriations bill, the House of Representatives promptly adjourned *sine die* at 4:21 a.m. The Senate—marking time in the early morning hours for the House to complete action on the measure so it could be brought up—was now stuck. If it rejected the conference report, the President would have to call a special session of the Congress.[14]

Senators were outraged. Democratic leader Mansfield denounced the House's lack of courtesy and complained that the Senate had taken a "shellacking." Republican leader Dirksen threatened a roll call showdown: "Are we a coordinate branch of the legislative establishment, or are we not?" Appropriations member Mundt decried the "shotgun held

14. Under Article 1, sec. 5, subsec. 4 of the Constitution, "Neither House, during the Session of Congress, shall, without the Consent of the other, adjourn for more than three days. . . ." In order to meet this requirement, a concurrent resolution is offered by the leaders in one house. When it is approved, it is forwarded to the other body. Once the other chamber accepts it, adjournment can occur. In 1961, Democratic leader Mansfield processed the concurrent resolution in the Senate early in the evening of the all-night session. Once the House had Senate approval to adjourn, it was free to do so at any time and did. Mansfield assured the Senate that he would not send a *sine die* adjournment resolution to the House the following year. *Congressional Record*, Vol. 107, Pt. 16, 87 Cong. 1 sess. (Sept. 26, 1961), pp. 21372, 21387, 21396.

at the head of the Senate by the House. . . ." Another GOP member of Appropriations, Hruska, exclaimed: ". . . by knuckling under . . . we are stultifying this branch of Congress." Although not all Senators agreed with these views, and cooler heads prevailed as the Senate approved the conference report and itself adjourned *sine die* at 6:16 a.m., many vowed it would never happen again.

Shortly after the second session got under way in January 1962,[15] Cannon informed Hayden that he wanted to alternate the location of conference meetings: one meeting to be held in the Senate wing of the Capitol, the next to be held on the House side. At the initial meeting of House Appropriations on January 31, 1962, Albert Thomas offered a resolution to alternate not only the meetings but also the conference chairmanships. While some members were not sympathetic with the proposal, no one opposed it. Hayden immediately consulted Russell and then called his committee together on February 9 to discuss Cannon's demand. By a unanimous vote, Hayden was instructed to inform Cannon that Senate Appropriations would like to have half of the appropriation bills originate in the Senate and half in the House. Once that was done, the Senate committee would be delighted to confer on the House side in connection with Senate-originated bills and on the Senate side (as had been the tradition) concerning bills initiated in the House.

Almost two months passed without further discussion of the issue. Then on the morning of April 10, House and Senate conferees assembled in Senate quarters—as they had for 173 years—to reconcile the differences in the regular Treasury–Post Office bill, which had passed the Senate two weeks before. As lunch time drew near, it was apparent that more work needed to be done. A House member indicated that there might be several roll calls in the House that afternoon. Senator Robertson, chairman of the Senate conferees, suggested that another meeting be held the next day. At that point the chairman of the House conferees, Democrat J. Vaughan Gary of Virginia, interrupted to

15. The chronology of the confrontation is based on interviews with leaders of both the Senate and the House who were active participants; relevant issues of the *New York Times;* the sequence of events detailed by Senator Robertson in the Senate, *Congressional Record,* Vol. 108, Pt. 10, 87 Cong. 2 sess. (July 9, 1962), pp. 12899–902; and an article by James C. Kirby, Jr., chief counsel of the Senate Judiciary Subcommittee on Constitutional Amendments, which was written for the December 1962 issue of the *American Bar Association Journal* and later reprinted in the *Congressional Record,* Vol. 109, Pt. 1, 88 Cong. 1 sess. (Jan. 28, 1963), pp. 1212–13.

explain that since the House committee had adopted a motion on the alternation of conference meetings, he would have to insist that the next meeting be held on the House side. "We'll trade meeting places with you when we originate appropriations bills," responded Robertson. "That will be never," said Gary as he and his colleagues left the room.

Within a week following the breakup of the Treasury–Post Office conference, the Senate requested a conference with the House on a supplemental bill. The following day, Senate Appropriations was informed that the House supplemental conferees would be willing to confer, provided that the conference was held in the space assigned to the House Appropriations Committee in the Capitol. In response, Hayden reminded Cannon of their conversation earlier in the year and renewed his offer to confer on the House side on those bills that the Senate originated.

Two months passed during which there were occasional hints of settlement. With less than three weeks remaining in the fiscal year, the pressure mounted sharply as the Senate approved the Interior appropriation bill on June 12 and the Defense bill the next day, and requested conferences on both. On June 14, the House passed a joint resolution that authorized the departments to continue their current level of spending and, in addition, included certain appropriations that were in the stalled supplemental. Early the following morning, Hayden wrote Cannon that it was the unanimous view of the Senate committee that the House action was "inadequate" in meeting "the pressing demands" of the government for funds prior to the close of the fiscal year. "In the public interest," Hayden invited Cannon and the other House supplemental conferees to meet the Senate conferees in the old Supreme Court chamber approximately midway between the two houses at 2 p.m. that afternoon. Hayden's plea went unanswered. Finally, on June 18, seven-man delegations from both House and Senate Appropriations met for an hour in the old Supreme Court chamber. On emerging, Hayden said, "We're right back where we started."

On June 22, Cannon added new fuel to the fire: he noted that the Senate had added $32 billion to House-passed appropriation bills in the previous decade—the exact amount of the increase in the public debt. On June 28, with the annual Fourth of July recess drawing near, a continuing resolution permitting the government to continue spending until July 31 was finally approved by both houses. By Friday, July 6, Senate Appropriations had counterattacked by issuing a unanimous resolution setting forth the background of the dispute, and noting that "the differences between the two bodies of Congress are not the minor question of the location of the room where conferences shall be held or the individual to preside, but involve the question of whether the Senate committee is coequal with the House committee in the consideration of appropriation bills." On Monday, July 9, the House committee replied with another resolution linking "the inequitable practice of conducting all conferences under the chairmanship of a Senator . . ." with the rise in the national debt, the increase in deficit spending, the upward pace of the cost-of-living index, the decline in the buying power of the dollar, and the loss of the nation's gold holdings. After receiving this missive, Hayden, speaking on the floor of the Senate, led his committee in refuting the House charges and stating their grievances against the House committee.

Despite the flurry and the fury, both sides were beginning to feel the pressures exerted by hard-pressed executive agencies, a needling press, and concerned colleagues. On July 11, Hayden agreed to negotiate, provided the Senate demand to originate half of the appropriation bills was also on the agenda. Cannon, with House members getting letters from home expressing concern that federal assistance to schools in impacted areas would be jeopardized, agreed to meet.[16] After several meetings in the old Supreme Court chamber, which was accepted as the meeting place without a formal agreement that might cause one side to lose face, an unsteady truce was reached on July 18 covering only the remainder of the session. The negotiators decided that a joint committee would present recommendations at the beginning of the next Congress and that in the meantime the question of who would preside over each conference would be decided by the subcommittee chairmen involved.[17]

With tranquillity partly restored, conferees displayed such an elaborate show of courtesy—the chairman of each group urging his counterpart to preside—that the meetings almost broke up again. Some con-

---

16. The Senate negotiating team was headed by Russell and included Hill, Pastore, Saltonstall, and Mundt. The House team was headed by Albert Thomas and included Democrats J. Vaughan Gary of Virginia and Michael J. Kirwan of Ohio, and Republicans Ben F. Jensen of Iowa and Gerald R. Ford of Michigan.

17. The joint committee was never appointed.

ferees agreed that nobody would preside; in other subcommittees they flipped a coin. Several subcommittee chairmen who had been amicably meeting with each other for years were keenly embarrassed by the whole affair. Others grumbled and soon went back to their old ways.

It was difficult to determine who emerged victorious from the conflict. The House secured a meeting place closer to its chamber and the alternating of conference chairmanships. The Senate failed to dent the long-standing House practice of originating all appropriation bills. In the long run, however, the House did not strengthen its position in terms of conference outcomes because the confrontation forced members of Senate Appropriations, consciously and unconsciously, to improve some of their practices. As senators returned to their subcommittees, many resolved to hold longer and more detailed hearings and never again to be embarrassed by the House.

Does a deep conflict remain between the House and Senate committees? Most senators and committee staff agree that irritations continue, though at a much more genteel level. There is disagreement, however, as to the extent of the rift. Many of the senior senators who were active participants in the 1962 confrontation support the view that "the controversy has washed on down the river."

With the succession of George Mahon, a mild-mannered, gentlemanly Texan, following Cannon's death on May 12, 1964, a new era between House and Senate Appropriations began. By 1965, it was hard to believe that less than three years earlier some government employees had gone without pay because of the bitter impasse between the two committees. A Senate subcommittee chairman, noting the change in attitude, remarked: "Mahon is easy to talk to and to cooperate with. The discussions in conference are now more rational. The decisions are based more on logic, whereas they used to be based just on obstinacy and we were often confronted with something on a 'take it or leave it' basis." Conferences that used to drag on for hours and days are now frequently completed in an hour. The Senate professional staff communicates more with its House counterpart prior to the meeting of the principals, and several of the subcommittee chairmen and ranking minority members also are increasingly in communication with their House counterparts. As a result, areas of agreement and of difference are more widely known, and the possibility for compromise enhanced.

* * *

As in the information-gathering process, at each stage of the decision-making process, from the pre-markup session through final conference and floor agreement, the subcommittee chairman dominates Senate action on a particular appropriation bill. With rare exceptions, he has the cooperation of the ranking minority member on his subcommittee. Because of the diligence of these men, committee colleagues and other senators usually defer to their recommendations. Checks do exist, however. In seeking the approval first of the subcommittee and then of the full committee and the floor, hurdles are encountered that encourage pause and deliberation. The greatest hurdle—and the basic institutional check—is the need to secure agreement in a House-Senate conference and then approval of the conference report by both chambers. It is a hurdle that ordinarily encourages a sense of responsibility in all participants in the congressional appropriations process.

CHAPTER SIX

The Committee
and the Executive

Committee Influence on the Executive

In his *Considerations on Representative Government,* John Stuart Mill eloquently argued that "instead of the function of governing, for which it is radically unfit, the proper office of a representative assembly is to watch and control the government: to throw the light of publicity on its acts; to compel a full exposition and justification of all of them which any one considers questionable; to censure them if found condemnable. . . ."[1] Although Mill was primarily concerned with the English parliamentary system, his views were influential in molding public opinion in America as well. There is no constitutional mandate requiring Congress to consider only broad matters of national policy and to leave their implementation to the discretion of the President and his subordinates. In the twentieth century, students of public administration have recognized that policy and administration are inseparable; American legislative practitioners have acted on this basis since the eighteenth century. Still, it is one thing for members of a legislative group to make decisions; it is quite another to see that they are effectively executed.[2]

1. John Stuart Mill, *Considerations on Representative Government* (London: Longmans, Green, Reader, and Dyer, 1878), People's ed., p. 42.
2. The literature on legislative oversight—or how Congress reviews and influences the implementation of statutes and programs—is extensive and growing. Two useful

The Question of Legislative Oversight

Budgets are designed to support policies, and in effect are descriptions of how the policies will be implemented. Because they review agency budgets on an annual basis, the Appropriations subcommittees possess more detailed program knowledge than do the legislative committees. From subcommittee actions on program details—questions at hearings, line item decisions, report directives—the executive agencies readily discern the nuances of approval and condemnation and make some accommodation to them. Many scholars and participants have agreed that the power to appropriate and "to specify the conditions under which public funds are to be spent" is "one of the most effective means available to Congress for accomplishing supervision and control of the bureaucracy in a sustained fashion. . . ."[3] Some scholars, however, have been alarmed at how the appropriations process has been used to influence executive policy. There is a valid disagreement regarding the type of control exerted by the Appropriations Committees and its actual effectiveness. Does control over detail rather than essentials lead to an influence on the administrative process that is in the public interest? Noting that "a hostile remark by a congressman in a committee hearing . . . induces tremors throughout the official world," Leonard D. White observed that "congressional wrath is not necessarily control, and official trepidation is not necessarily conformity." White believed that Congress could "make its greatest contribution [to ensuring high standards of administrative performance] by building up the administrative system and by depending largely on its internal controls."[4] On the other hand, many scholars believe, as one has argued,

---

books, which represent, in part, the executive and legislative schools of thought on the problems involved, are Joseph P. Harris's *Congressional Control of Administration* (Brookings Institution, 1964) and Charles S. Hyneman's *Bureaucracy in a Democracy* (Harper & Brothers, 1950). See especially Hyneman's perceptive Chap. 9, "Reviewing the Action of the Bureaucracy." A shorter but equally perceptive study is Cornelius P. Cotter's "Legislative Oversight" in *Congress: The First Branch of Government* (American Enterprise Institute for Public Policy Research, 1966), pp. 25–81. Few attempts have been made to explore the nonstatutory means by which a legislative body influences and controls executive policy. An interesting beginning has been made by Michael W. Kirst, *Government Without Passing Laws: Congress' Nonstatutory Techniques for Appropriations Control* (University of North Carolina Press, 1969).

3. L. Dwaine Marvick, "Congressional Appropriation Politics: A Study of Institutional Conditions for Expressing Supply Intent" (Ph.D. thesis, Columbia University, 1952), p. 2.

4. Leonard D. White, "Congressional Control of the Public Service," *The American Political Science Review*, Vol. 39 (February 1945), p. 7. White states that his sug-

"that the review of operations should play a far more effective role in the budget process than it has in the past."[5]

In recent years, as government regulation has spread throughout the American economy and increasingly affected the livelihood of the citizens, new emphasis has been given to legislative oversight as a major role for Congress to pursue. Confronted with the vast expansion of the American bureaucracy resulting from the depression and the Second World War, the Legislative Reorganization Act of 1946 directed each standing committee of the Senate and the House of Representatives to exercise "continuous watchfulness of the execution by the administrative agencies concerned of any laws . . ." for which they were responsible. What later became the Committees on Government Operations in both houses were also granted a broad mandate by the 1946 act, including, in part, "studying the operation of Government activities at all levels with a view to determining its economy and efficiency. . . ."[6] Despite this wide-ranging jurisdiction, however, the Senate Committee on Government Operations has only sporadically reviewed even part of the work of the executive branch. The standing committees with much narrower jurisdiction have done little more. The spectacular investigation has excited interest; the dull, detailed work needed to keep abreast of how the executive administers legislative enactments and carries out congressional intent has generally been avoided.

In 1966, twenty years after the first major attempt at congressional reorganization in this century, another Joint Committee on the Organization of Congress reported and once again urged that

> The responsibilities of Congress extend beyond the passage of new legislation. One of the most important of these is to scrutinize continuously existing programs to determine whether they are being administered in accordance with congressional intent, whether amendments are desirable, or whether the program has outlived its purpose.[7]

---

gestions are premised on reform of the committee system and seniority, something not likely to occur soon. Perhaps the basic difficulty is that such internal controls are more likely to result from an administrative class similar to that of the British higher civil service than from the diverse and mobile administrative and technical talents called upon to operate the vast American governmental machinery.

5. Arthur Smithies, *The Budgetary Process in the United States* (McGraw-Hill, 1955), pp. 49–50.

6. 60 Stat. 816 and *Senate Manual,* S. Doc. 1, 89 Cong. 1 sess. (Government Printing Office, 1965), Rule 25, sec. 1 (j) (2) (B), p. 34.

7. *Organization of Congress,* Final Report of the Joint Committee on the Organization of the Congress, S. Rept. 1414, 89 Cong. 2 sess. (July 28, 1966), p. 23.

Recalling that the 1946 act recognized the need for continuous review, the joint committee concluded that it "has failed to achieve the desired result." In suggesting that "review" would be a more accurate description of the function than "oversight," the joint committee recommended that each standing committee be authorized one additional permanent professional staff member "who shall be designated a review specialist and who shall be assigned exclusively to performance of review (oversight)." The review specialist was urged to inspect and analyze the General Accounting Office reports submitted to the committee. In addition, the joint committee recommended that each standing committee, other than Appropriations, file an annual report on the review activities it had conducted during the year, with copies of the reports going to the President and the Bureau of the Budget, as well as to the two houses of Congress.

Having enacted a mass of Great Society proposals—some of which had been before Congress for almost two decades—legislators in the mid-1960s expressed interest in following up on their handiwork. Thoughout the Eighty-ninth Congress, Democratic leader Mansfield urged his colleagues to engage in a careful review of these programs. In a letter to each of the Senate's standing committee chairmen prior to the opening of the Ninetieth Congress, Mansfield noted that the time seemed "ripe" for such a "concentrated reexamination." Not only should the more recent programs be reviewed, said the majority leader, but also the older ones—such as agricultural subsidies, foreign aid, income taxes, and the military draft—which had not had a "thoroughgoing second look for many years." He believed that " a complete restudy by the Senate could provide not only a basis for adjustment of legislation, as necessary to the current needs of the nation, but also a check on the equity and efficacy of the administrative interpretations and practices which have developed."[8]

Despite the urging of the joint committee and congressional leaders, legislative review by most standing committees has not been pursued. Most committees do not require the agencies to review their conduct of a specific program on an annual basis. For the few, such as the ones on armed services, that are an exception to this rule, the annual review has come to resemble the detailed review long carried on by the various Appropriations subcommittees. Although there has been a growing tendency to limit legislative authorizations to one year, pro-

8. *New York Times,* Dec. 28, 1966.

grams are usually authorized for two, three, four or more years, with review hearings seldom held in the interim. Some programs have blanket authorizations. Legislators whose responsibility it is to authorize or appropriate funds for agency programs often acquire vested interests in the programs and policies of the agency—just as do the agency administrators. Public and private partisans of particular goals or viewpoints strive for ready access to those legislators who are in a position to help or hinder a program. Often the legislator finds himself not an advocate of a particular course of action, but rather a reconciler of diverging interests—within the agency, among several agencies, and even between the agency and the constituency it serves.[9]

Scholars who have examined the hearings and reports and have interviewed members of various legislative committees conclude that committee members, on the whole, value legislative and constituent-service activity more than they do participation in oversight activity. House members and those senators with an election less than two years away are likely to spend time on what will bring immediate publicity and constituent recognition. Plodding research and concentrated study of agency activities with no likelihood of headlines are unappealing—and especially so to some legislators who feel that the bureaucracy is an impenetrable maze. Since those on legislative committees usually have easy access to agency officials and as a result can more readily serve their constituency, they are unlikely to disturb a pleasant relationship by undertaking an investigation. Dampers on effective agency review also include possible retribution by interest groups that enjoy the status quo and by the administration in power, which resents criticism, especially from members of its own party. Conversely, oversight is more likely to occur if those in control of the legislative committee and those in control of the administration belong to different political parties. If, as individuals, the committee leaders have failed to achieve their aims or those of powerful constituent interests, then committee review might also be used. Presidential tampering with the regulatory agen-

9. In a 1943 essay, a political scientist from Columbia University wrote one of the most frequently quoted paragraphs in the literature on congressional oversight. Referring to the oversight function conducted by the two Appropriations Committees, he observed: "It is not Congress, not the House or Senate, not even the appropriations committee as a whole that should be thought of as abstractions, set against administration. The reality is a handful of men from particular states or districts, working with a particular committee clerk on a multitude of details." Arthur W. Macmahon, "Congressional Oversight of Administration: The Power of the Purse I," *Political Science Quarterly*, Vol. 58 (June 1943), p. 181.

cies, which have a historic position as an arm of Congress, is likely to elicit a sharp legislative response.[10]

The attitude of the committee chairman and his relations with his subcommittee chairmen help to determine the vigor with which legislative review is pursued. So does the professional staff available to the committee. No matter how competent, a small, overburdened staff does not have time for detailed study and review. Staff review of agency activity is not a simple task, since what is waste to one senator is often worthwhile to another. It has also been suggested that oversight suffers because committees with low prestige do not attract member interest in their work.[11]

The problems of the legislative committees in achieving effective oversight—and the opportunity for the Appropriations Committees— were aptly noted during the 1966 debate on creating a nine-member Senate Committee on Intelligence Operations. Senator Russell led the opposition to formation of the new group. He observed that those who wanted to make the Senate's scrutiny of the Central Intelligence Agency more formal seemed "to have the idea that legislative oversight means that a legislative committee which is oversighting has some control over the administration of that agency." In Russell's judgment, nothing could be further from the facts. He explained:

> All that we can do by oversighting is to keep ourselves informed as to what an agency is doing, with the exception of the Committee on Appropriations. I want to make that exception. They have the power of the purse. If they feel disposed, they can reduce the appropriation. But the other standing committees, when they are exercising legislative oversight, cannot control the operations of the agency.[12]

10. Most of the propositions in this paragraph that identify the conditions under which committee review is likely to occur or not occur are based on Seymour Scher's thoughtful study of two House committees (Interstate and Foreign Commerce, and Education and Labor) and one Senate committee (Labor and Public Welfare) and their relations with the various regulatory commissions over which they maintain legislative jurisdiction. Scher views "Congressional committee leaders and members . . . as people who act on the basis of rational estimates of their situation. The decision to initiate, participate actively in or avoid committee inquiry into agency performance is understood by the Congressman as one involving costs and gains." Seymour Scher, "Conditions for Legislative Control," *The Journal of Politics,* Vol. 25 (August 1963), pp. 526–51.

11. John F. Bibby, "Committee Characteristics and Legislative Oversight of Administration," *Midwest Journal of Political Science,* Vol. 10 (February 1966), pp. 78–98.

12. *Congressional Record,* Vol. 112, Pt. 12, 89 Cong. 2 sess. (1966), p. 15676.

Has the Senate Committee on Appropriations been effective in reviewing agency activities? With one exception, the members of the committee in 1966 described their review efforts as "weak," "poor," "ineffective," "erratic," "spasmodic," or "nonexistent." Most members and staff on the committee are convinced that additional staff is needed to perform effective followup. Subcommittees with one and usually not more than two professional staff members are besieged with the daily problems relating to a particular agency's programs. Little time is available for the research, meetings, and field trips necessary for effective review. Seldom discussed, however, is the basic point raised by Budget Director Harold D. Smith when he testified before the Joint Committee on the Organization of Congress in 1945. He decried the emphasis on the hiring of staff experts as a cure-all for congressional problems:

> What we want is the common sense and judgment of the elected representatives upon the issues of policy which come before the Congress. . . . His judgment is a composite of all of his experience, plus a sensitivity to the reaction of the people who elected him to Congress. Experts can have blind spots and be short-sighted.[13]

And there is still another aspect to ineffective legislative review. A knowledgeable staff member suggested it: "I think the committee is just as effective as it wants to be, and this is also true of Congress. Congress has control of the purse if it wants to control it. If its power has diminished, it is because Congress has preferred it that way."

Statutory Controls

Historically, through the appropriations process Congress has exerted its influence on the executive branch, first, by detailing a specific level of funding to be expended on a given governmental function and, second, by imposing prohibitions and limitations on that spending. The appropriation of funds for specific purposes rather than in a lump sum dates back to the founding of the nation and the victory of the legislatively oriented Jeffersonians over the executive-oriented Hamiltonians. With the impetus given by the Hoover Commission in 1949 to the concept of performance budgeting (budgeting based on functions, activities, and projects—the work to be done—rather than on things to be acquired, such as personal services, equipment, and supplies), and the beginning made in modernizing the budget document,

13. *Organization of Congress*, Hearings before the Joint Committee on the Organization of Congress (May 28, 1945), Pt. 3, p. 684.

some headway has occurred in recent years in granting larger or lump sums for programs and reducing the emphasis on minute and specific statutory detail.[14] (See Table 6–1.) The tendency of Congress to appropriate for broad categories of services within a given appropriation bill has increased executive flexibility and supposedly provided for more effective use of resources by those Congress holds responsible for carrying out a particular program.

With larger and larger line item appropriations, there can be only a tacit understanding between committee and administrator about legislative preferences. It is generally understood that a program will seek to achieve the goals expressed in the agency justifications and the congressional hearings on which the committee's decision was based. In some programs, however, not even that much is guaranteed. With foreign aid, for example, the Agency for International Development has traditionally presented an illustrative program, and neither Appropriations Committee expects the justifications to be rigorously adhered to in their original form. Given shifting strategic requirements, changing technologies, an evolving international situation, and varying costs in human and material resources, line item appropriations in the Defense appropriation bill are particularly meaningless.

What statutory control Congress exerts beyond the initial authorization and annual line item appropriations consists mainly of specific prohibitions and limitations inserted into the appropriation acts. Although much less so than in past years, appropriation acts are sprinkled with prohibitions and limitations restricting executive action. Traditionally, these apply to administrative as opposed to program expenditures. They usually specify the amount that can be spent for the purchase of newspapers and periodicals and an agency's printing and travel costs; the number of automobiles that can be replaced; the total

14. After reviewing the efforts of Congress to control expenditures from 1789 to the Second World War, one scholar concluded that "the multiplication of appropriations, far from securing to Congress that completeness of financial control which is, so to speak, its constitutional birthright, has served only to make the law less certain and to satisfy Congress with the name, rather than the substance, of power." Lucius Wilmerding, Jr., *The Spending Power: A History of the Efforts of Congress to Control Expenditures* (Yale University Press, 1943), p. 195. The Hoover Commission noted that "there is no uniformity in the schedules of appropriations. Some appropriations represent huge sums, others small amounts. Appropriations for the same service appear in many different places. Much of this results from historical accident." *Budgeting and Accounting*, A Report to the Congress by the Commission on Organization of the Executive Branch of the Government (February 1949), p. 7.

Table 6–1. Number of Line Item Appropriations, Limitations, and Prohibitions in Regular General Appropriation Acts, Classified by Dollar Amount, 1946 and 1965

	Amount class (millions of dollars)													Percentage change, 1946-65
	Less than 0.1		0.1–0.9		1.0–9.9		10–99		100–999		More than 1,000		Total		
Act	1946	1965	1946	1965	1946	1965	1946	1965	1946	1965	1946	1965	1946	1965	
Agriculture	49	17	51	14	43	34	12	27	4	12	...	2	159	106	−33.3
Defense	37	3	36	4	51	10	30	20	34	21	3	16	191	74	−61.3
District of Columbia	119	18	59	12	26	16	1	11	...	...	...	...	205	57	−72.2
Foreign Assistance	...	1	...	...	...	5	...	10	...	9	...	2	...	27	...
Independent Offices	99	22	37	40	47	51	16	45	5	13	2	3	206	174	−15.5
Interior	209	18	86	23	43	33	6	26	...	2	...	...	344	102	−70.3
Labor-HEW	54	9	55	17	25	70	17	61	2	20	...	1	153	178	+14.0
Legislative	759	78	46	38	7	26	2	5	...	...	...	...	814	147	−81.9
Military Construction	...	...	...	1	...	5	...	11	...	5	...	...	...	22	...
Public Works	31	7	44	10	40	8	10	15	3	5	...	1	128	46	−64.1
State-Justice	137	35	59	32	45	61	8	29	...	7	...	2	249	166	−33.3
Treasury-Post Office	65	7	51	9	35	11	13	11	5	7	...	2	169	47	−72.2
Total	1,559	215	524	200	362	330	115	271	53	101	5	29	2,618	1,146	...
Percentage change, 1946-65	−86.2		−61.8		−8.8		+57.6		+47.5		+82.8		−56.2		−56.2

personnel, information, or legislative liaison officials who may be hired; the number of experts and consultants who may be retained; and the funds available for entertainment. Mainly because there is a lack of full committee coordination of the provisions in the various subcommittee bills, such restrictions frequently vary from agency to agency. In addition, each appropriation act has its own unique prohibitions and limitations. Some are enacted following legislative or interest group agitation, while others are included for reasons long since forgotten. In the Agricultural Appropriation Act for 1966, for example, Congress provided that except for materials required in research or experimental work, "no part of the funds appropriated by this Act shall be expended in the purchase of twine manufactured from commodities or materials produced outside of the United States." The private and public shipyards of America have secured more up-to-date restrictions: the Defense Appropriation Act of 1966 contained a paragraph that appropriated more than $1.5 billion in a lump sum for Navy shipbuilding and conversion, but Congress also declared that "none of the funds herein provided for the construction or conversion of any naval vessel to be constructed in shipyards in the United States shall be expended in foreign shipyards for the construction of major components of the hull or superstructure of such a vessel." Despite a continuing concern with administrative minutiae, Congress also enacts prohibitions and limitations that can have a decided policy impact. Although both the Senate and House Appropriations Committees have attempted to restrict executive discretion on domestic policies, the Senate and its Appropriations Committee have usually been more willing than the House to provide leeway for the President in foreign and national security policy matters.

Prohibitions and limitations have been used by the Appropriations Committees of both houses to circumvent the rule against legislation in a general appropriation bill. Strictly speaking, under the precedents of the House of Representatives, "A proper limitation is negative and in the nature of a veto, and when it assumes affirmative form by direction to an executive in the discharge of his duties under existing law it ceases to be a limitation and becomes legislation."[15] Yet in the Inde-

15. From Hinds' Precedents, 4, 3967, 3975; 7, 1606, as cited in Clarence Cannon, *Cannon's Procedure in the House of Representatives*, H. Doc. 610, 87 Cong. 2 sess. (Government Printing Office, 1963), p. 64. See the section on "Limitations" in

pendent Offices Appropriation Act for 1966 funding the activities of the Interstate Commerce Commission, a provision was inserted to provide that "$35,000 shall be available for establishment of a motor carrier office in Wyoming. . . ."[16] In its report for the previous year, Senate Appropriations had directed the commission to open such an office, but to no avail. With a statutory mandate, the office opened in Casper, Wyoming, on October 15, 1965. Of much greater policy impact is the provision annually renewed in the Defense Appropriation Act "that no funds herein appropriated shall be used for the payment of a price differential on contracts hereafter made for the purpose of relieving economic dislocations." The act further provides that ". . . so far as practicable, all contracts shall be awarded on a formally advertised competitive bid basis to the lowest responsible bidder."[17] To the chagrin of senators from the Midwest and Northeast, that language has maintained the preeminence of California in defense procurement against large-scale attempts to distribute defense contracts according to the level of unemployment in an area.

Congress has used many statutory devices to exert control over various aspects of the federal administration. Beginning in the late 1930s, increasing numbers of statutes have been enacted providing that either one or both houses of Congress may disapprove, end, or ratify executive actions taken under them. Typical of such statutes are the reorganization acts by which Congress authorizes the President to submit reorganization plans that will go into effect after a given period of time, provided that neither house has passed a resolution of disapproval. During the Second World War several emergency statutes —such as those relating to price control—contained provisions permitting Congress to terminate them by concurrent resolution. With the Greek-Turkish Aid Act of 1947, Congress provided that assistance under the act could be ended by concurrent resolution unless it were terminated sooner by the President. The provisions of the Neutrality Act

---

Cannon's Procedure, pp. 63–71. According to Hinds, "The purpose rather than the form of a proposed limitation is the proper criterion by which its admissibility should be judged, and if its purpose appears to be a restriction of executive discretion to a degree that may be fairly termed a change in policy rather than a matter of administrative detail it is not in order (7, 1691)." *Cannon's Procedure,* p. 65. "A limitation must apply solely to the present appropriation, and may not be made as a permanent provision of law (4, 3929)." *Cannon's Procedure,* p. 65. According to Hinds, where the limitation has applied to funds other than those in the pending bill, it has been construed as legislation and not admitted. *Cannon's Procedure,* p. 69.

16. 79 Stat. 533.
17. 79 Stat. 877.

of 1939 could be invoked either by the President or a concurrent resolution of Congress. In the case of the Tennessee Valley Authority, Congress even provided that members of the TVA Board could be removed at any time by concurrent resolution. In these instances, there is no opportunity for amendment. Congress decides the issue on an all-or-nothing basis. The simple or concurrent resolution is not subject to a presidential veto.

In twelve instances during 1965, Congress required in the various appropriation acts that an executive official report his actions to both the House and Senate Committees on Appropriations. Five of the twelve instances involved the secretary of defense; five, foreign assistance; one, the Atomic Energy Commission; and one, the attorney general. In all but one case, the committees merely required notification after the executive had acted. The exception was the use of unobligated balances for foreign economic assistance. The law provided that these balances could be continued if they were applied to purposes that had been previously justified before the Appropriations Committees, and the committees were "notified prior to the reobligation of funds for such projects or programs."[18] In the other cases, the time limit for notification and reports ranged from "shall immediately advise" (as when Defense funds were expended on an airborne alert) to a semiannual basis (as when AID paid an individual or group more than $25,000 in engineering and architectural fees on any single project). Whatever the particular requirement, it was abundantly clear that departments and agencies were to consult with the committees before undertaking various programs.

Senators recognize that presidents—regardless of party—are reluctant to approve any measure requiring an agency of government to consult with Congress before it takes action. But despite occasional presidential vetoes and preachments on the separation of powers, consultation between the executive departments and Congress does take place prior to the implementation of many administrative decisions. The agencies wish to maintain a semblance of harmony with the committees whose decisions can drastically affect their level of expenditure.[19]

18. 79 Stat. 1003.
19. For a lucid discussion of both the constitutional and the political problems involved in the various kinds of committee clearance devices, and the judgment that they are constitutional, see Richard T. Greer, "Control of Administration by Congressional Committees" (master's thesis, Georgetown University, 1959). Also see Joseph and Ann Cooper, "The Legislative Veto and the Constitution," *The George Washington Law Review*, Vol. 30 (March 1962), pp. 467–516 at pp. 514–15.

Nonstatutory Controls: The Report

The forms of nonstatutory control over an agency are many: a letter or telephone call from the subcommittee chairman to the program director, a private meeting between the subcommittee chairman (perhaps including the ranking minority member) and the cabinet officer or bureau chief concerned, language in the committee or conference report, or a colloquy on the floor to develop the legislative history interpreting a provision in a report or bill that affects an agency's activities. Of all these forms, the most important is the language in the committee or conference report.

Although senators seldom take the time to read committee hearings, most at least glance at the report that accompanies each appropriation bill. The appropriation of larger and larger amounts with fewer statutory limitations has resulted in more detailed committee reports. The reports are designed to inform the nonmembers who pass judgment on the committee's work, and the executive officials in charge of a program, of the reasons for recommending a given level of appropriations or advocating a specific course of action. They are an important vehicle for conveying committee instructions to the executive. In its reports, Senate Appropriations "is pleased" or "was disturbed." The committee —more particularly, its subcommittee chairmen and influential members—"agrees," "approves," "asks," "believes," "feels," "finds," "instructs," "protests," "requests," "recommends," "suggests," and "urges." Report language attempts congressional control before the fact and permits criticism after the fact.

Report language has many sources. Government departments, interest groups, expert witnesses, legislators and their staffs, all press suggested paragraphs on the chairman and his subcommittee clerk. Much of the language comes from the departments and agencies concerned. A close liaison between the committee staff and departmental budget officers elicits the necessary program description to support a committee recommendation. Although the committee itself usually makes the suggestions and caustic comments, on occasion departmental officials have secretly offered appropriate language in order to chastise a bureau with which the cabinet officer and his budget director have had difficulty. The bureaus also maintain working relations with the subcommittee to secure the insertion of committee praise and direction that will give them some leverage against any central control exerted by either the department or the White House. But usually the department and the bureau are allied in seeking nonstatutory language to support the detailed implementation of a program for which they might have only broad—and vague—authority.

Report language primarily specifies how a line item appropriation is to be expended, without tying the agency's hands with inflexible statutory language. For example, a paragraph in the public works appropriation bill for fiscal year 1966 appropriated $993,279,000 for general construction, to remain available until expended. In the "Statement of the Managers on the Part of the House" accompanying the conference report, twenty-nine pages were devoted to specifying, by state and project, the exact amounts allocated to 315 construction projects and 134 planning studies.[20] But a report does much more than merely allocate the funds granted in a lump-sum appropriation. It also gives direction to the agency by indicating the budget procedures to be followed, the management practices to be employed, and the emphasis to be given various programs. For instance, in the District of Columbia appropriation bill for 1966, funds were allowed to provide day care services for children, but by Senate report language, which was strictly adhered to by the District Department of Public Welfare, the funds were "restricted to mothers while in [job] training, and mothers who have completed training, and for 3 months thereafter."[21] Not infrequently, basic authorizing legislation is approved without much thought about the administrative implementation of a program. Thus, ironically, to avoid what might be an embarrassing showdown at the time of enactment, the legislative committees leave the job of filling in congressional intent to the Appropriations Committees.

In 1965, through the medium of the committee report, the various subcommittees of Senate Appropriations issued a total of 150 nonstatutory directives and suggestions to the agencies under their jurisdiction. (See Table 6–2.) These were in addition to the hundreds of directives that simply allocated a lump-sum appropriation among programs and projects. The directives pertained mainly to the goals and emphasis of agency activity (program), the distribution of costs among programs and groups (budget procedure), and the administrative means to implement the activity (management). As might be expected of a committee

20. *Public Works Appropriation Bill, 1966* [Conference Report to Accompany H.R. 9220], H. Rept. 1163, 89 Cong. 1 sess. (Oct. 13, 1965), pp. 7–35.

21. Statement of Donald D. Brewer, Director, Department of Public Welfare, District of Columbia, in *District of Columbia Appropriations, 1966,* Hearings before the Senate Appropriations Subcommittee, 89 Cong. 1 sess. (May 10, 1965), p. 908.

Table 6-2. Number of Report Directives, by Category, Issued by Senate Appropriations Subcommittees, 1965

| Subcommittee | *Category of nonstatutory directive* | | | |
	Program	*Budget procedure*	*Management*	*Total*
Agriculture	14	12	3	29
Defense	4	3	1	8
District of Columbia	1	2	2	5
Foreign Operations	1	. . .	. . .	1
Independent Offices	13	2	2	17
Interior	7	2	1	10
Labor-HEW	34	4	2	40
Legislative	6	3	. . .	9
Military Construction	. . .	1	. . .	1
Public Works	7	6	6	19
State-Justice	3	2	. . .	5
Treasury–Post Office	3	2	. . .	5
Supplementals[a]	. . .	. . .	1	1
Total	93	39	18	150

a. In 1965, there were four supplemental bills. With the exception of a nonstatutory directive pertaining to the Office of Economic Opportunity, whose budget requests were exclusively handled by the Supplementals Subcommittee during the Eighty-ninth Congress, all other supplemental nonstatutory directives were counted with those of the relevant subcommittees. The four supplementals contained twenty-five directives in all; ten pertained to program, eight to budget procedure, and seven to management.

that is policy oriented, 62 percent of the directives were concerned with program.

Report language often provides an opportunity for accommodating senatorial interests without changing the statutory content of a bill. Skillfully developed wording can soothe ruffled feelings in a markup session and aid in achieving committee unity. For example, to head off Senator Allott's efforts to add funds for hospital construction to the Labor-HEW bill for 1966—an addition that would have been subject to a point of order—Senate Appropriations agreed to the following paragraph in its report:

> The committee in its discussions felt there is an urgent need, in view of the enactment of the Social Security Amendments of 1965, for a restudy of the Hill-Burton program, looking toward the possibility of increasing the authorizations for general hospital construction and long-term-care facilities. The attention of the committees having jurisdiction in these matters is invited to this comment. The chairman of the Committee on Appropriations

was asked to send a copy of the committee report to the President of the United States.[22]

These words dissipated one of the rare partisan clashes within the committee—a confrontation that, if carried through, would have placed Democrats in the embarrassing position of voting against a liberalizing Republican amendment. Frequently, of course, the accommodation of colleagues relates less to partisanship or ideology than to the service of constituents.

Sometimes the report ratifies agreements the committee has extracted from executive representatives during the formal hearings or in private meetings. In the 1965 report on supplemental funds for the Office of Education, for instance, the following appeared:

> In conformity with the assurances given to the committee by the Commissioner of Education during hearings on the bill, the committee recommends that the Office of Education take no steps toward any national testing program, directly or by contract, until the Congress has had an opportunity to determine [whether] such a policy is advisable through its regular legislative committees.[23]

Lobbyists increasingly recognize that the appropriations report offers a possible vehicle for influencing not only the activities of executive departments and agencies, but also those of the semiautonomous regulatory bodies. Although a senator and his staff usually avoid pressing an independent regulatory commission, a congressional committee has no such compunction in dealing with what has been called the "fourth branch of government." The annual appropriations hearing provides an opportunity to expose the various commissioners to a give-and-take session with the people's representatives and the constituent groups they represent. Thus, in 1965, a nationwide automobile rental firm, faced with competition in the Midwest from a small, subsidized airline that also rented cars to its passengers at various airports, successfully secured report language directing the Civil Aeronautics Board's attention to "the practice of certain air carriers to engage in noncarrier ac-

22. *Departments of Labor, and Health, Education, and Welfare, and Related Agencies Appropriation Bill, 1966* [Report to accompany H.R. 7765], S. Rept. 537, 89 Cong. 1 sess. (Aug. 3, 1965), p. 23.

23. *Departments of Labor, and Health, Education, and Welfare Supplemental Appropriation Bill, 1966* [Report to accompany H.R. 10586], S. Rept. 680, 89 Cong. 1 sess. (Sept. 2, 1965), p. 6.

tivities. . . ." The Senate subcommittee admonished the board to "continue to supervise these activities vigorously to make sure that such noncarrier operations are not being subsidized."[24]

On occasion, Senate and House Appropriations use a directive in the committee report to block attempts at executive reorganization. In the budget proposals for fiscal 1966, Secretary of Labor W. Willard Wirtz sought to consolidate the separate accounts of the long-established Bureau of Employment Security and Bureau of Apprenticeship and Training (BAT) with the account of the Manpower Administration, which he had established early in 1963. The reaction from clients served by the two well-entrenched bureaus was immediate and clamorous. Building trades unions had long considered BAT their own fiefdom within the government. Over the years, many of their key members had retired to a BAT sinecure. Now these long-existing and pleasant relations between the bureau and the unions would possibly be disrupted both in Washington and in the field. Hugh C. Murphy, BAT administrator, happened to be a member of the Bricklayers' Union. So was John E. Fogarty, chairman of the House Appropriations Subcommittee on Labor-HEW. This coincidence killed Secretary Wirtz's proposed reorganization. In its report, the House committee warned that it "would be strongly opposed to any proposition to revive the plan for this reorganization."[25] The Senate committee readily concurred.

The Senate committee, however, has not unduly hampered executive reorganization. It has generally supported the reforms, begun by Eisenhower's last secretary of defense, Thomas S. Gates, and continued by Robert S. McNamara, that have strengthened the management role of the secretary and consolidated various service functions such as atomic support, communications, contract audit, intelligence, and supply. But the closing of federal facilities is another matter. Reorganization in Washington is tolerated as long as it does not hurt friends or constituents. Reorganization in a state or congressional district can be painful.

THE EFFECTIVENESS OF THE REPORT. The Senate rule that prohibits legislation in any general appropriation bill does not apply to the directions and instructions the Committee on Appropriations regularly

24. *Independent Offices Appropriation Bill, 1966* [Report to accompany H.R. 7997], S. Rept. 384, 89 Cong. 1 sess. (June 30, 1965), p. 5.

25. *Departments of Labor, and Health, Education, and Welfare, and Related Agencies Appropriation Bill, 1966* [Report to accompany H.R. 7765], H. Rept. 272, 89 Cong. 1 sess. (April 29, 1965), p. 4.

offers in its reports. Mandates in a report are not subject to a point of order. Although the direction might have come more properly from the legislative committee concerned, the executive departments are unlikely to quibble, knowing that they face an Appropriations subcommittee at least annually. In the Senate, where there are dual chairmanships between some legislative committees and the related Appropriations subcommittees, to object would be particularly pointless. In addition, time can be saved by clarifying statutory intent in an appropriations report. Otherwise amendments would have to be introduced and approved by the relevant legislative committees and their parent chambers.[26]

The executive agencies and the federal courts have mixed feelings as to the "binding" nature of directives expressed in the committee report or on the floor. While report language does not have the force of law, the fact that the General Accounting Office—with its sanction of disallowance—will adhere to a committee directive as indicative of legislative intent substantiates its restrictions on executive action. Moreover, executive officials know that their disobedience could be subject to question by the Appropriations subcommittee, and that it might result in a reduction in the level of appropriations for favored programs.

Nonetheless, the members and staff of the Senate Appropriations Committee remain doubtful about the effectiveness of report language. Some departments do implement the committee's instructions "to the gnat's eyebrow," as one high official expressed it. The Department of Defense has perhaps the most elaborate machinery for following up on nonstatutory directives. Once the committee report is received and analyzed in the general counsel's office, it is turned over to an action group in the office of the assistant secretary of defense (comptroller), where responsibility for looking into each criticism or suggestion is assigned to the appropriate agency within the Department of Defense. Prior to

26. For example, in the 1965 Senate report on the Defense appropriation bill, a single sentence—"Such funds as may be required may be used to restore lands under jurisdiction of other Government agencies, damaged while being used for military training purposes under agreement with such agencies"—was sufficient for the General Accounting Office to permit the Army to make funds available in cases of damage caused by military maneuvers on federally owned lands. *Department of Defense Appropriation Bill, 1966* [Report to accompany H.R. 9221], S. Rept. 625, 89 Cong. 1 sess. (Aug. 18, 1965), p. 23. On May 7, 1965, the comptroller general had ruled [Decision B-106776, 44 *Comp. Gen.* 693] that military funds could not be made available to reimburse other federal agencies in the absence of a clear expression of congressional intent. If the committee directive had been placed in the Defense appropriation bill, it would have been subject to a point of order.

the secretary's next appearance before Senate Appropriations, the necessary data are gathered and coordinated, decisions made, and the secretary briefed to answer questions about the disposition of each directive. Other departments are less cooperative. Most "play it by ear." The bureaucracy seems to have an uncanny way of determining which sections of the report represent the views of the subcommittee chairman and which sections reflect the opinions of less influential committee members. A close liaison between agency budget officer and subcommittee staff sometimes makes it possible for the agency to relegate the concerns of even the ranking minority member to the "ignore" category. Although subcommittee chairmen, in an effort at accommodation, frequently encourage the ranking minority member and other interested senators to express their feelings in the report, their views have slight effect if the chairman disagrees. For it is the chairman's ill will the agency fears.

If an agency sees that the reports of House and Senate Appropriations are in disagreement, the conferees will often be asked to resolve the issue. A distinct disadvantage for the Senate is that the House conferees are required under their rules to prepare a statement to accompany the conference report they submit to the House of Representatives. Although Senate and House conferees often agree on the nonstatutory directives made in this statement, the fact remains that the content and nuances of the language are under the complete control of the House chairman and his colleagues. Frequently the conferees do not reconcile the differences arising from the nonstatutory language that has been adopted by the two committees. If an agency wants to avoid a clear mandate and take the consequences, it can.

Although most departmental budget officers believe that they comply with nonstatutory directives, a number of them are surprised that once the committee report has been issued, so little is done to see whether the agency has conformed. While the committee often requests departmental compliance by a specified date, many of the nonstatutory injunctions, once delivered, go unreviewed even in the appropriations hearing the following year.

Nonstatutory Controls: Reprogramming Procedures

The Appropriations subcommittees, especially those concerned with defense and military construction, recognize that some reprogramming —the shifting of funds to other purposes than were justified by the agency before receiving its appropriations from Congress—is almost inevitable because of the time lag (often amounting to a year and a half or more) that exists between the preparation of the program justifications, the passage of the appropriations act, and the expenditure of the funds. During the Second World War, transferability clauses were added to the various war and navy appropriation bills to permit the departments to readjust rapidly to shifts in national security policy. Throughout the emergency period, however, House Appropriations, in particular, cautioned the executive departments to avoid taking advantage of this prerogative. By the early 1950s an informal procedure had been worked out to clear program changes with the chairmen and ranking minority members of the relevant Senate and House Appropriations subcommittees. At that time, as a result of the Hoover Commission recommendations, the Department of Defense appropriation accounts were reduced from over one hundred to about forty multibillion dollar accounts encompassing large areas such as personnel and procurement. In 1955, the House Appropriations Committee—in admonishing the Department of Defense to "keep faith" with the committee—called for semiannual reports detailing all major reprogrammings of funds. By 1959, both Senate and House Appropriations wanted more than semiannual reporting. The committees were to be informed of all "operation and maintenance" and "research, development, test, and evaluation" reprogrammings above $1 million and all procurement changes exceeding $5 million. In the early 1960s, the Committees on Armed Services began to authorize first procurement and later research, development, test, and evaluation projects on an annual basis. On March 4, 1963, the Department of Defense issued new reprogramming procedures that provided for even closer congressional control. Regardless of amount, prior approval of the committees was required if the reprogramming involved an increase in the procurement quantity of aircraft, missiles, or naval vessels, or the application of funds to a program reduced, rejected, or not previously approved by Congress. The amount of funds involved in Defense reprogramming is substantial. Over $8.8 billion in Defense reprogramming actions occurred during the four fiscal years 1961 through 1964 for missiles, ships, research, development, test, and evaluation alone. The figures for many millions more were not even known to the interested congressional committees.[27]

27. *Department of Defense Reprogramming of Appropriated Funds: A Case Study,* Report of the Subcommittee for Special Investigations of the Committee on Armed Services, House of Representatives, 89 Cong. 1 sess. (July 8, 1965).

Many of the Defense reprogrammings—as is true of reprogrammings by the other departments—are handled at the staff level by the subcommittee clerks. They check with the interested senators if an action affects a particular state—as in the case of construction projects—and then clear the documents with the subcommittee chairman and ranking minority member concerned. Reprogramming is regarded strictly as a subcommittee matter that does not even require clearance with the full committee chairman. When clearance difficulties arise in one or the other body, the papers are simply delayed until the issue is resolved in order that the House and Senate committees can act on a united basis. Most of the junior members on Senate Appropriations are unaware of the vast reprogramming responsibilities held by their senior colleagues, who make the decisions for them and for the Senate by virtue of their subcommittee positions. While the subcommittee chairmen, ranking minority members, and their staff conscientiously scrutinize reprogramming requests, the requests and the disposition of them almost never become known to others on the subcommittees or full committee, let alone to all members of the Senate. Although the senators not on the committee do have the opportunity to review the appropriations processed by Senate Appropriations if they inspect the printed hearings, reports, bills, and amendments submitted for their approval, the billions of dollars annually reprogrammed never come under similar examination. The opportunity simply does not arise.

Reprogramming is primarily an agency-committee matter. The Bureau of the Budget has no government-wide budget circular to standardize the process. While departmental officials might check with the budget examiner responsible for reviewing their requests, or with the budget director himself if the magnitude of the reprogramming seems to warrant it, this procedure is not mandatory. There is no record of the total reprogrammings that occur within the executive branch in a given fiscal year.

In all, in the 1955–65 decade only a handful of reprogramming requests were turned down by the Appropriations Committees. The major turndown came early in 1965 when, after a special hearing, the Defense Subcommittee rejected a $3.1 million reprogramming request, strongly supported by the Johnson administration, to begin a special training enlistment program (STEP), which was described as "an experimental program of military training, education, and physical rehabilitation for men who cannot meet current mental or medical standards for regular enlistment in the Army." At the special hearings, after listening to Democratic leader Mansfield's strong opposition to STEP, Senator Staltonstall asked what might well be asked, given the billions of dollars annually involved in the reprogramming process: "Would not the Senator agree that, if this program is to be put into existence, the whole Congress should know it, that it should not be passed on by this subcommittee as a reprogramming procedure without further consideration by the Congress?"[28] As Senator Saltonstall's comments suggest, even senior members of Senate Appropriations worry about the ramifications of reprogramming. They are disturbed that some departments defer congressionally approved projects by using the reprogramming process to substitute new ones not brought before Congress in the regular appropriations cycle. The subcommittee chairmen and members want the agencies to consult them. They want the opportunity to make their views known prior to executive implementation of a reprogramming decision. "Their goal," said one member, "is to try and keep the funds going for the purpose for which they were intended."

Executive Influence on the Committee

The President, the Cabinet, and Agency Officials

All members of Senate Appropriations admit that a call from the President is usually effective in winning support for the administration position, regardless of a senator's party affiliation. But the President himself does not always call. In fact, with the exception of Defense, foreign aid, and space programs, personal requests from the Chief Executive are few. Primarily this is a question of tactics. No President wants to commit his prestige and then suffer a rebuff. White House staff and cabinet officers alike try to keep the President in reserve for only the most crucial situations. They also have a vested interest in persuading legislators that they can speak for the President. On occasion, however, they are unaware of the President's activity on behalf of legislation: a call direct from his office, a few whispered comments at a White House reception or a bill signing ceremony, a quiet huddle with an old colleague.

As a man trained in the ways of the Senate establishment, Lyndon B.

28. *Department of Defense Reprogramming, 1965*, Hearings before the Senate Appropriations Subcommittee, 89 Cong. 1 sess. (Jan. 26, 1965), p. 16.

Johnson called Hayden, Russell, or Stennis with ease. John F. Kennedy felt more comfortable contacting the junior Democratic and Republican senators on the committee, as well as his senior Massachusetts colleague, ranking Republican Leverett Saltonstall. While Dwight D. Eisenhower also called Hayden and various senior Republican members, he regularly saw Styles Bridges, who served as the committee's chairman for two years and ranking Republican for six years during his administration. But when Bridges voiced the President's opinion during a markup, it was often: "Eisenhower said this, but I don't agree." Many committee members believe that the Eisenhower congressional liaison staff (primarily Bryce N. Harlow and Major General Wilton B. Persons), which had long prior experience on the Hill, was much more effective than the Kennedy staff, which had little prior experience working with Congress. Most also volunteered that Johnson really did not need a staff.[29]

More persistent—and quite effective—is the influence exerted on Senate Appropriations by various members of the cabinet and their subordinates. Breakfast with the secretary of state, luncheon with the secretary of defense in his massive Pentagon office, a private briefing on the Hill by AID administrators on the proposed foreign aid program, a quiet office visit from the secretary of agriculture to discuss his department's agricultural research activities—these are only a few of the many settings in which contact between the members of Senate Appropriations and high officials in the executive branch occur. Most of the interchange between legislators and their staffs and the political and career appointees of the administration takes place during office hours. While occasionally a senator might invite an executive witness to lunch in the senators' dining room or staff members might meet agency officials in the Senate cafeteria, most committee-agency contact takes place in the office or by telephone. Social wooing or the exchange of hospitality at each other's homes seldom occurs, and many members of Senate Appropriations long ago decided to forsake the Washington cocktail circuit.

A leading Republican member of Appropriations noted in 1965 that although Johnson administration officials were unhappy with

29. Beginning with the Eisenhower administration, the congressional liaison function was institutionalized within the White House. Although President Kennedy initially wanted to abolish most of the Eisenhower innovations, he was encouraged to keep and appropriately staff the liaison office. No President, Johnson included, could do without such an office, given the demands placed on it and the expectations of legislators for service.

some of the policy positions he had taken, they regularly came to hold his hand on Appropriations. He was convinced that agencies "must keep a list of the Appropriations members right by the telephone" since he never had any difficulty speaking with the officials he desired. His experience illustrates the old Capitol Hill maxim that members of Appropriations have easier access to agency officials than do senators generally. Senator Allen J. Ellender, then the third-ranking Democrat on Appropriations, recalled: "When I first came to Washington [1937], I couldn't talk to a member of the cabinet. But after I got on the Appropriations Committee, they hunted me up." However, a junior Democrat found that "the higher up you get on the subcommittee that affects the agency, the quicker you have access to the head of the department or bureau." Agency officials only came to see him immediately before the subcommittee markup and then they went away for another year. He was surprised that they did not do more to win support from members of Appropriations. "Frankly," the senator added, "I think they run a slovenly, haphazard, and sloppy operation. I am really amazed they don't do more."

While the executive agencies are sometimes direct and vigorous in the pursuit of their interests, they often mobilize constituent supporters to conduct the frontal assault. When outside witnesses appear at hearings, they frequently just happen to be from the states of the senators active on the subcommittee. Annually, during gatherings of the legislative committees of various agricultural, business, commodity, labor, and user groups, delegates from many states are turned loose to prowl the halls of the Capitol and the two Senate office buildings in search of their senator and his staff. Constituent reports on those legislators considered friendly or unfriendly are often coordinated with an agency or White House liaison officer.

Illustrative of the close agency-private interest group coordination that can exist on some issues was Secretary of Defense McNamara's successful effort to allow the British to bid on United States ship construction. During the summer of 1965, negotiations between the Department of Defense and the British government had led to firm orders for the sale to Britain of almost a billion dollars' worth of U.S.-manufactured military aircraft and other equipment and options for the sale of several hundred million dollars more. To assure the success of the negotiations, which were important in alleviating American balance of payments problems, Secretary McNamara had agreed to consider approximately

$50 million to $60 million of ship purchases (minesweepers, tugboats, and small craft) from British suppliers, provided they were fully competitive with American manufacturers in both quality and cost. But this aroused the Shipbuilders Council of America, representing the domestic private shipyards. The domestic aircraft industry, as might be expected, lined up with the Pentagon. Until a week before the August 16 subcommittee markup session on the Defense appropriation bill, most members of the Defense Subcommittee were opposed to the Pentagon position. In a short period before the markup, McNamara personally contacted almost all committee members. Representatives of the aircraft industry, coordinating their efforts with McNamara's staff, also made known their interest. Potential subcontractor suppliers of various parts were enlisted in the cause. When the showdown came in the full committee, McNamara's personal effort, combined with his skilled use of a rival segment of the private economy, paid off.

Administration Spokesmen within the Committee

Senators and staff agree that no single senator on the committee is the spokesman for an administration all of the time. But some senators are readily recognized by their colleagues as more willing than others to assume this role. During the Johnson administration, Senator Pastore headed the list of administration spokesmen, leading the fight for foreign aid and rent supplements, as well as for many other measures of concern to the President. Perhaps next in line was Senator Magnuson, followed by Senator Monroney. Foreign aid—often described as an orphan without a constituency, despite the fact that most of the procurement funds are spent in the United States—has always needed help within the committee. During the Kennedy administration, when Senator Gale W. McGee managed the foreign aid appropriation bill, he had the vigorous backing within the committee of Hubert H. Humphrey. Prior to that time, administration spokesmen for foreign aid included Lyndon B. Johnson, Leverett Saltonstall, and Everett M. Dirksen, who were all members of Senate Appropriations during most of Eisenhower's second term.

Whoever plays the role of administration spokesman always walks a delicate line in maintaining his loyalties to the Senate and the committee as he attempts to advance the President's cause. Some of the senior senators in both parties resent undue executive intrusion into the markup process, since they deeply believe that there must be at least one place where a legislator is free to express his views without the eyes of the White House or lobbyists following his every move. Nevertheless, most of the senators who have acted as administration spokesmen for a time seem to have avoided any permanent stigma.

A committed administration spokesman can wield great influence within the committee, especially if he happens to be a subcommittee chairman and uses the power available to him. In 1965, the Senate's passage of the foreign aid appropriation bill demonstrated both the parliamentary prerogatives that a subcommittee chairman can use in markup and in conference to further an administration cause, and the coordinated effort that an administration can undertake in securing passage of its legislation.

When Senate Appropriations met in executive session on September 10, 1965 to mark up the foreign aid appropriation bill, members knew that something was different. For several years, a triumvirate of Hayden, Saltonstall, and first McGee and then Pastore had fought together to pass the Kennedy and Johnson administrations' foreign aid requests after drastic cuts had been made in the budget estimates by the House Appropriations Subcommittee on Foreign Operations. Now Senator Saltonstall, the committee's ranking Republican, demanded a $100 million cut before he would support the bill. Deeply concerned with the rising costs of the Vietnam conflict, he wanted retrenchment wherever it could be achieved, and he wanted it rapidly. All but one of the Republicans were known to be in support of his proposal. This relative GOP solidarity, combined with the votes of various southern and mountain state Democrats at the markup session, seemed to assure adoption of the Saltonstall amendment.

Sensing an impending defeat, Pastore, who was presiding, hurriedly gathered proxies for the showdown roll call, which Saltonstall narrowly won. Pastore then suggested that since the vote was so important, all members of the committee should have an opportunity to record themselves on the question. While such an unusual procedure bothered Saltonstall, "being a gentlemen," as one senator later observed, "he did not object." With that, the markup was recessed for the weekend. Within a few hours, Saltonstall was informed that at a Monday session of the committee another vote would be permitted. He then told some of the southern Democrats who were not at the markup what had happened and solicited their support.

With the closeness of the vote, both the White House and AID realized that the bill was in serious trouble. Secretary of State Dean Rusk and AID Administrator David E. Bell had been cultivating Saltonstall and committee Republicans for several weeks. Mansfield and other Democrats also had been sounding out GOP members one by one on the floor to see if they could encourage any defections from the position taken by the committee's ranking Republican. Over the weekend, the President and the White House staff redoubled their pressure on committee members. The President personally telephoned a few southern Democrats and encouraged them to stay away from the Monday markup session.

AID officials were divided in their views as to the proper strategy. One view held that Saltonstall should be accommodated in committee so that he would not take his fight to the floor and set off an avalanche of cuts. Another view, however, was that Senate Appropriations should not cut the President's budget estimates since they would be cut on the floor anyhow. Pastore, responsible for managing the bill, was ready to agree to some cuts in committee.

When the committee met, Saltonstall's $100 million cut was defeated by one vote. Despite this narrow markup victory, however, a cut of $50 million was made. When this amount was added to other decreases, it meant that Senate Appropriations had slashed $94,265,000 out of the $4 billion House-passed foreign aid bill. The administration could ill afford additional major floor cuts. President Johnson wanted no repetition of the Kennedy administration's experience, when a foreign aid budget of $4.9 billion was submitted with the knowledge that it would be cut—which it was, in 1963, to $3 billion. He had determined to give Congress a "barebones" budget—and then fight for it.

For the next week, while the Senate was occupied with other legislation, every possible vote was sought. The administration brought to a head its efforts, begun the preceding February, to educate the Congress about the workings of the foreign aid program. On September 20, three days prior to floor consideration, Vice President Humphrey held a meeting to which all Senate Democrats were invited. (About thirty were able to attend.) An AID official has described this meeting as "the most effective session ever held in the Senate on foreign aid." Pastore, the bill's manager, and Holland, a leading southern Democrat, spoke up strongly for the measure that had been reported by Senate Appropriations. Russell, who had not attended the markup session and was soon to vote for the Saltonstall amendment in the Senate, urged his colleagues to uphold the President on Vietnam.

On September 23, Saltonstall offered his amendment to cut an additional $50 million from the bill. It was the first one to be voted on. As senators argued its merits in the chamber, Secretary of State Rusk, AID Administrator Bell, and Vice President Humphrey saw an endless stream of Democrats in the latter's office just off the chamber. A few who had indicated to Saltonstall that they might vote with him now told him that they had to switch. Until shortly before the roll call began, Saltonstall was convinced that he would lose. However, Democratic leaders noted that some of their party's key foreign aid supporters were absent: for example, both Edward M. Kennedy of Massachusetts and Robert F. Kennedy of New York were out of town. The Kennedy brothers, some senators thought, were reluctant to vote against Saltonstall—a pillar of the Bay State who had had close working relations with their late brother. In addition, the chairman of the Foreign Relations Committee, William Fulbright, increasingly disturbed by the administration's foreign policy and especially its military assistance programs, was nowhere to be found.

While Saltonstall worried that his amendment would not carry, Pastore, who was keeping a careful head count, was certain of its adoption. Fearful that its passage would begin a tidal wave against the bill, Pastore made one more attempt to persuade Saltonstall not to push his amendment. Saltonstall refused, but assured Pastore (as he had Rusk) that he would help him hold the line against any further cuts, and that he thought a number of Republicans would join him. The Senate then approved the Saltonstall amendment by a vote of 54 to 35.[30]

The next vote was crucial. Wayne Morse offered an amendment to reduce funds for military assistance to various Latin American countries by $25 million. Led by Saltonstall, eleven Republicans who had supported the Saltonstall amendment voted against Morse's proposal, which was defeated 43 to 41. Other cuts were rejected by much larger margins. The real fight on the amendments over, the bill was approved later that day by a vote of 59 to 22. Because of the President's persua-

---

30. Both Kennedys and three other absent Democrats were announced against the Saltonstall amendment. There were five absent Republicans who were announced for Saltonstall. Ten Senators, however, were absent and took no position. One was a Republican; nine were Democrats; all but one (Stennis) had supported the authorization bill, the Foreign Assistance Act of 1965, when the Senate approved it on June 14, 1965—which might lead one to query the effectiveness of the administration's lobbying effort. Some of the senators such as Fulbright, who were absent on the Saltonstall roll call, wandered in later in the afternoon to vote on some of the other amendments.

sion and Pastore's skillful prodding, the conferees later restored $75 million of the $144 million the Senate had cut from the House bill. The administration's effort had been, on the whole, successful.

* * *

In the continuing process of interaction between the Appropriations Committee and the executive branch, the powers of the President to persuade, the Bureau of the Budget to recommend, and the agency head to advocate are great. So are the powers of sanction held by those in key committee positions. While the balance often lies with those who hold the purse strings, their controls are frequently applied only to administrative details. Subcommittee reports contain instructions for executive agencies on a range of policy, budget, and managerial matters, but whether those instructions are followed is checked haphazardly at best. The committee has not yet taken up the powers of legislative oversight that its appropriations functions make available to it.

CHAPTER SEVEN

The Need for Change

The Committee on Appropriations, as the Senate's agent in appropriations matters and the repository of the Senate's budgetary expertise, has the triple role of gathering and imparting information, making judgments, and implementing the Senate's will. If the Senate is to fulfill its responsibilities as a working partner in the federal appropriations process, then its committee must have appropriate procedures and structures for carrying out each part of its role with maximum effectiveness. Ideally, the committee should make independent decisions after reviewing the budgetary proposals submitted by the President. It is important that the committee and the Senate be able to make reasonable judgments between presidential advocacy and House economy.

In reaching its conclusions, the committee needs pertinent information. The values held by each member will determine whether he explores a program's ends as well as its means, but it is assumed that in the committee as a whole both means and ends will be regularly scrutinized to some degree. Before reaching a decision in allocating budgetary resources, however, the committee members should also attain an overview of various programs, judge the alternatives, and weigh the consequences not only for their immediate constituents, but for the whole nation as well.

One premise of a democratic system is that a representative is ultimately answerable to those he represents for his conduct in office. Senators who seek reelection at the end of their six-year term do face the judgment of the people. A more immediate sanction on a senator's decisions is the reaction of his colleagues. In this sense, during markup the members of the full committee have an opportunity to judge the work of their subcommittees, and during floor consideration all senators have an opportunity to judge the work of the full committee. But just as committee members need relevant information if they are to choose wisely among alternatives, so senators generally must have adequate information in order to evaluate the work of their committee. Senators—many of whom have state constituencies sufficiently broad to mirror the problems of the United States as a whole—also need an informed constituency if some sense of responsibility and responsiveness is to be maintained between the elected and the elector, and ultimately—on the elector's behalf —between the elected and the bureaucracy. Accordingly, the recommendations for change in Senate appropriations procedures set forth in this chapter place emphasis on communicating information to decision makers, and on communicating the decisions to those who carry them out.

The purposes of a legislative body can include law-making, representation, consensus-building, legitimizing, policy clarification, and legislative oversight; but in considering institutions and procedures, it is necessary to remember that neither Congress, the Senate, nor the committee agree on the emphasis to be given any of these purposes at any particular time. What each member seeks to accomplish on the Committee on Appropriations depends on his view of himself, the demands of his constituency and his party, the pressures of the administration and of outside lobbies, and the nature of the issue before him. As a result, members pursue various purposes depending on their personal model of Congress and themselves. Given on the one hand the varying institutional and personal goals, and on the other certain structural rigidities that appear unlikely to change—such as committee selection and advancement based essentially on seniority—the task of this chapter is to propose ways in which the committee might more effectively and responsibly meet its needs and the needs of the Senate and the public.

In brief, specific recommendations are intended to help fulfill one or more of the following ideals of committee operation:

1. Before making its decisions, the committee should have available

to it accurate, relevant, unbiased, and complete information regarding the goals and implementation of governmental programs. There should be ample access for diverse viewpoints to help assure that such information is produced.

2. As much as possible, committee activity should bring together related governmental programs so that alternatives and their consequences can be weighed before a decision is reached.

3. In making its decisions and communicating them, the committee should make explicit its premises for action so that those who pass judgment on the work of the committee, or look to the committee for legislative intent, can be aware of the basis for a particular decision.

4. The committee should so act on behalf of the parent body as to fulfill the Senate's constitutional position as a coequal partner in the appropriations responsibilities of the legislative branch.

5. Committee and staff leadership should be exercised to achieve the maximum development, utilization, and coordination of members and staff.

What Is Wrong with the Senate Appropriations Process?

Before discussing what is wrong with the Senate appropriations process, it is important to note some limiting factors over which the Committee on Appropriations has little control. The first is the constitutional tradition that sanctions the origination of all general appropriation bills in the House of Representatives. The Senate does not mark up an appropriation bill in committee or consider it on the floor until the House has acted. The second limitation—which applies equally to the House committee—is the tendency of various legislative committees to require annual authorizations for the programs under their jurisdiction. For example, in the administrative budget requests for fiscal year 1968, almost $37 billion, or 28 percent of the total, was subject to the annual authorization process before funds could be appropriated.[1] If an authorization bill must first clear the Congress—as is true of the

1. "Congress and the Budget," *Staff Papers and Other Materials Reviewed by the President's Commission on Budget Concepts* (Government Printing Office, 1967), p. 13.

atomic energy, foreign aid, space, military procurement and research programs, and many others—this inevitably delays the initial markup in House Appropriations and retards action in the Senate.

The third factor affecting the work of both Appropriations Committees is that much of the budget cannot really be controlled by them. The salaries of federal employees, the costs of completing projects already begun, permanent appropriations for paying the interest on the national debt, and trust fund expenditures for social security and highways, among others, leave little room for discretion. Moreover, Congress has agreed to finance some government activities by other than annual appropriation acts—the so-called "backdoor financing" that takes place when legislative committees authorize public debt transactions to fund programs.

But many practices that are within the committee's capacity to modify stand in the way of committee and Senate attainment of the ideal. Clear recognition of them is essential if reasonable changes are to be made.

A Broad Range of Relevant Information Is Lacking

Most of the committee's information comes from one source—the executive department or agency seeking the funds. Witnesses at hearings, whether they represent a government agency or a private group, are almost always advocates of the agency's spending proposals. If knowledgeable outsiders testify, they are usually private consultants or members of government advisory committees with ties to the programs on which they are testifying. Their participation provides an "end run" on behalf of the agency executives whose own testimony is subject to the limitations on advocacy imposed by the Bureau of the Budget. Seldom does a witness oppose a budget request.

Since the hearings are dominated by department and agency advocates, the committee lacks the opportunity to become aware of the President's perspective and reasons—except as they are revealed in the budget documents—for making a particular decision on program expenditures. The President's expenditure perspective is best represented by the director of the budget, and his revenue perspective by the secretary of the treasury and the chairman of the Council of Economic Advisers. For several years, the House Appropriations Committee under Chairman Mahon has held background sessions with the Treasury and Budget officials before considering the appropriations requests at subcommittee level. For four years—1963 through 1966—the Senate committee held no overall review with any of these key presidential advisers. Finally, in 1967 Senate Appropriations began to call the secretary of the treasury and the director of the budget for annual briefings.

No institutionalized "nay-sayers" are regularly available to tell the committee why some project should not be undertaken or why one alternative might be better than another. The professional staff finds it difficult to make time available for the long-term studies that should be made on many programs and projects if pertinent information and alternatives are to be developed. The long-term investigating effort of Senate Appropriations is now handled by one counsel. The minority does not have a large enough staff to fulfill its role as responsible critic. Even if the present committee and minority staff could make sufficient time available for in-depth studies, they lack some of the analytic skills necessary for such undertakings.

The committee has also failed to make effective use of the noncommittee staff resources available to it. Few subcommittees have requested the General Accounting Office to undertake studies that would be helpful in making appropriations decisions. The House Committee on Appropriations has made increasing use of the vast amount of program knowledge GAO experts possess. Before reviewing some agency budgets, a few House subcommittees have held a session with the GAO's substantive review staff responsible for auditing a particular agency's activities. But the Senate has not made a similar initiative. Nor has the committee worked out a procedure for bringing to the attention of its members those reports on agency activities regularly issued by the GAO. Despite a mandate in the Legislative Reorganization Act of 1946 for the General Accounting Office to conduct expenditure analyses, Congress—as a result of action by House Appropriations—has never appropriated funds to enable the GAO to undertake such studies.

An insufficient effort is made before the hearing and the markup to inform senators of the nature of the agency's budget requests and the main policy issues involved. Although justifications are submitted by each agency, and memoranda are prepared by the professional staff for the subcommittee chairmen who conduct the hearings, there is no uniform effort to bring all committee participants up to date on agency goals, activities, and budget requests. The burden of subcommittee questioning is left with the chairman and, if he is interested, the ranking minority member. Moreover, there is no prior committee consensus on the areas of questioning and investigation that should be developed if the subcommittee is to have the information it needs to evaluate an agency's requests.

With the barring of the senatorial office staff from committee mark-up sessions, a member who is neither a subcommittee chairman nor a ranking minority member lacks adequate staff assistance when the decisions are being made. The regular committee staff—despite its general claim that it aids all committee members on a nonpartisan basis—owes its principal allegiance to the subcommittee chairmen; the minority staff has a similar relation with the ranking minority members. Indeed, it could not be otherwise. Even with a willingness to help all members, a staff professional with expertise on a given subject can advise only a small number of senators in the sometimes hurly-burly atmosphere of a markup session. And it should not seem strange if he advises the most senior senators more often than he does the others. The result is that the bipartisan leaders of the committee and their staff usually have a monopoly of knowledge on each appropriation bill. Yet policy disputes do arise between senior and junior members in both parties, as well as between senators who have different regional stakes. For a senator to have his legislative assistant (who often has a security clearance equal to those of many on the committee staff, and who may have spent months dealing with the issue under consideration) barred from the markup session is a great handicap.

The Present Subcommittee Structure Prevents a Unified Analysis of Separate but Related Programs

The subcommittee structure is based on the appropriation bills the committee is called upon to review. Although the President submits his requests for new obligational authority in a single budget, the appropriation authority granted by Congress is contained in a dozen or more annual bills. Since, by custom, general appropriation bills originate in the House of Representatives, the basic decision as to their number, content, and format has been made by House Appropriations. Appropriation bills have been created to relieve the load on an already overworked subcommittee, as when the military construction bill was carved out of the Defense appropriation bill. Sometimes they have been created to provide closer scrutiny for a particular area of governmental activity. On other occasions, a separate bill has been drawn and a subcommittee established simply to provide a chairmanship for a deserving member of the majority party. Or an independent agency is allotted to a particular appropriation bill because of the subcommittee chairman's enthusiasm for it—and it remains there without logic or reason for years after the protective chairman has passed from the scene.

The misallocation of agencies to particular appropriation bills is widespread. A few examples will suffice. For the Smithsonian Institution—an agency deeply involved in scientific research and the diffusion of knowledge in many fields—to be carried in the Interior appropriation bill makes little sense. The Bureau of the Budget has recognized the purpose of the Smithsonian by assigning review of its estimates to the Economics, Science, and Technology Programs Division of the bureau, rather than to the Natural Resources Programs Division. Similarly, existing procedure places the civil defense activities of the Department of the Army in the Independent Offices bill rather than the Defense bill. Yet, in the Budget Bureau those estimates are quite properly reviewed by the National Security Programs Division. The budget requests of the Selective Service System are also reviewed by the Independent Offices Subcommittee, yet the activities of Selective Service are intimately related to defense manpower needs and might more properly be considered by either the Defense or Labor-HEW Subcommittee.

Because the appropriation bills are considered solely on an individual basis by the various subcommittees, wide discrepancies occur not only in the logic of agency assignment, but also in the varying administrative provisions included in the bills. The inconsistent treatment of representation allowances and employment of consultants are two of many cases in point. If Congress wishes to control administration through detailed provisions and limitations, that is its privilege; but with the present lack of coordination among appropriation bills, the legislative branch frequently appears uncertain of what it is controlling. In a 1949 report, the Hoover Commission expressed the hope that the performance budget approach, which bases the budget on functions, activities, and projects, rather than on the services and equipment to be acquired, would enable the Appropriations Committees "more easily to decide the basic expenditure issue each year; namely, just what should be the magnitude of the many Federal programs."[2] The commission found the appropriation structure underlying the budget "a patchwork affair" that had evolved over a great many years and followed no rational pattern. While progress has been made since 1949 in reducing the degree of specificity in appropriation bills, they are still a "patchwork."

As a result of this fragmentation, and the full committee's practice of marking up and reporting an appropriation bill soon after receiving it from the subcommittee, there is no opportunity to evaluate similar programs and processes contained in several bills. Seven subcommittees —Agriculture, Defense, Independent Offices, Interior, Labor-HEW, Public Works, and State-Justice—consider substantial research and development programs. Currently, no evaluation is made of the various standards that each agency uses in allocating funds to in-house and contracted-out research. No comparisons are made of the medical research programs conducted by the various military services (Defense Subcommittee), the National Aeronautics and Space Administration and the Veterans Administration (both reviewed by the Independent Offices Subcommittee), and the National Institutes of Health (Labor-HEW Subcommittee). The sixteen-agency oceanographic effort is another example of a government program that cuts across numerous departments and agencies—and appropriation bills.

In an effort to achieve unity in one area, the committee has established a single subcommittee to handle all deficiency and supplemental appropriation bills, but this device often falters. The subcommittee is composed of all subcommittee chairmen and most of the ranking minority members—a group that should know the background of most items brought before it, since it has considered them in hearings on the regular budget requests. The usefulness of such a group is limited, however, because the major supplemental bill usually comes to the Senate in the closing days of the session, and there is simply not enough time for a single subcommittee to review the numerous agency requests. During the last week of the 1965 session, the Senate had to review a supplemental appropriation bill for 1966 totaling almost $5 billion. The lack of time and the size of the bill necessitated the parceling out of various parts to six of the substantive subcommittees.

---

2. *Budgeting and Accounting*, A Report to the Congress by the Commission on Organization of the Executive Branch of the Government (February 1949), p. 11.

Full, Consistent Disclosure of the Premises and Results
of Committee Decisions Is Lacking

Only on the floor of each house is there a possibility of bringing some consistency of treatment to measures authorizing the expenditure of public funds. Since not all of these measures are reported by the Committee on Appropriations—for example, the backdoor financing provisions reported by some of the legislative committees—this is a trying task. It is even more distressing when the parent body has difficulty reviewing those matters that do come from a single Appropriations Committee.

The President's budget specifies his requests in terms of the new obligational authority that is sought. The budget requests also note the actual expenditures for the completed fiscal year and the estimated expenditures for the coming fiscal year. Yet the decisions in the committee reports on the various appropriation bills are expressed primarily in terms of appropriations. Seldom are actual expenditures for past fiscal years or estimated expenditures for the coming fiscal year included in the summary page of the report. At present, the report does not differentiate between the portion of an appropriation that will be spent during the coming fiscal year and the portion that will be spent later. Without such information, those interested in fiscal considerations have difficulty ascertaining the economic impact of a given level of government appropriations.

The committee report also fails to make explicit the nonstatutory directives that the subcommittee has given to an agency. A careful reading will reveal many of them. But the report usually does not receive such a reading, even from committee members. (Often the subcommittee's draft report is not available to the committee members until they enter the markup. In the give and take of that environment, it is difficult to go over the report thoroughly before final action on the bill.) The informal agreements entered into by the subcommittee leaders and the agency administrators as the hearings progress are unknown not only to nonmembers, but to many on the full committee as well.

Also unknown to both nonmembers and many on the committee are the reprogrammings of appropriated funds by the agencies, either with the consent of the subcommittee leaders or under the general authority granted to them. It is incongruous that the committee spends days, weeks, or even months holding hearings to review a particular budget—and additional time in markups and on the floor and in conference, arguing the merits of various appropriations—only to have one or two members months later approve an agency's request to shift funds often amounting to many millions of dollars from one purpose to another. Billions of dollars are reprogrammed annually in the Department of Defense alone. Not only do members of the subcommittee and full committee have a right to know of these reprogrammings, but so do members of the Senate and the public—unless national security requires secrecy.

For many senators, another difficulty is the lack of time between the availability of the report and printed hearings, and the consideration of the bill on the floor. In 1966, when such important bills as District of Columbia ($460 million), Interior ($1.3 billion), State-Justice ($2.3 billion), Second Supplemental for 1966 ($2.8 billion), and the Supplemental for 1967 ($5.1 billion) were reported one day and passed within forty-eight hours, there was little time for a senator to review the committee's work. Although a senator can raise a point of order to enforce the rule that no general appropriation bill shall be considered unless "printed committee hearings and reports on such bill have been available for at least three calendar days . . . ,"[3] in the rush for adjournment, with a steady stream of long-delayed appropriation bills and House-Senate conferences still ahead, procedural safeguards often go unenforced.

The Senate's often hasty acceptance of appropriation bills can suggest great faith in the hard work and diligence of a committee of influential members. It can also imply widespread unwillingness to accept responsibility for budgetary control. A comment by Senator Stennis during consideration of the Legislative Reorganization Act of 1967 is indicative:

> Last year I saw appropriation bills sail through this chamber with $4 billion to $6 billion in them. They were reported one night and passed the next morning. I recall in the case of one bill that was brought in of about that magnitude, the report was not filed until the next morning around 10 or 11 o'clock. There was not a scintilla of testimony from the hearings until just before the bill was voted on; still it sailed through the Senate like a kite.[4]

3. 60 Stat. 833 (The Legislative Reorganization Act of 1946).
4. *Congressional Record*, Vol. 113, Pt. 4, 90 Cong. 1 sess. (1967), pp. 5543–44.

Capacities for Meeting the Senate's Appropriations Responsibilities Have Not Been Improved or Fully Used

By tradition all general appropriation bills originate in the House of Representatives, but once the Senate participates in the process both bodies are equal. Each has one vote in conference. The bargaining can be as vigorous as the conferees desire. Eventually, by a give-and-take process, an accommodation is reached on the differences between the two houses. Yet the interpretation of the conference decisions is based on the report and statement of the House conferees. Under the rules of the House of Representatives, no conference report on an appropriation bill can be considered unless a report by the House conferees is submitted in writing. The House conferees also submit a statement explaining their decisions in a narrative fashion. In some instances, this statement—which is viewed by the executive agencies as indicative of ultimate congressional intent—represents the opinions of the Senate conferees as well; in other cases, it does not. The House statement also compares the conference decisions with the amounts originally approved by the House. No similar report and statement prepared by the Senate conferees is available to guide the Senate when it is asked to accept or reject the conference report.

Although the Senate has done well in many of its appropriations conferences with the House in recent years, this has frequently resulted from happenstance and a tendency of the House to yield on matters it was not very serious about in the first place. In considering crucial issues, senators have sometimes not been well prepared and have had to yield to House demands. Occasionally, some senators have undercut their committee's bargaining position in conference. Unlike their House counterparts, members of Senate Appropriations do not hold preconference sessions to review and agree upon their strategy, tactics, and position.

The possibilities for meeting the Senate's appropriations responsibilities more fully have also been neglected at earlier stages in the appropriations process. The division between authorization and appropriations committees has resulted in congressional failure to examine on a government-wide basis the institutional arrangements for managing and implementing public policy and programs. Even in the face of this lack, what annual review the Senate Appropriations Committee conducts is usually limited—especially in nondefense programs—to an examination of the incremental changes recommended in the budget estimates. Many programs continue from year to year with little thought given to their current necessity or priority. Once the appropriations base is secured, the agency and the committee—often by default when confronted with a jumble of budgetary data—limit their exchange, if any, to differences among the past, present, and coming fiscal years.

The Resources of Members and Staff Are Not Fully Developed and Used

There is no overall attempt by the chairman—or the chief clerk on his behalf—to pool committee and noncommittee (such as GAO) resources to conduct an effective program review. There is little overall coordination of member and staff activity and travel. No attempt is made to encourage senators and staff members to visit particular federal activities at home and abroad. Program review is dependent solely upon the desires of each subcommittee chairman and the initiative of his professional staff.

An imbalance in committee assignments undoubtedly prevents an efficient distribution of work among the members, and to some extent inhibits their participation. Senior members, by virtue of the committee's adherence to the seniority system, are able to serve on the more important and prestigious subcommittees. These subcommittees—such as Public Works, Defense, Agriculture, and Independent Offices—not only consider a greater portion of the President's budget, but in doing so hold a greater number of hearings than the less prestigious subcommittees, such as District of Columbia, Legislative, and Treasury–Post Office. Since those with low seniority usually serve on more of the less prestigious subcommittees, and these subcommittees have fewer hearings, the employment of junior members in the overall work of the committee is low. For example, in 1965 Senator Russell, who was then the second most senior Democrat, was assigned to eight subcommittees. Senator Bartlett, then third from the bottom in Democratic seniority, was assigned to five subcommittees. Senator Russell's subcommittees held a total of 204 hearings; Senator Bartlett's subcommittees held only 63. Junior members could devote more time to committee business, but they lack the subcommittee assignments permitting them to do so.

Senate leaders with floor responsibilities find it particularly difficult to participate in subcommittee hearings. In 1965, a year that saw extended floor debate before passage of the Voting Rights Act and much of the Great Society legislation, neither Democratic leader Mansfield nor assistant Republican leader Kuchel was able to participate in the hearings of his Appropriations subcommittees more than 8 percent of the time—the lowest participation rate for any senator who was not ill during the session. Yet Senator Mansfield was assigned to five subcommittees and Senator Kuchel to six. Both were on Defense, Interior, and Military Construction. Junior members were precluded from participating in these subcommittees because the seats were held by senior members, yet some of the senior members had institutional responsibilities that meant that their seats, in effect, were vacant.

In the Senate, as opposed to the House of Representatives, members always serve on two or more standing committees. Consequently, a senator on Appropriations must frequently weigh the need to attend a hearing of his legislative committee (and perhaps one or more of its subcommittees) against the need to attend a hearing of one of the Appropriations subcommittees to which he is assigned. But just as there are frequently conflicting meetings between the legislative committees and Appropriations, there are conflicting meetings between Appropriations subcommittees. Of the 241 Appropriations subcommittee hearings held in 1965, 153 or 63.5 percent of them competed with other Appropriations hearings.

The large size of some Appropriations subcommittees also lowers the degree of participation by subcommittee members. In 1965, the Public Works Subcommittee comprised twenty-one senators. When it sat as the Army Civil Functions Panel, three ex officio members from the Committee on Public Works were added to consider rivers and harbors items. The regular members of this panel alone made it a larger group than any other Senate committee except Appropriations itself. Yet for all practical purposes, broad membership was of little value in developing the hearing record. Most members would attend the subcommittee's markup session; but for the hearing process, most were members in name only.

The use of proxies in subcommittee and committee markups also diminishes senatorial participation, as well as reduces a senator's sense of responsibility. By giving his proxy to the subcommittee chairman, the ranking minority member, or a colleague without specific instructions, a senator avoids the necessity of studying an issue and participating in the decision-making process. He avoids his responsibilities.

No attempt is made to encourage career development of the professional staff. Unfortunately, Congress as a whole has failed its professional employees by not including them within the provisions of the Government Employees' Training Act so that they could further their education and training at full salary. Unlike members of other committee staffs, no member of the Appropriations staff has applied for one of the congressional staff fellowships granted since 1963 by the American Political Science Association. It is, of course, difficult for staff members to absent themselves from their responsibilities for the minimum of six months such a fellowship would involve, since backup employees are not readily available. But the committee leaders have not sought to overcome these difficulties by arranging for outside experts to brief the professional staff. Particularly disturbing is the leaders' failure to encourage the staff to participate in programs designed to improve their ability to use the new analytic techniques increasingly employed by the executive branch as a result of the emphasis on planning, programming, and budgeting (PPB). No effort has yet been made to prepare the staff for evaluating a budget prepared according to the PPB system.

The Strategy of Reform

Reformers of the congressional appropriations process have long had a fascination with proposals embodying broad structural changes. Under the Legislative Reorganization Act of 1946, a legislative budget was tried and found wanting. During the first two months of each session, Congress was to establish an expenditure ceiling for the ensuing fiscal year that would limit the appropriations approved later in the session. In 1950, an omnibus appropriation bill that consolidated all of the subcommittee bills was tried and abandoned. Since 1952, legislation to establish a joint committee on the budget has repeatedly been approved by the Senate, only to die in the House of Representatives. This joint committee, consisting of the senior members from the Appropriations Committees in both houses, would supervise an expert staff whose purpose would be to analyze the budget and investigate federal operations.

In addition, some legislators have favored granting the President an item veto on appropriation bills. These proposals have been as unsuccessful as those calling for the Senate to originate at least half of the appropriation bills. The idea of considering appropriation bills in a special session has gained few supporters. In an attempt to secure some overall view of the budget, others have suggested strengthening the Joint Economic Committee. Suggestions that the committee alone could adopt have included providing additional staff assistance for each committee member and more time for review of a bill between the subcommittee and full committee markups.

Appendix C indicates the attitudes of committee members during the Eighty-ninth Congress toward these proposals. The members expressed wide support for establishing a joint committee on the budget, for originating at least half of the appropriation bills, and—especially among the less senior members—for securing an additional staff assistant. This response indicates the desire of many members to play a more active role in the appropriations process and reflects in part two deeply felt frustrations repeatedly expressed by most senators on the committee: unhappiness with the lack of internal coordination of committee activity; and dissatisfaction with the quantity, and occasionally even the quality, of existing staff support. Members recognize that additional staff needs must be met if the committee is to fulfill its responsibilities properly.

Subcommittee chairmen are not opposed to changes that will benefit the Senate and the public—if they believe the changes will also benefit themselves. They expressed support for the establishment of a joint budget committee, which they would dominate, and were evenly divided on originating half of the appropriation bills and on having a specified layover period between subcommittee and full committee markup. But by a two-to-one margin, subcommittee chairmen opposed the provision of an additional office assistant for each committee member. The chairmen already have staff support, and the addition of other staff members who would be responsible solely to junior members might undermine their monopoly of knowledge. They also overwhelmingly objected to a presidential item veto and were unanimously against a single omnibus appropriation bill that would bring all recommendations from each subcommittee before the full committee at the same time.

Although most of these and other suggestions have come and gone, a glimmer of support for each remains. In suggesting their schemes of order and rationality for what they view with alarm as a fragmented, imperfect, and uncoordinated legislative system, reformers in and out of Congress have often failed to give much thought to the full ramifications of the intended, let alone the unintended, consequences. Yet those particularly affected, such as subcommittee chairmen and senior members generally, are usually keenly aware of the effect that specific reforms would have on their power.

Barring extensive dissatisfaction of nonmembers with the work of the committee, proposals for change must attract substantial support from within the Committee on Appropriations to be successful. Since the members constitute almost a quarter of the Senate, their attitudes can substantially further or hinder any attempt at reform. Therefore, recommendations should be designed to encourage, not discourage, the support of many senior members who have often been suspicious of any reform. Senior members are not above pleas to strengthen the role of the Senate in the appropriations process. If they realize that they will not lose and might possibly gain power—for example, by having more important subcommittees over which to preside—the transition might be relatively easy. But if the proposals are to have any chance for adoption, they must be grounded in practical, not utopian, considerations.

Some reforms do not warrant the effort necessary to adopt them. For example, it would not be worthwhile to try to eliminate the ex officio members who can participate in some work of Senate Appropriations as representatives from certain legislative committees. Many senators on the Appropriations Committee, probably correctly, see little value in retaining these ex officio members. Yet some senators not on the committee would like to add still more ex officio members from other legislative committees. For Senate Appropriations suddenly to undertake an effort to change the rules and eliminate ex officio membership would elicit cries of outrage from the affected committees. Ex officio members—as was apparent from an examination of their participation during the Eighty-ninth Congress—do little harm. A wise policy therefore would be to let the present ex officio members continue in their nonattendance, and to try to prevent more from being added.

Similarly fruitless are the proposals that challenge the House's acquired prerogative to originate all general appropriation bills, and that seek to establish a joint committee on the budget. When it comes to preserving the appropriation prerogative, House sentiment is adamant. To achieve some of the goals that underlie both of these proposals, however, Senate Appropriations might broaden the scope of its hearings and have *all* of its subcommittees hold them earlier in the year. The Senate might also intensify its efforts in policy and program review—an area that the House Committee on Appropriations, with its concentration on personnel and on objects of expenditure, frequently ignores. Some of the advantages of extra staff, which a joint committee on the budget would assure, can be achieved within Senate Appropriations if its members really want to remedy existing deficiencies.

In the recommendations that follow, an attempt is made to suggest evolutionary, rather than radical, changes in existing institutions. Implementation would depend primarily on the actions of either the committee or the Senate. In some cases, of course, the cooperation of House Appropriations would be required. A strengthened Senate Committee on Appropriations might well elicit that cooperation.

What Should Be Done?

The Quality and Objectivity of Committee Information Should Be Improved

The imaginative overhaul and better use of existing institutions and resources, and the creation of some new ones, could help committee members to become aware of program and management alternatives—and their consequences—before the markup. Diverse sources of information and expertise are necessary if the advocacy of executive agencies is to be weighed with care. It is not simply more information, but also an analytical evaluation of that information, that is essential.

In addition to the program review conducted by the substantive subcommittees, there is need for a special investigative group with appropriate staff support to conduct detailed studies encompassing government-wide programs. This subcommittee—possibly of eight senators—ideally should be headed by a member of the party not in control of the presidency. (In the 1920s, the so-called Teapot Dome investigation of a Republican administration was headed by a Democrat in a Republican Senate.) The chairman could be designated by the ranking senator on the full committee from the party out of power. Membership could be equally divided between the two political parties. The subcommittee would have the authority to hold hearings, issue subpoenas, and make recommendations to the full committee. Its inquiries should not be limited to instances of incompetence and mismanagement, which are regularly revealed in reports from the comptroller general. Although it should not be precluded from such inquiries, it would more usefully pursue in-depth studies of various programs and their management.

The staff should be directed by a person skilled in program and management analysis. Whether that person has been a lawyer, political scientist, economist, or investigator is less important than his ability to understand the complexities of modern government, to define problems and formulate questions, and to use the latest analytical methods in eliciting answers on which legislative decisions can be based. Unfortunately, the Senate's self-imposed salary restrictions might prevent the attraction of the analytical talent often available in the private economy. The staff director should be appointed by the subcommittee as a whole. He in turn would appoint members of the professional staff, subject to guidelines laid down and funds approved by the full committee. The supporting staff should be nonpartisan in spirit and broad in experience and knowledge.

If a separate investigating subcommittee is not established, at the very least a greatly enlarged investigative staff should function under the joint direction of the committee chairman and the ranking minority member, much as does House Appropriations' surveys and investigations staff. Regardless of its organizational location, the staff might well come to fill the role of legislative auditor so successfully used by the California legislature.[5] This is a difficult role—especially when a com-

5. In 1941, in California, a Republican legislature confronted the first Democratic governor since 1899. Losing confidence in the governor's budget recommendations, the legislature created a joint committee on the budget, with a nonpartisan staff headed by a legislative auditor, to review executive estimates. The legislative auditor makes a detailed analysis of the governor's budget and submits specific recommendations in an annual report of more than a thousand pages. His staff attends the hearings of the two appropriations committees and, until the early 1960s, even participated in the agency hearings held by the Department of Finance before the governor made his decisions.

mittee member's pet project is involved. Considerable self-restraint and forbearance would be needed on the part of some committee members. But the staff should be willing to testify in support of its recommendations.

In addition to an enlarged investigative staff, the committee needs an increase in its minority staff. An increase of six members, from the present four to ten, would encourage the minority to conduct adequate studies by permitting the assignment of at least one professional to each of the following subcommittee groups that now exist: Agriculture; Foreign Operations and State-Justice; Independent Offices, District of Columbia, and Transportation; Interior and Public Works; Labor-HEW; and Treasury–Post Office and Legislative. Three minority staff members could be assigned to Defense and Military Construction. The minority staff director should not have specific subcommittee responsibilities, but should devote his efforts to staff coordination and direction. There should be no separate assignment to the Supplementals Subcommittee; those staff members responsible for particular program areas should be used as needed on supplemental bills.

If the work of the Appropriations subcommittees is reorganized on a program basis—a reform proposed in the next section—minority staff assignments would be simplified, and particular specialties could be stressed in recruitment. Under the guidance of an effective staff director, greater coordination of staff skills could result. If a person with experience in engineering analysis were hired, his abilities could be used on the Military Construction, Independent Offices (housing and federal buildings construction), and Public Works Subcommittees. Similarly, analysts with competence in scientific program evaluation could help the several subcommittees that review research and development programs.

But, as has been suggested, more personnel alone will not overcome the lack of analysis and information. The expansion of the minority staff would provide a unique opportunity to develop a professional group thoroughly competent to deal with the complexities of PPB and the capabilities of automatic data processing. But so should the regular, or majority, staff develop in this direction. Especially needed are political scientists and economists who understand not only the fundamentals of the budgetary process, but also the program and management problems of the federal establishment. Both the majority and minority staffs could not go far wrong if they were to seek out young professionals who have had experience in the executive branch as management interns and program analysts. With new analytic techniques and computers that permit access to data never before used, a staff skilled in problem definition and solution would greatly strengthen the Senate's contribution to the appropriations process.

Whether or not the Appropriations Committee provides adequate professional staff assistance for individual senators, members of a senator's personal staff who are responsible for appropriations matters should be permitted to attend markup meetings. (If markup sessions are to be closed to office staff on the ground of potential security or publicity leaks over which the committee has no control—and which to date have not occurred—then, to lessen further such a potential risk, committee staff members who do not have a substantive responsibility on the appropriation bill under consideration should also be excluded.) Better use of each member's office staff is one readily available way to enlarge the committee's resources. Special briefings by various federal agencies for these legislative assistants would be particularly useful. Both the Agency for International Development and the Alliance for Progress have successfully provided such briefings from time to time for key legislative assistants in both parties—including critics and supporters. That effort should be broadened.

Another useful congressional resource would become available to the committee if the Joint Committee on the Reduction of Nonessential Federal Expenditures were revitalized. This group was long known as the Byrd committee because it was chaired from its founding in 1941 until 1965 by the late Senator Harry F. Byrd of Virginia. A novel aspect of this joint committee is that its statutory members include both the secretary of the treasury and the director of the budget. In addition, it includes three members from each of the Senate and House revenue and appropriations committees. All but Senate Appropriations have assigned to it their chairman, a senior majority member, and their ranking minority member. In the Eighty-ninth Congress, Senators Ellender and Holland were the two majority members from Senate Appropriations, while ranking Republican Saltonstall represented the minority. In the Ninetieth Congress, Senator Allott succeeded Saltonstall. The committee is authorized "to make a full and complete study and investigation of all expenditures of the Federal Government with a view to recommending the elimination or reduction of all such expenditures deemed by the committee to be nonessential."[6] Hearings can be held, experts employed, subpoenas issued, agency services used, recommendations made, and reports filed.

But giving substance to this structure is a problem. In the later years of Byrd's chairmanship, the committee did little more than serve as a means of providing extra staff for the chairman. For years, it seldom met. Following Byrd's retirement from the Senate, the legislative members of the committee met in March 1966 to select House Appropriations Chairman Mahon as the new chairman. Some senators, led by Ellender, thought this "was a golden opportunity," as one expressed it, "to have a joint committee which is already in existence start to do a job." But Mahon—remembering that Clarence Cannon and House Appropriations had traditionally resisted joint budget committees from fear of an increased role for the Senate—would agree only to study the matter. The joint committee thus remains, as it has been for years, a minor statistics-gathering operation producing material of little relevance in resolving the real budgetary problems that confront the Congress.

An even more important source of information and analysis that should be used more effectively is the General Accounting Office. As a matter of regular procedure before holding the formal agency hearing, each subcommittee chairman should schedule a closed session with the substantive review staff in the GAO responsible for auditing that agency's activities. The committee needs expert witnesses who do not have the vested interests of the President or his Bureau of the Budget, or of the executive departments and agencies. The only informed witnesses readily available are those employed by the General Accounting Office. Information developed by the GAO would be invaluable in educating subcommittee members.

Also, as a matter of regular procedure, the appropriate subcommittee staff should summarize the comptroller general's reports examining and reviewing agency actions.[7] The full committee chairman should

6. 55 Stat. 726.

7. The Joint [Monroney-Madden] Committee on the Organization of the Congress recommended in its 1966 report that the GAO undertake the expenditure analyses originally authorized in 1946. Clarence Cannon and his House Appropriations Committee consistently opposed granting funds for such studies. These analyses would have to be more than the traditional audit or review reports. They should include at least an evaluation of the management and organization used in carrying out a program, an assessment of the degree to which legislative intent has been fulfilled,

then circulate the summary and report on a priority basis to the affected subcommittee members. Although senators on Appropriations generally have a high regard for the work of the GAO, many do not have the opportunity to see its reports. Sometimes this is the fault of the GAO in its routing; on other occasions it is the fault of the senator's office staff in not bringing the report to the senator's attention. A priority memorandum from Appropriations' chairman might secure for these reports the attention they deserve.

Still another step the committee should take is to gain a presidential perspective on the budget. Following the submission of the President's budget, the committee should invite the director of the budget, the chairman of the Council of Economic Advisers, and the secretary of the treasury to testify on the overall fiscal implications of the budget as to estimated revenue and expenditures. The budget director and his staff should be asked to elaborate on the cross-sectional special analyses— now a regular part of the annual budget document—that show similar activities in different agencies. In addition, a special meeting should be held with the director of the Office of Science and Technology to discuss the research and development aspects of the budget, which cut across many agency jurisdictions. The director should brief the committee on the priorities and interrelationships in his functional area so the members can understand the degree of coordination, if any, that has occurred within the executive branch among these costly, but necessary, programs. These are the President's men. They have been intimately involved in the decisions that have shaped the budget recommendations for the coming fiscal year. If Congress, which now handles the budget on a piecemeal basis, is to perceive the budget as a whole, there should be a face-to-face exchange between those who share the presidential perspective and those who share responsibility for making legislative decisions on the budget.

After the agency presentation, questions often arise requiring clarification in terms of the overall administration program. The budget director, or a representative designated by him, should be available to answer this kind of question for the record. If the responsible bureau officials appear, such an exchange might prove useful. For the career

---

and an independent judgment as to the adequacy of the agency criteria used in formulating the budget requests for a particular program. If the GAO were to assume responsibility for this type of evaluation, it would require the addition of staff with sufficiently broad qualifications to render such judgments.

budget examiners to appear would probably invite unnecessary harassment; however, officials at the assistant director level and above already appear before various congressional committees and should not find the practice unusual.[8]

Subcommittee chairmen might also experiment with scheduling prehearing conferences in which members of the regular and minority staff could examine responsible agency officials on the budget justifications to be considered. Time is saved in regulatory or judicial proceedings by the appointment of a hearing examiner or master to take testimony from witnesses and to sift through that testimony to focus the issues and aid the administrator, board, or court in making a decision. This device might prove useful in clarifying the issues for congressional hearings. To permit a free exchange, the pre-hearing conference should be closed. Perhaps a transcript could be taken for later use by the committee. A pre-hearing conference would have advantages for both the legislative and executive branches. Administration officials would improve their understanding of congressional concerns because the regular and minority staffs would reflect the views of their principals during the questioning. Consequently, an agency would have the opportunity to tighten its presentation before the appearance of its chief executive at the hearing. Such a small group would also be able to develop a specific policy issue at length, which, as the many disjointed hearing records indicate, frequently is not the case at hearings, where senators are limited to ten minutes on a round.

Finally, a briefing on agency goals, activities, and budget requests should be given before the hearing by the regular staff responsible for a bill. Invitations should be extended not only to the committee members concerned, but also to each member's legislative assistant. The briefing would also serve as a focal point for planning the investigation strategy to be pursued in the hearing. The regular staff briefing for members of both parties might be followed by a smaller session held by the minority in order to develop its own hearing strategy.

Written memoranda extracting relevant House testimony might be circulated. Certainly no hearing by the subcommittee should be held

8. Suggestions have been made from time to time that the budget examiners attend Appropriations Committee sessions to clarify on the spot any questions the members might have. This proposal has been rejected on the plausible ground that the presence of the budget examiners would inhibit agency frankness with the committee. Similar proposals that the Appropriations staff sit in on Budget Bureau sessions reviewing an agency's budget requests have been given an equally cool reception—but this time by the executive branch.

until the prepared testimony of agency officials has been received. The testimony should be in hand for at least three working days in advance of the hearing if both the committee and office staffs are to have sufficient time to formulate questions for senators to use during the hearing. The result would be a more productive session and the development of a more useful public record.

Appropriations Requests Should Be Considered Comprehensively

Given the powerful position of each subcommittee chairman, efforts to secure an overall view through a single omnibus appropriation bill will probably fail. Some fragmentation will continue. What might be possible, however, is a reorganization of the fragments so that an overall view can occur within each of several consolidated areas—although in many cases, at the present time, not even that is possible.

By 1969 there were fourteen regular appropriation bills considered by as many subcommittees. These bills and subcommittees should be consolidated into five groups that, while not perfect, would more accurately reflect federal executive activity: (1) *Agricultural and Natural Resources,* to include most of the present Agriculture, Interior, and Public Works bills; (2) *General Government,* to include many of the traditional agencies in the Independent Offices bill, the Department of Justice and the Judiciary from the present State-Justice bill, and the agencies contained in the Legislative and Treasury–Post Office–Executive Office bills; (3) *Human Resources,* to include several of the major agencies such as the Department of Housing and Urban Development and the Veterans Administration now carried in the Independent Offices bill, as well as most of the present District of Columbia and Labor-HEW bills; (4) *National Security,* to include most of the activities in the Defense, Foreign Operations, and Military Construction bills, as well as the Department of State and United States Information Agency currently found in the State-Justice bill; and (5) *Science and Technology,* to include the Department of Commerce, the Department of Transportation, the National Aeronautics and Space Administration, the National Science Foundation, and the Smithsonian Institution, among other agencies whose requests are now reviewed by at least four different subcommittees.[9]

9. See Appendix D, which lists for each federal agency the appropriation bill from which it received funds in the Ninetieth Congress, the Bureau of the Budget division that currently reviews its estimates, and the consolidated bill to which the agency would be assigned if the proposed reorganization were to occur.

A special comment should be made about the work of the District of Columbia Subcommittee. An assignment to this group is not high on any senator's list. The subcommittee's hearings seldom last more than a week. Yet Washington, D.C. suffers as do few other cities the complex problems of urban America: inadequate public schools, crime, slums, Negro ghettos, whites fleeing to the suburbs, and so on. As long as Congress desires to play city council, it should at least play its role well. With vast governmental undertakings being spawned to aid America's cities, certainly the Senate Appropriations subcommittee reviewing these education, housing, and job opportunity programs should also review the city government for which Congress is directly responsible—and make it a showcase in the process.

If the present uncoordinated subcommittee structure is maintained, perhaps the number and size of the subcommittees could be reduced, and at least there should be a better balance of subcommittee assignments to provide greater opportunity for participation by the less senior members in both parties. The principal subcommittees should be limited to ten members and no member should have more than three major subcommittee assignments. Both Democrats and Republicans on Appropriations should adopt a variation of the so-called Johnson Rule for committee assignments, which Senate Democrats have used on and off since 1953 and which the Senate Republican Conference formally adopted in 1965. The rule might be that no senator on Appropriations can receive a third major subcommittee assignment until all other members have received at least two major subcommittee assignments.

A corollary of such a rule should be that no member would be assigned to more than one of the following subcommittees: District of Columbia, Legislative, and Treasury–Post Office. Perhaps the work of these three subcommittees could be combined with some of the more active subcommittees. If the work of the District of Columbia Subcommittee were consolidated with the Independent Offices Subcommittee (which now reviews the programs of the Department of Housing and Urban Development) or in the proposed Subcommittee on Human Resources, one minor subcommittee could be eliminated. There is no reason why a new subcommittee could not pass on the programs of both the Department of Housing and Urban Development and the District of Columbia, even if House Appropriations decided to maintain separate bills and subcommittees. By reassigning budget review of several of the independent financial agencies (such as the Federal Home Loan

Bank Board and the Federal Savings and Loan Insurance Corporation, among others) from Independent Offices to Treasury–Post Office, the jurisdiction of the latter committee would be strengthened. The Legislative bill might be absorbed by a subcommittee that considered all of the more traditional governmental functions.

The Foreign Operations hearings that until 1969 were held by the full committee (to prevent senior conservatives from dominating a subcommittee and cutting back the program) could again be held at that level. Because national security matters account for such a large proportion of the annual budget, perhaps the defense posture hearings should also be held at the full committee level, and an exception be made to the limitation on members to permit fifteen on the Defense Subcommittee.

A subcommittee on research and development would improve committee review and aid in overcoming the effects of the dispersal of scientific programs among several subcommittees. It should consist of the chairman and ranking minority member from each of the existing subcommittees that have large scientific programs under their jurisdiction: Agriculture, Defense, Independent Offices, Interior, Labor-HEW, Public Works, and State-Justice. If scheduling difficulties prevent the director of the Office of Science and Technology from meeting with the full committee at the beginning of a session, he and his supporting staff should brief the leaders of these seven subcommittees on the executive judgments involved in deciding priorities among the various research and development programs.

In 1965, Senator Stennis, as acting chairman of the Armed Services–Defense Appropriations joint subcommittee, created an ad hoc group on research and development under Senator Symington, an ex officio member from Armed Services. The Symington group was able to scrutinize the "R&D" component in greater detail than would have been possible before the regular subcommittee as a whole. Other subcommittee chairmen might well consider the advisability of appointing such ad hoc groups, which could go deeply into the scientific program and report their findings to the subcommittee and full committee. The subcommittee on research and development would not be responsible for an individual appropriation bill, but for comprehensive review and comparison. Research and development items should not be separated from the major programs of which they are a fundamental part.

Instead of a permanent Deficiencies and Supplementals Subcommittee, an ad hoc subcommittee—consisting of the subcommittee chairman, a majority member, and the ranking minority member from the regular subcommittees under whose jurisdiction the items in a particular supplemental bill fall—should be established as needed. Individual items would be heard by the regular substantive subcommittees. House Appropriations has returned to this latter procedure. In this way, the decisions made on supplemental requests would be related to the earlier decisions each subcommittee made on the regular bill. Once each subcommittee has reviewed the supplemental requests, the bill should be brought together either at the full committee level or by having the ad hoc group meet in advance of the full committee meeting. The chairman of the full committee could designate the chairman and Senate conferees on the basis of the major issues involved in a particular supplemental bill.

The Senate Should Construe Its Appropriations Responsibilities More Broadly and Improve Its Fulfillment of Them

For Congress to make permanent appropriations to carry out any executive function, without providing that such authority can be canceled by the passage of a concurrent resolution not subject to a presidential veto, is for the legislative branch to abdicate its responsibility. At a minimum, programs implemented as a result of permanent appropriations should be subject to some form of annual legislative review.

The Senate as a whole has a vested interest in seeing that executive agencies and programs are subject to annual review. If that review is to be effective, and if there is to be an opportunity for comparisons among different but related programs, then the Committee on Appropriations, with government-wide jurisdiction and the power of the purse, is the most logical place for it to occur. Since the rivalry in the Senate between the legislative committees and Appropriations has never reached the bitterness that it has in the House, there is a distinct possibility that the Committee on Appropriations could undertake this task. The need is not only to bring under review some programs that have not been subject to an annual appropriations review, but also to examine periodically the appropriations base of many programs already annually reviewed. Often, decisions have been based on the increments from one year to the next rather than on a reassessment of the basic need for—or validity of—a particular program. The existence of various trust fund expenditures and other kinds of permanent appropriations should not preclude the Committee on Appropriations from examining an agency's appropriations base.

In addition, at least once every five years Congress, through its Committees on Appropriations and Government Operations, should commission a management review of each executive department and agency, as well as of the legislative and judicial branches. Although it might be more feasible to contract with outside consultants to perform such studies, consideration should be given to the establishment in the legislative branch of a high quality management review staff to undertake this work. This staff could also serve various legislative committees as the occasion demanded. Such a staff might be established on Capitol Hill in a RAND type of institution that would be free to accept federal and foundation funds. Since the management studies would be a continuing undertaking, with different agencies scheduled for review each year, there would be an opportunity to assemble and retain a staff of highly qualified professionals in program and management analysis.

Competent management of public programs remains one of the great challenges confronting the executive branch. By associating the review of administrative management more closely with the annual appropriations process, Congress would increase its ability to improve institutional efficiency. Such studies would also educate legislators in administrative problems. The regularity of the budget process and the congressional power of the purse are powerful sanctions—if effectively used—against executive mismanagement.

There should also be more control of reprogramming. It could be argued that because Congress approves each appropriation bill, it is Congress as a whole—not a committee, subcommittee, or one or two members of either—that should approve any major shifting of funds. All major reprogramming requests might be submitted to the president of the Senate and the speaker of the House to lie on the table for a two-week period. As in the reorganization plan procedure, unless a resolution of disapproval passed either house during that period, the reprogrammings would be carried out. If both House and Senate Appropriations confronted the reprogramming problem in an open manner however, and acquainted their colleagues with their decisions, perhaps this more complicated alternative would not be necessary. At a minimum, the Committee on Appropriations should develop broad criteria as to amount, program, and timing that would determine which agency reprogrammings require the attention of the full committee, and which could be delegated to the subcommittee chairman and ranking minority member to consider on the committee's behalf. Proposed reprogrammings might be routed to all committee members; then, any objections could be brought up in a twice-monthly executive session. On a monthly basis, a compilation of the reprogrammings approved by Senate Appropriations should be published either in the *Congressional Record* or the *Budget Register* that is proposed below. On a quarterly basis, those reprogrammings that did not require committee action should be published. The executive branch needs reprogramming authority especially in the national security field, where changing requirements and technology demand flexibility. Perhaps the reprogramming authority that exists in various domestic programs is needed there as well. What is essential is that the committee recognize the issue.

Either alone or in conjunction with House Appropriations, the Committee on Appropriations should publish a monthly *Budget Register* detailing significant aspects of federal revenue and appropriations. This publication would be a cross between the monthly *Economic Indicators,*[10] which the Council of Economic Advisers prepares for the Joint Economic Committee, and the *Federal Register,* which is a daily publication recording the executive orders and administrative regulations issued by the President and agency heads. The *Budget Register* should include at least (1) a monthly statement of federal revenues by source; (2) a monthly statement of federal expenditures and remaining obligational authority by department and broad program category (including both administrative budget and consolidated cash budget items such as trust funds);[11] (3) a monthly statement of the reprogrammings, by agency, approved by the two Appropriations Committees; (4) a quarterly statement of the reprogrammings, by agency, that did not require the clearance of either committee; (5) a status report on the

10. *Economic Indicators* includes charts on federal budget receipts, expenditures, and net lending; federal budget receipts by source and outlays by function; and the federal sector on the basis of national income accounts.

11. Based on the state of the economy, and especially on the revenue collections resulting from the April 15 income tax payments, a midsummer revision of revenue estimates for the coming fiscal year should be made by the President and submitted to Congress. The executive should also make an effort to update cost estimates so that Congress does not take testimony on budget estimates that are clearly out of date. A midsummer projection of revised budget estimates by the President would also be useful to Congress and the public.

appropriation bills before Congress as to hearings, subcommittee, full committee, and conference action; (6) a list of the nonstatutory directives made in House, Senate, and conference reports on appropriation bills; (7) a summary of the estimated first-year and five-year cost, if fully funded, of legislative measures approved by Congress during the month;[12] (8) a list of the comptroller general's reports issued during the month, with an annual summary of agency action on each report; and (9) a list of subcommittee assignments or transfers occurring within either House or Senate Appropriations. Such a publication would be immensely useful not only to members of both Appropriations Committees, but to all legislators, administrators, the news media, and interested citizens as well. It would bring some order to the many sources of information now available and would assure that members of both committees obtain needed data that they do not now receive.

Finally, if the chain of responsibility from subcommittee through Senate to electorate is to be maintained, the Committee on Appropriations has an obligation to make its decisions explicit and to state them with consistency. A uniform format should be developed and used in all the reports of the committee so that senators wishing to make comparisons between bills may do so easily. The reports should specify not only the amount of appropriations, but also the carryover of obligational authority and the estimated expenditures for each agency or pro-

12. The Joint Committee on the Organization of the Congress suggested that a point of order lie against consideration of any new legislation that did not include cost projections for five years or the duration of the program, whichever is less. Budget Bureau officials, however, have expressed doubt as to the wisdom of blanket five-year projections. Their argument is that the President would be reluctant to commit himself to a specific figure so far in advance. Most legislators realize, however, that any such projection would not be binding, but would simply be an indicator. For those programs, such as grants-in-aid, that depend on formula and on state approval, there is always a degree of uncertainty as to what will happen until some experience has been gained. But even though many projections would be only approximations, having such forecasts would help to improve the degree of fiscal consciousness within Congress, and among its legislative committees in particular, by showing the possible size of various programs. Public Law 801, enacted in 1956, requires that official reports from the executive branch (except the CIA) on legislation that would result in the annual expenditure of more than a million dollars include a statement for each of the first five years of the program as to the estimated maximum additional man-years of civilian employment, the expenditures for personal services, and the expenditures for all other purposes (70 Stat. 652). But there is no requirement that a congressional committee relay these estimates in its report on a bill, or make its own estimate as to the probable cost of a program.

gram during the coming fiscal year. A summary sheet of nonstatutory agency directives should also be part of each report. The committee might well discuss what other information would be most useful to members and nonmembers who want to comprehend quickly the gross dimensions of agency spending.

Making explicit nonstatutory report directives would not preclude the continuation of unwritten agreements between agency administrators and Appropriations subcommittees. But Congress and the executive branch would mutually benefit from a clearer understanding of legislative expectations. Although still not statutorily binding, those directives would have greater sanction behind them after being presented to Congress in the committee report when consideration was given to an agency's appropriations.

Senate conferees should also be required to submit a statement to the Senate explaining the results of appropriations conferences held with the House. The filing of a Senate report and explanatory statement would make explicit the decisions that were reached and the interpretation the Senate conferees believe should be given to them.

The Role of Members and Staff Should Be Improved

Improving the quality of committee information, the comprehensiveness of budget review, and the fulfillment of broadly construed responsibilities requires a more effective employment of members and staff. Some recommendations that have already been made—such as reorganizing the subcommittees and their membership—would lead to the participation of more members, but additional efforts are needed if this goal is to be attained.

While serving as party floor leaders, committee members should not carry a full subcommittee load. However, to protect their seniority in anticipation of the day when they might no longer be a part of the leadership, they should not lose subcommittee ranking. The floor leaders could still participate in a full committee markup on behalf of their state or in furtherance of their policy preferences. But by permitting others in their party to take their place on all but two of their subcommittees, added committee resources would be made available during the hearing process. Such a procedure would also provide a greater opportunity for subcommittee participation and the assumption of responsibility by junior members, since it would free some of the choice assignments now monopolized by senior members.

Prohibiting the use of proxies might increase attendance at markup sessions and thus lead to a more thorough and responsible consideration of appropriation measures. Although in a review of the 1965 session there was no evidence that proxies had been consciously misused, there was evidence that proxies had been inadvertently cast in ways they might not have been if the senators who left their proxies had been present. The use of proxies occasionally has affected the outcome of a vote within the committee. Their elimination would do much to increase senatorial and committee responsibility.[13]

If the role of the staff is also to improve, staff members must be urged to familiarize themselves with the fundamentals and limitations of the various tools of economics and political science to which the executive branch has made such a strong commitment. Congress should amend the Government Employees' Training Act to permit its own employees to add to their professional skills at full salary, just as it does professionals in the executive branch.

Perhaps most important of all, the committee needs strong leadership. If there is to be any effective review of agency activities, there must be greater coordination of member and staff activity, a planned pooling of committee and noncommittee resources directed toward specific ends, and a balanced and coordinated plan of domestic and foreign travel for both members and staff. Clearly, a revitalized committee would require substantially more time from the chairman. Time, of course, is the commodity that any senator finds difficult to make available, given the demands of his office staff and the pressures of his noncommittee responsibilities. When a senator has become chairman of the Committee on Appropriations, however, few can equal him in the Senate's power structure. He does not need to have his energies dissipated on other committee assignments. The chairman should be given some

---

13. As originally reported to the Senate, the proposed Legislative Reorganization Act of 1967 (S. 355) prohibited proxy voting. But on Jan. 26, 1967, early in floor consideration, this provision was modified so that proxies could be used in all cases but the final reporting of the bill. On Feb. 7, 1967, Democrat Russell B. Long of Louisiana, chairman of the Finance Committee, successfully modified even that compromise to permit each committee to allow the use of proxies in reporting a measure, provided the absentee was informed of the matter and affirmatively requested to be so recorded. The result was to ban only general proxies. Long's modification was adopted by a vote of 48 to 38. Fourteen members of Appropriations supported Long; twelve were opposed. Eight of the Appropriations subcommittee chairmen favored a less restrictive proxy policy; five, including Chairman Hayden, were opposed. S. 355 was never approved by the House of Representatives.

formal relief from other assignments—with self-restraint serving as perhaps the best interim solution.

* * *

Each year, the President requests additional billions of dollars to carry on the functions of a powerful nation with world-wide commitments. Each year, the Congress approves in one form or another the appropriation bills that grant needed financial resources to the national administration. In this annual budgetary-appropriations process, presidential priorities are not immutable. The executive budget is correctly a political document—the financial program for the future operations of an administration holding temporary political power. The budgetary checks and balances of a legislative branch confronting an executive branch, and of competing committees within a bicameral Congress, help assure that despite frustrating obstacles, some sort of operational consensus does emerge. Competing forces within society presumably have had their chance and been meshed together in a consensus as best a diverse, democratic polity can mesh them. Through the representative process, Congress attempts to assure the continued responsibility of the executive to the people. The recommendations in this chapter are aimed at strengthening that assurance, and also at providing institutional and political accountability in the budgetary process within the legislative branch and its subgroups.

But implementation of these recommendations, as was indicated earlier, is not likely to occur smoothly or easily. Evolution and quiet adjustment are one thing. Mobilizing committee and Senate sentiment to accomplish a specific change at a particular time is quite another.

It is easy for those within the legislative institution to dismiss the critics. For despite the critics both within and without, Congress does work. Before 1964, few Americans would have believed that two-thirds of the senators present and voting would invoke cloture to shut off a filibuster against civil rights legislation, yet it happened. Congress is sensitive to change if the nation is aroused. The movement of Negroes to large urban centers, the rise of suburbia, the industrialization of the South, the increased two-party competition throughout the land, the almost instant communication of issues and events through the medium of television, the mobilization of constituent opinion by various interest groups, and the changes resulting from reapportionment have all acted to increase legislative sensitivity and to disturb entrenched seats of congressional power—and the attitudes that often accompany them. In the appropriation process, however, the legislative branch does not face strong external pressure to mend its ways.

The nature of an institution can greatly affect substantive ends. Would a strengthened committee increase the leverage exercised by some forces in the Senate so that the result would be unrepresentative of the Senate as a whole? It might—temporarily. At the end of the 1960s, membership on Appropriations still proportionately favored southern as opposed to northern Democrats. The key subcommittee chairmanships were still dominated by southern Democrats. In addition, there was a regional imbalance in favor of the South and the West. Yet change was occurring. Of those on the committee in 1965, four were not present in 1969. Two had been defeated in party primaries (Robertson in 1966 and Kuchel in 1968) and two (Hayden and Hill) had decided not to run for another term in 1968. But because it is composed of relatively senior members, the committee is more insulated and stable than the Senate as a whole. Consequently, a strengthened Appropriations Committee might be less responsive than other groups of senators to legitimate pressures.

But the committee is not a separate entity immune to the sanctions of its creator. If the Senate differs with Appropriations, it can make its views prevail. Appropriation bills and conference reports must still clear the parent chamber. Amendments can be offered and adopted. The opportunity to overrule the committee does exist—although unless the Senate has the necessary information and the time in which to act, it is a limited opportunity at best.

The Senate Committee on Appropriations has not done badly, but it could do better. Its power to affect the appropriation process and to focus the Senate's energies on the administrative and budgetary problems of the nation is largely unused. If the Senate is to make full use of its unused power as a constitutional partner in making appropriations, then the time has come to reorganize its most prestigious committee. Such a reorganization would go far toward assuring both legislative and executive responsiveness—a result that should be welcomed by all who value effective representative government.

Members of the Senate Committee on Appropriations and Their Assignments, 1965–66

Table A–1. Members of the Senate Committee on Appropriations and Their Assignments, 1965–66

See notes at end of table

Name, tenure, and positions in Senate and party	Legislative committee membership and subcommittee leadership assignments[a]	Appropriations subcommittee and panel assignments[a,b]
DEMOCRATS		
Carl Hayden of Arizona 39 years on committee 39 years in Senate 88 years of age President pro tempore Policy Committee Democratic Steering Committee	Interior and Insular Affairs Rules and Administration ★ *Standing Rules Subcommittee* ★ *Printing Subcommittee*	★ Full committee ★ Foreign Operations ★ Interior and Related Agencies Public Works ★ *Panel on Bureau of Reclamation and Interior Power Marketing Agencies* Defense Deficiencies and Supplementals District of Columbia All other subcommittees—ex officio as chairman
Richard B. Russell of Georgia 33 years on committee 33 years in Senate 68 years of age Policy Committee Democratic Steering Committee	★ Armed Services ★ *CIA Subcommittee* Aeronautical and Space Sciences Joint Committee on Atomic Energy	★ Defense Agriculture and Related Agencies Deficiencies and Supplementals Independent Offices Interior and Related Agencies Labor, HEW, and Related Agencies Military Construction Public Works

Allen J. Ellender of Louisiana
17 years on committee
29 years in Senate
75 years of age
Democratic Steering Committee

★ Agriculture and Forestry

★ Public Works
★ *Panel on Army Civil Functions*
Defense
Deficiencies and Supplementals
Independent Offices
Military Construction
State, Justice, Commerce, the Judiciary, and Related Agencies

---

Lister Hill of Alabama
17 years on committee
28 years in Senate
71 years of age
Policy Committee

★ Labor and Public Welfare
★ *Health Subcommittee*

★ Labor, HEW, and Related Agencies
Public Works
★ *Panel on AEC-TVA*
Agriculture and Related Agencies
Defense
Deficiencies and Supplementals
Independent Offices

John L. McClellan of Arkansas
17 years on committee
23 years in Senate
69 years of age
Democratic Steering Committee

★ Government Operations
★ *Permanent Subcommittee on Investigations*
Judiciary
★ *Patents, Trademarks, and Copyrights Subcommittee*

★ State, Justice, Commerce, the Judiciary, and Related Agencies
Defense
Deficiencies and Supplementals
Interior and Related Agencies
Public Works
Treasury, Post Office, and Executive Office

A. Willis Robertson of Virginia
17 years on committee
20 years in Senate
78 years of age
Democratic Steering Committee

★ Banking and Currency
★ *Financial Institutions Subcommittee*

★ Treasury, Post Office, and Executive Office
Agriculture and Related Agencies
Defense
Deficiencies and Supplementals
Independent Offices
Public Works

Table A–1 (Continued)

Name, tenure, and positions in Senate and party	Legislative committee membership and subcommittee leadership assignments[a]	Appropriations subcommittee and panel assignments[b]
Warren A. Magnuson of Washington 13 years on committee 21 years in Senate 60 years of age Policy Committee ★ Democratic Senatorial Campaign Committee	★ Commerce ★ Merchant Marine and Fisheries Subcommittee Aeronautical and Space Sciences	★ Independent Offices Defense Deficiencies and Supplementals Labor, HEW, and Related Agencies Public Works State, Justice, Commerce, the Judiciary, and Related Agencies
Spessard L. Holland of Florida 11 years on committee 20 years in Senate 73 years of age Democratic Steering Committee	★ Agriculture and Forestry ★ Agricultural Credit and Rural Electrification Subcommittee [1965] ★ Agricultural Production, Marketing, and Stabilization of Prices Subcommittee [1966] Aeronautical and Space Sciences	★ Agriculture and Related Agencies Deficiencies and Supplementals Independent Offices Labor, HEW, and Related Agencies Public Works State, Justice, Commerce, the Judiciary, and Related Agencies
John Stennis of Mississippi 11 years on committee 19 years in Senate 64 years of age ★ Select Committee on Standards and Conduct	Aeronautical and Space Sciences Armed Services ★ Preparedness Subcommittee ★ Officer Grade Limitations Subcommittee	★ Military Construction Agriculture and Related Agencies Defense (acting chairman during 1965) Deficiencies and Supplementals Independent Offices Labor, HEW, and Related Agencies Public Works

John O. Pastore of Rhode Island
9 years on committee
15 years in Senate
58 years of age
Policy Committee

● Joint Committee on Atomic Energy
★ *Legislation Subcommittee*
Commerce
★ *Communications Subcommittee*

★ Deficiencies and Supplementals
Defense
Independent Offices
Labor, HEW, and Related Agencies
Public Works
State, Justice, Commerce, the Judiciary, and Related Agencies

· · · · · · · · · ·

A. S. Mike Monroney of Oklahoma
7 years on committee
15 years in Senate
63 years of age
● Joint Committee on the Organization of the Congress

Commerce
★ *Aviation Subcommittee*
★ Post Office and Civil Service [1966]
★ *Postal Affairs Subcommittee*

★ Legislative
Defense
Deficiencies and Supplementals
Independent Offices
Public Works
Treasury, Post Office, and Executive Office

· · · · · · · · · ·

Alan Bible of Nevada
7 years on committee
11 years in Senate
56 years of age
Democratic Steering Committee

District of Columbia
★ *Fiscal Affairs Subcommittee*
Interior and Insular Affairs
★ *Parks and Recreation Subcommittee*

Interior and Related Agencies
Labor, HEW, and Related Agencies
Military Construction
Public Works
State, Justice, Commerce, the Judiciary, and Related Agencies

· · · · · · · · · ·

Robert C. Byrd of West Virginia
7 years on committee
7 years in Senate
47 years of age

Armed Services
Rules and Administration
★ *Restaurant Subcommittee*

★ District of Columbia
Deficiencies and Supplementals
Interior and Related Agencies
Labor, HEW, and Related Agencies
Public Works
State, Justice, Commerce, the Judiciary, and Related Agencies

Table A-1 (Continued)

Name, tenure, and positions in Senate and party	Legislative committee membership and subcommittee leadership assignments[a]	Appropriations subcommittee and panel assignments[b]
Gale W. McGee of Wyoming 7 years on committee 7 years in Senate 50 years of age	Commerce Post Office and Civil Service ★ *Retirement Subcommittee*	Agriculture and Related Agencies Interior and Related Agencies Labor, HEW, and Related Agencies Public Works State, Justice, Commerce, the Judiciary, and Related Agencies
Mike Mansfield of Montana 3 years on committee 13 years in Senate 62 years of age Majority floor leader ★ Policy Committee ★ Democratic Steering Committee	Foreign Relations ★ *State Department Organization and Public Affairs Subcommittee*	Agriculture and Related Agencies Defense Interior and Related Agencies Military Construction State, Justice, Commerce, the Judiciary, and Related Agencies
E. L. Bartlett of Alaska 3 years on committee 7 years in Senate 61 years of age	Commerce	District of Columbia Interior and Related Agencies Labor, HEW, and Related Agencies Legislative Treasury, Post Office, and Executive Office
William Proxmire of Wisconsin 3 years on committee 9 years in Senate 50 years of age	Banking and Currency ★ *Small Business Subcommittee*	Agriculture and Related Agencies District of Columbia Interior and Related Agencies Legislative Military Construction

Ralph Yarborough of Texas
1 year on committee
9 years in Senate
62 years of age

Labor and Public Welfare
★ *Veterans Affairs Subcommittee*
Post Office and Civil Service
★ *Civil Service Subcommittee*

Agriculture and Related Agencies
District of Columbia
Legislative
Military Construction
Treasury, Post Office, and Executive Office

REPUBLICANS

Leverett Saltonstall
of Massachusetts
19 years on committee
21 years in Senate
73 years of age
★ Republican Conference
Policy Committee

☆ Armed Services
☆ *Preparedness Investigation Subcommittee*
☆ *CIA Subcommittee*

☆ Full committee
☆ Defense
☆ Foreign Operations
☆ Legislative
Deficiencies and Supplementals
District of Columbia (ex officio)
Independent Offices
Labor, HEW, and Related Agencies (ex officio)
Military Construction
State, Justice, Commerce, the Judiciary, and Related Agencies

Milton R. Young of North Dakota
19 years on committee
21 years in Senate
68 years of age
Secretary, Republican Conference
Policy Committee

Agriculture and Forestry
☆ *Agricultural Production, Marketing, and Stabilization of Prices Subcommittee*
☆ *Agricultural Research and General Legislation Subcommittee*

☆ Agriculture and Related Agencies
☆ Deficiencies and Supplementals
Defense
Independent Offices
Interior and Related Agencies
Legislative
Public Works

Table A–1 (*Continued*)

Name, tenure, and positions in Senate and party	Legislative committee membership and subcommittee leadership assignments[a]	Appropriations subcommittee and panel assignments[b]
Karl E. Mundt of South Dakota 13 years on committee 17 years in Senate 65 years of age Policy Committee	☆ Government Operations ☆ Permanent Subcommittee on Investigations ☆ National Security International Operations Subcommittee ☆ Foreign Aid Expenditures Subcommittee ☆ Intergovernmental Relations Subcommittee Foreign Relations	☆ Interior and Related Agencies Public Works ☆ Panel on Bureau of Reclamation and Interior Power Marketing Agencies Agriculture and Related Agencies Defense Deficiencies and Supplementals State, Justice, Commerce, the Judiciary, and Related Agencies
Margaret Chase Smith of Maine 13 years on committee 17 years in Senate 68 years of age Policy Committee	☆ Aeronautical and Space Sciences Armed Services ☆ Officer Grade Limitations Subcommittee	☆ State, Justice, Commerce, the Judiciary, and Related Agencies Defense Deficiencies and Supplementals Independent Offices Labor, HEW, and Related Agencies Public Works
Thomas H. Kuchel of California 7 years on committee 13 years in Senate 55 years of age Minority Whip Policy Committee	☆ Interior and Insular Affairs ☆ Irrigation and Reclamation Subcommittee	☆ Military Construction Defense Deficiencies and Supplementals Interior and Related Agencies Legislative Public Works

Roman L. Hruska of Nebraska
7 years on committee
12 years in Senate
61 years of age
Republican Senatorial
  Campaign Committee

Judiciary
☆ *Constitutional Rights Subcommittee*
☆ *Improvements in Judicial Machinery Subcommittee*
☆ *National Penitentiaries Subcommittee*
☆ *Internal Security Subcommittee*
☆ *Juvenile Delinquency Subcommittee*

☆ Public Works
☆ *Panel on Army Civil Functions*
☆ *Panel on AEC-TVA*
Agriculture and Related Agencies
Deficiencies and Supplementals
Independent Offices
Military Construction
State, Justice, Commerce, the Judiciary, and Related Agencies

- - - - - - - - - - - - - - - - - - - -

Gordon Allott of Colorado
7 years on committee
11 years in Senate
58 years of age
Republican Committee on Committees

Interior and Insular Affairs
☆ *Public Lands Subcommittee*

☆ Independent Offices
Defense
Labor, HEW, and Related Agencies
Public Works
Treasury, Post Office, and Executive Office

- - - - - - - - - - - - - - - - - - - -

Norris Cotton of New Hampshire
4 years on committee
12 years in Senate
65 years of age
Policy Committee

☆ Commerce
☆ *Aviation Subcommittee*

☆ Labor, HEW, and Related Agencies
District of Columbia
Independent Offices
Public Works
State, Justice, Commerce, the Judiciary, and Related Agencies

- - - - - - - - - - - - - - - - - - - -

Clifford P. Case of New Jersey
4 years on committee
11 years in Senate
61 years of age
Policy Committee

Foreign Relations

☆ District of Columbia
☆ Treasury, Post Office, and Executive Office
Agriculture and Related Agencies
Labor, HEW, and Related Agencies
State, Justice, Commerce, the Judiciary, and Related Agencies

---

★ denotes chairman; ● denotes vice- or co-chairman; ☆ denotes ranking minority member.
a. Does not include membership on joint, select, or special committees that do not have legislative authority. Italics denote subcommittee of preceding committee.
b. The Foreign Operations Subcommittee includes all members of the full committee; hence the members of this group are not separately identified except for the chairman and ranking minority member. Italics denote panel of preceding subcommittee.

APPENDIX B

The Origination of Appropriation Bills, 1787–1861

The Constitutional Convention of 1787

The actual sequence of votes in the Constitutional Convention began on May 29, 1787, when Edmund Randolph of Virginia offered the so-called Virginia Plan for consideration of his colleagues: Number 6 of its fifteen resolutions was that "each branch [of the legislature] ought to possess the right of originating acts."[1] That same day Charles Pinckney of South Carolina submitted various proposals, including the proposition that all money bills originate in "the House of Delegates and shall not be altered by the Senate."[2] (Yet by August 8, Pinckney was to say that such a provision gave no advantage to the House of Representatives and would "clog" the government: "If the Senate can be trusted with the many great powers proposed, it surely may be trusted with that of originating money bills.")[3]

On May 31, Randolph's resolution that each chamber would be equal in origination was unanimously agreed to in the Committee of the Whole without debate. On June 13, Elbridge Gerry of Massachusetts moved to amend the Randolph proposal to provide an exception for "money bills, which shall originate in the first branch [i.e., the House] of the national Legislature."[4] James Madison of Virginia and others opposed Gerry's amendment and it was voted down with seven states against it and only three for it. On June 26, the Constitutional Convention unanimously agreed to the Randolph proposal. Then the question of representation for large and small states came to the fore.

On July 5, a special committee headed by Gerry reported and urged the

1. Max Farrand (ed.), *The Records of the Federal Convention of 1787* (Yale University Press, 1911), Vol. 1, p. 21.
2. *Records*, Vol. 3, p. 596.
3. *Records*, Vol. 2, p. 224.
4. *Records*, Vol. 1, p. 224.

Convention to allow one member in the House for every 40,000 inhabitants. It also recommended that all bills for raising or appropriating money and for fixing the salaries of the federal officers originate in the House, and not be altered or amended by the Senate. No money was to be drawn from the treasury except in pursuance of appropriations originated by the House. Each state was to have an equal vote in the Senate. On July 6, after considerable discussion, five states voted to keep the clause pertaining to money bills in the report, three were opposed, and three divided.

On July 16, a select committee—to which the whole question of legislative representation had once again been referred—recommended that all bills for raising or appropriating money originate in the House and not be altered or amended by the Senate. Five states agreed to the package including this proposal, four were opposed, and one divided.

On July 26, all of the propositions previously adopted were referred to the Committee on Detail. On August 6, this committee reported with a draft of the Constitution providing that all bills for raising or appropriating money shall originate in the House "and shall not be altered or amended by the Senate."[5] On August 8, however, that language was stricken by a vote of seven states to four. The vote was reconsidered and, on August 13, Randolph moved to amend the clause so that "Bills for raising money for the purposes of revenue, or for appropriating the same, shall originate in the House of representatives; and shall not be so altered or amended by the Senate as to encrease or diminish the sum to be raised, or change the mode of raising or the objects of its appropriation."[6] This was in exact accordance with the privilege as exercised in the English House of Commons. Four states favored the House's having exclusive origination of money bills; seven states were opposed. On the vote to agree to the section as reported, only three states favored excluding the Senate from the right to alter or amend, and eight were opposed. Only one state favored exclusive origination of appropriation bills in the House; ten were opposed.

On August 15, the issue again came before the Convention in the form of language providing that the House originate bills "for raising money for the purposes of revenue or for appropriating the same" and permitting the Senate to "propose or concur with amendments."[7] Consideration of this proposal was postponed until after the Senate's powers were considered.

On September 5, in the spirit of compromise, the Committee of Eleven reported a substitute: "All Bills for raising revenue shall originate in the House of representatives and shall be subject to alterations and amendments by the Senate: No money shall be drawn from the Treasury, but in consequence of appropriations made by law."[8] A clear distinction had been made between the revenue and appropriation functions. On September 8, the Convention agreed by a vote of 9 to 2 that the House would originate all bills

5. *Records*, Vol. 2, p. 178.
6. *Records*, Vol. 2, p. 266.
7. *Records*, Vol. 2, p. 294.
8. *Records*, Vol. 2, p. 505.

for raising revenue. As a compromise between the small and large states, it was then unanimously agreed to strike the next phrase and insert the words used in the Massachusetts constitution: "but the Senate may propose or concur with amendments as on other bills."[9] With that change the language became the first clause of the seventh section of Article 1 of the Constitution, while the last clause—"No money shall be drawn from the Treasury, but in consequence of Appropriations made by Law"—was transferred to the ninth section of Article 1.

The Role of James Madison

James Madison, who is generally regarded as "the Father of the Constitution," repeatedly fought the attempt by Gerry and George Mason of Virginia to prohibit the Senate from originating money bills. Madison and other delegates held that there was no analogy between the House of Lords and the Senate. Madison stated that commentators on the British Constitution did not agree on the reason for restricting the House of Lords in money bills. He thought it was meaningless to argue that the House should exclusively originate money bills since the states in the Senate were also represented in the House, and "they might surely find some member from some of the same States in the lower branch who would originate it."[10] Such a provision, Madison said, would be "a source of injurious altercations between the two Houses."[11] Madison clearly understood that revenue meant the levying of taxes.

The Virginia delegation, however, was split on the provision. On August 13, 1787, by a vote of 3 to 2, Virginia was one of four states that voted to confine the origination of money bills exclusively to the House. Delegates John Blair and Madison were opposed, but Randolph—who had switched his position since May 29, when he had offered the Virginia Plan that allowed both houses to originate bills—and Mason gained the support of George Washington. In a note, Madison said that Washington "disapproved & till now voted agst., the exclusive privilege, he gave up his judgment he said, because it was not of very material weight with him & was made an essential point with others, who if disappointed, might be less cordial in other points of real weight."[12] With rare exception, the delegates who assembled in Philadelphia were not ideologues. They were very practical men who saw that their mission was "to form a more perfect union" and were willing to accommodate each others' views to achieve that purpose.

Throughout the Constitutional Convention, delegates showed awareness of state experience with similar provisions. John Dickinson of Delaware noted that eight states provided for the exclusive origination of money bills in the "popular" branch, but that most of them allowed the other branch to amend, which he also favored allowing the Senate. John Rutledge of South Carolina responded that "these clauses in the Constitution of the States had been put

9. *Records,* Vol. 3, pp. 148–49.
10. *Records,* Vol. 1, p. 527.
11. *Records,* Vol. 2, p. 224.
12. *Records,* Vol. 2, p. 280.

in through a blind adherence to the British model. If the work was to be done over now, they would be omitted."[13] Madison thought Virginia was wrong to prohibit its state senate from originating a bill.

Yet when it came time to ratify the Constitution, Madison's views seemed to change. One of the most difficult battles over ratification occurred in New York. To rally public support for ratification, Madison joined with Alexander Hamilton and John Jay in writing a series of articles under the pseudonym Publius in the *New York Packet*. These became *The Federalist Papers*. On February 22, 1788, what has become known as Federalist paper No. 58 appeared. Hamilton later claimed authorship of this article, although some scholars have attributed it to Madison.

Number 58 of *The Federalist Papers*, designed to secure the support of a large state, held that

> a constitutional and infallible resource still remains with the larger States, by which they will be able at all times to accomplish their just purposes. The House of Representatives cannot only refuse, but they alone can propose, the supplies requisite for the support of government. They, in a word, hold the purse—that powerful instrument by which we behold, in the history of the British Constitution, an infant and humble representation of the people gradually enlarging the sphere of its activity and importance, and finally reducing, as far as it seems to have wished, all the overgrown prerogatives of the other branches of the government. This power over the purse may, in fact, be regarded as the most complete and effectual weapon with which any constitution can arm the immediate representatives of the people, for obtaining a redress of every grievance, and for carrying into effect every just and salutary measure.

On June 14, 1788, in the Virginia Convention called to consider ratifying the Constitution, Madison responded to criticism that "there is an ambiguity in the words" as to "where the origination of money bills may take place." He held that "the first part of the clause is sufficiently expressed to exclude all doubts." Noting that the Constitutional Convention had been divided on "the utility of confining this to any particular branch," he added: "Whatever it be in Great Britain, there is a sufficient difference between us and them to render it inapplicable to this country." Citing the problems that had arisen in various states, Madison concluded: "The power of [the Senate] proposing alterations removes this inconvenience, and does not appear to me at all objectionable. I should have no objection to their [the Senate] having a right of originating such bills."[14]

The Early Congresses

Confusion between money bills and revenue measures is evident in the sketchy records of the First Congress. On May 15, 1789, the House of Representatives began to consider a bill for levying a duty on goods, wares, and merchandise imported into the United States. Madison agreed with a member who stated: "The Constitution . . . authorized the House of Representatives

13. *Records*, Vol. 2, p. 279.
14. *Records*, Vol. 3, pp. 317–18.

alone to originate money bills. . . ."[15] The discussion concerned the advisability of passing a perpetual revenue law or placing a time limit on the measure so that the Senate and the President would not have undue power because the House had acted. Representative John Laurance of New York asked: "Where must the bill for the appropriation originate? It must be here."[16] His colleague, Theodorick Bland of Virginia, who had opposed ratification in the Virginia state convention, urged that the House must preserve "inviolate" the privilege of raising money and added that "the importance of the House itself depended upon their holding the purse strings; if they once part with this power, they would become insignificant, and the other branch of the Legislature might become altogether independent of them."[17] The next day, however, Elias Boudinot of New Jersey commented: "It was contended that the House were relinquishing their right to the purse strings; what was their right? They can originate a money bill, but the Senate can alter and amend it; they can negative it altogether; the system of finance is under the mutual inspection and direction of both Houses."[18] Whether money bills included both taxes and appropriations remained unclear.

Eight years later, on March 3, 1797, the House-passed military and naval establishment appropriation bill for 1797 was reported in the Senate with amendments. It was the last day of the session and the bill had just reached the Senate from the House of Representatives. Some senators were outraged, and a motion was made denouncing the House practice of withholding bills and thus preventing Senate investigation and deliberation. One of the resolves provided that

> the Senate of the United States will not hereafter originate any bill for appropriating moneys for the support of government, or of the military and naval establishments, nor any law of general importance to the public, at any time after ten days (Sundays excluded) before the day on which the second session of any Congress of the United States will expire under the constitution; nor will the Senate receive, and act upon, any such bills, if originated in the House of Representatives of the United States, at a day later than is herein before prescribed; . . .[19]

A motion to postpone the consideration of this resolution until the next session of Congress carried by a vote of 18 to 8. The Senate was not willing to fight.

1816

On April 12, 1816, Senator Abner Lacock of Pennsylvania obtained permission to bring in a bill making further appropriations for the year 1816. After consideration, it was passed on April 27. The House received and amended the Senate bill, the Senate accepted the House amendments, and

15. *Annals of Congress*, 1 Cong. 1 sess. (May 15, 1789), p. 345.
16. *Annals*, p. 349.
17. *Annals*, pp. 349–50.
18. *Annals* (May 16, 1789), p. 364.
19. *Journal of the Senate of the United States of America*, 4 Cong. 2 sess., Vol. 2 (March 3, 1797), pp. 347–48.

the President signed the bill on April 30—the last day of the session. While this was not one of the regular general appropriation bills, it was a major supplemental. It encountered no known opposition in the House.

1837–38

During the Andrew Jackson administration, legislators had become embroiled over revenue questions involving the Bank of the United States, the distribution of the surplus in the Treasury to the states, and the tariff. Under Jackson's successor, Martin Van Buren, relations were strained between Senate Finance and House Ways and Means. On September 18, 1837, House Ways and Means reported a $1.6 million appropriation bill providing additional funds to prosecute the war against the Seminole Indians in Florida. On September 21, Senate Finance reported a similar measure to the Senate, which was approved on September 26. Next day the Senate bill was referred in the House to the Committee of the Whole on the State of the Union, where the House bill was already pending. On October 14, the House approved its own bill. When the House bill reached the Senate late that evening, it was noted that the House had retained "the precise words of the Senate bill." Senator Daniel Webster of Massachusetts objected to the bill and the whole proceeding as being "improper and unparliamentary, as the House had given no account of the Senate bill on their table. . . ." Clement C. Clay of Alabama, a former Indian fighter who had served in the Senate just over a month, noted that the House had taken the Senate "to task . . . for usurping their prerogative in originating these bills . . . [but] . . . at this time, and on this subject, he was not disposed . . . to be ceremonious." He wanted the bill "passed at once" since "Florida had been bleeding at every pore for the last two years. . . ." James Buchanan of Pennsylvania agreed: ". . . he was not disposed at this time of night, and with the present state of the Senate, to stand upon its dignity. . . ." But for Webster it was "not a matter of dignity at all, but of regularity of business. . . ." Letting the House bill pass, he served notice that at the next session he would object to any such proceedings.[20]

During the next session, no general appropriation bills were reported by Senate Finance, but a bill making appropriations for Wisconsin roads and one providing appropriations for work on the Red River were reported by the Senate Committee on Roads and Canals. Both passed the Senate and House and were signed by the President. Similarly, the Senate Committee on Commerce reported an appropriation bill for lighthouses, lightboats, beacon lights, buoys, and surveys for fiscal year 1838 that passed both houses and became law.

1855–56

On December 11, 1855, Senator Richard Brodhead of Pennsylvania, a member of the Committee on Finance, which then handled appropriation bills in the Senate, informed his colleagues that he would "ask the Senate to con-

20. *The Congressional Globe,* 25 Cong. 1 sess. (1837), pp. 38, 82, 85, 139, 142–43.

sider the question of the power and the right of this body to originate the general appropriation bills. . . ." He explained that his object was "to avoid the evils of night sittings at the close of each session." His resolution proposed "That the Committee on Finance be directed to inquire into the expediency of reporting the appropriations bills for the support of the government, or adopting other measures with a view of obtaining more speedy action on said bills."[21]

On January 7, 1856, the Brodhead resolution came up for consideration. Brodhead reviewed the handling between 1842 and 1855 of the three principal appropriation bills—civil and diplomatic, army, and navy—and noted that the House of Representatives retained them "for generally two hundred days, and leaves the Senate about ten days to consider them." Other senators, including Robert M. T. Hunter of Virginia, the chairman of Senate Finance, generally concurred. A notable exception was New York's William H. Seward, a rising leader in the new Republican Party. He admitted that by the letter of the Constitution appropriation bills were not revenue bills, but thought that "in point of fact, they have come into the place of revenue bills." Seward believed that "this great branch of business . . . properly belongs to the commons of the country—the House of Representatives—according to the previous settled habit of the country." Not so James A. Bayard, Jr., of Delaware, who berated Seward for indulging "in a line of remark calculated to impair the dignity and proper weight" of the Senate. Glaring at Seward, Bayard declared: "Sir, I hold . . . that the Senate of the United States stands on a footing of equality with the House of Representatives of the United States." With that the resolution was adopted.[22]

Less than a month later, on February 4, 1856, Chairman Hunter reported that senators on Finance had considered the Brodhead resolution "and they have come to the conclusion that it would, perhaps, be better that they should be directed to prepare such of those appropriation bills as they may deem expedient, and report them to the Senate." Hunter thought it was probable that this would "expedite the business of the two Houses; and it may be that the committees of the House and of the Senate will agree on some distribution of this business, which will promote the convenience of both Houses."[23] An objection by Seward, however, postponed further consideration. Finally, on February 7, the confrontation came. Seward launched into an extended speech reviewing the history of the Constitutional Convention. Hunter responded that Seward's remarks were based "partly upon some fancied analogies, which really do not exist, between this body and the English House of Lords. . . ." Hunter granted that with passage of the resolution, general appropriation bills would be originated in the Senate for the first time. But he noted that earlier in the day the Senate had approved an individual relief bill, and he asked: "If we may relieve one individual by a special appropriation bill, why may we not relieve many by a general appropriation bill?"[24]

21. *The Congressional Globe,* 34 Cong. 1 sess., Pt. 1 (Dec. 11, 1855), p. 16.
22. *Globe,* pp. 160–63.
23. *Globe,* p. 349.
24. *Globe,* p. 377.

Seward's only allies were the two antislavery, soon-to-be Republican, senators from Massachusetts, Charles Sumner and Henry Wilson. Sumner, whose words and deeds were causing institutions to crumble about him, began on a cautious note: "The proposition is a clear departure from usage and on this account must be regarded with suspicion." He reminded his colleagues that according to Benjamin Franklin, the House prerogative on revenue matters was an integral part of the compromise that granted the small states equal representation in the Senate. Like Seward, Sumner looked, in part, to the English analogy and the prerogative of the House of Commons over money bills "by which the Government is carried on." He did admit that "the language in the Constitution seemed to me indefinite. It is not, on the face of it, clear." But the resolution was approved.[25]

The Finance Committee, which had asked for an expression of the Senate on the matter, was composed of six members; five of them had previous service in the House.

On February 27, 1856, the Senate passed an invalids' pension appropriation bill for fiscal 1857. The day before, House Ways and Means had reported a similar bill, which passed the House on March 6 and was approved by the Senate on March 27. On April 17, Representative George W. Jones of Tennessee, a member of the Select Committee on Rules, successfully moved to table the Senate bill, which had never been referred to committee. On March 6, the Senate had sent a second appropriation bill to the House, the fortifications appropriation bill for fiscal 1857. That, too, was tabled on April 17. The House version of the fortification bill had been reported on March 17. After heated debate between pro- and antislavery forces, the measure passed the House on August 2 and the Senate willingly approved it on August 16.

On August 5, 1856, a bill making additional appropriations for the support of the army for fiscal 1857 was reported from the Committee on Military Affairs and referred to Finance, which reported the measure to the Senate on August 15. The bill was tabled the next day. On January 22, 1857, the Senate considered and postponed a bill making appropriations for certain fortifications.

1861

On August 1, 1861, with Congress responding vigorously to President Lincoln's initiatives to save the Union, the Senate Committee on Military Affairs and Militia—chaired by Senator Wilson, who had sided with Seward in the 1856 dispute—reported a bill that appropriated $100,000 for contingencies in constructing fortifications. After brief floor consideration and the acceptance of an amendment to abolish flogging for military crimes, the bill was approved with no reference to Finance. It was referred to House Ways and Means the same day. On August 3, the House approved the Senate-initiated appropriation bill.

From the time of this bill until the dispute between the House and Senate Appropriations Committees in 1962, the Senate showed no particular interest in originating the annual general appropriation bills or the deficiencies or supplementals related to them.

25. *Globe,* pp. 379–81.

APPENDIX C

Attitudes of Senate Appropriations Members toward Eight Proposed Reforms, 1965–66

Figures C–1 through C–8 show the attitudes of the twenty-seven members of the Senate Committee on Appropriations during the Eighty-ninth Congress toward eight proposals offered by various senators to improve the appropriations process. Member attitudes are shown by party, committee position, and ideology. Senior members were defined as those who had served on the committee for nine years or more as of 1965; junior members were those who had served for eight years or less. Liberals and conservatives were identified by using a combination of the 1965 conservative coalition, presidential support, and expanded federal role scores compiled by *Congressional Quarterly*.[1]

Only one senator, a senior Democrat, was opposed to all eight proposals. Among Democrats, the range of support for the eight reforms extended from zero to seven, with a median of three. For Republicans, the range was from two to six, with a median of four. On the whole, the Republican minority on the committee—regardless of ideology or seniority—was more interested in reform than the Democrats. This might have resulted in part from a feeling of helplessness after being in the minority for more than a decade. However, some of the strongest proponents of reform were those ranking Republican members who did exert a major influence on the decisions made by their subcommittees.

1. See *Congressional Quarterly*, Vol. 23 (Nov. 12, 1965), p. 2306; (Nov. 26, 1965), p. 2389; (Dec. 3, 1965), p. 2421.

Figure C–1. Should Congress Establish a Joint Committee on the Budget?

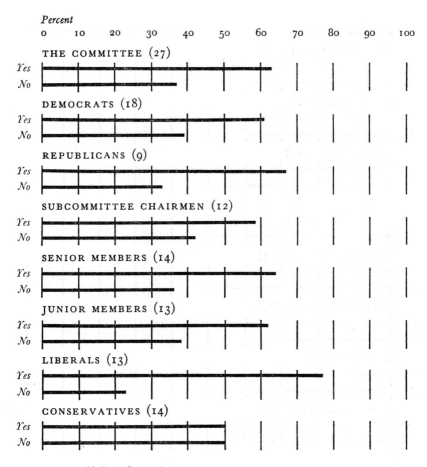

Senator McClellan first advanced this idea in 1950, although similar proposals had been suggested from time to time for several decades. The primary purpose of the McClellan approach, which has been approved by the Senate in every Congress since 1952, is to bring together an expert staff to analyze the budget and investigate federal operations. In 1965, McClellan's bill to establish a joint committee was sponsored by twenty-seven senators. Eighteen were from Senate Appropriations—although notably absent were Chairman Hayden and the next senior Democrat, Richard Russell. Some opponents thought the joint committee would be competitive and would duplicate the work of existing committees. Others argued that senior members were already overburdened with meetings and that the joint committee would thus be primarily a staff operation. They believed that any additional staff should be added to the two Appropriations Committees.

Figure C–2. Should the Senate Originate at Least Half of the General Appropriation Bills Each Year?

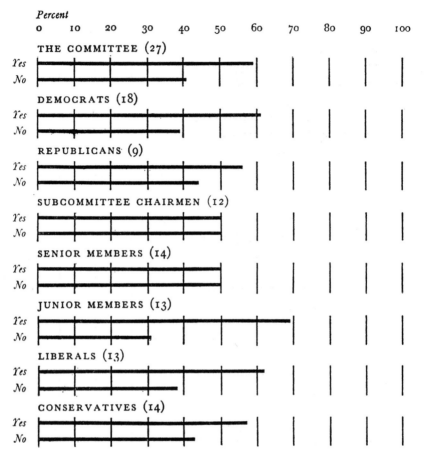

Although almost three-fifths of the committee members believed the Senate should originate at least half of the general appropriation bills each year, most realized—as one subcommittee chairman gloomily remarked—that "it will never happen." They knew that the House was adamant about preserving its traditional prerogative in this area, regardless of its questionable constitutional validity. Both proponents and opponents, however, thought such a procedure would speed congressional action on appropriations because the Senate committee could be more productive than the House at the beginning of a session and would not have to wait four or five months for the House to clear the first appropriation bills. But the fact that the senior members and subcommittee chairmen were equally divided on the suggestion was an indication that the committee leaders would not wage a vigorous fight for this change.

Figure C–3. Should Each Committee Member Have an Additional Staff Assistant in His Office for Appropriations Matters?

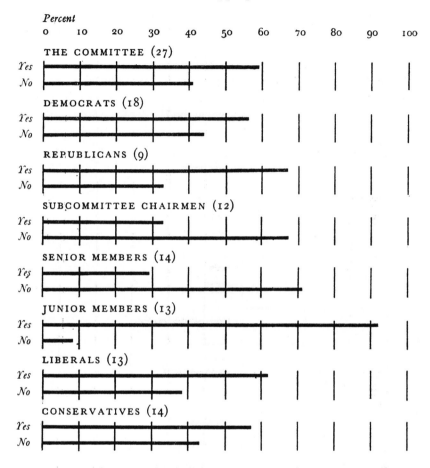

Percent

This question disclosed sharp differences within the committee. Although three-fifths of the whole committee favored the idea, subcommittee chairmen and senior members were opposed by more than 2 to 1. All but one of the junior members, however, favored the proposal. Senior members in both parties already had their staff needs met by the regular committee or minority staff. They saw little need for additional assistance for their junior colleagues. Revealing perhaps more than he intended, one subcommittee chairman expressed it this way: "I think it would be better to have more people on the committee staff following up on the executive agencies than to have a man in my office writing memos to me so I can go down to the committee and stir up trouble." If additional staff were assigned to the committee, they would be under the control of the leaders; in an office, they might "stir up trouble." The senior members had strong allies among the committee staff, who were not eager to see an additional hurdle interposed between them and the members. During the Eighty-ninth Congress, only four members—two in each party—had one of their principal assistants devoting as much as half of his time to Appropriations work. The others depended primarily on the committee staff.

Figure C–4. Should There Be a Specified Layover Period between the Subcommittee and Full Committee Markups to Allow Members of the Full Committee More Time to Review the Work of the Subcommittee?

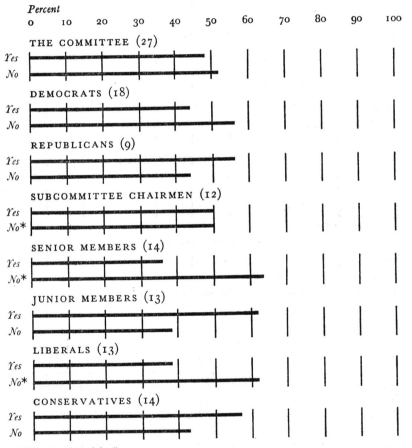

* Includes one "no opinion."

By a narrow margin, the committee as a whole did not favor having a specified layover period between the subcommittee and full committee markups. Some of those opposed emphasized that in the last few days of a session there was simply no time to observe a specified layover. The subcommittee chairmen, who might expect to gain an advantage from being able to speed a measure through the full committee, were themselves evenly divided on the proposal, but junior members, especially among the Republican minority, were convinced that a specified layover was needed.

Figure C–5. Should the Joint Economic Committee Be Reorganized to Include the Senior Members from Both Appropriations Committees?

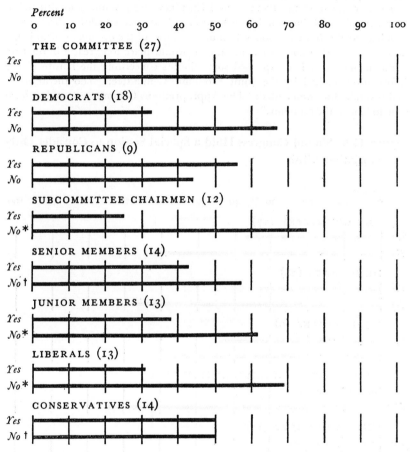

* Includes two "no opinions."   † Includes one "no opinion."

Repeatedly some who have sought to reform the appropriations process have suggested that Congress needs to look at the budget as a whole. They have sought a weighing of economic, fiscal, and revenue considerations before Congress makes its decisions on appropriations. To this end, Senator Kuchel urged in 1965 that the Joint Economic Committee be reconstituted to consist of the chairman, ranking minority member, and a majority member from the Appropriations, Banking and Currency, and revenue committees of both houses, as well as from the Armed Services and Public Works Committees. Since its creation by the Employment Act of 1946, the Joint Economic Committee has evolved as a forum in which many economic and budgetary issues have been discussed. But the committee is handicapped because it can only hold hearings and issue reports; it cannot report legislation.

When the Joint Economic Committee began, three of the seven Senate members were also on Senate Appropriations. By 1965, of the eight senators on the joint committee, only William Proxmire served on Appropriations. In 1967, Proxmire became chairman and Jacob K. Javits was again on both committees. House Appropriations continued to be unrepresented, however. Most of the members came from the Banking and Currency and revenue committees. Almost three-fifths of those on Senate Appropriations opposed adding three senior members to the Joint Economic Committee. Most of the opponents simply believed that another committee assignment would place too great a burden on senior members. A few expressed some doubts concerning the nature of the information elicited by the Joint Economic Committee: "Too theoretical," said several. One commented: "The Appropriations Committee wouldn't have time to look at the economy."

Figure C–6. Should Congress Hold a Special Session to Consider Only Appropriation Bills?

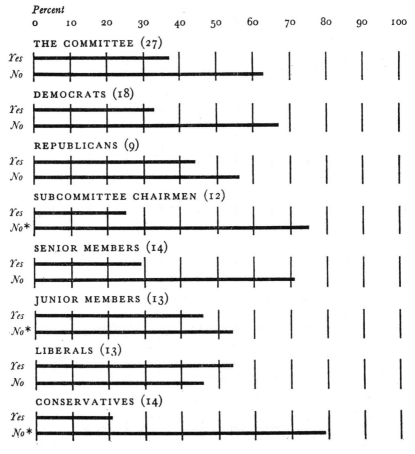

* Includes one "no opinion."

In 1957, Senator Warren Magnuson first offered a bill providing for a regular annual fiscal session from the second Monday in November to December 31 during which legislative committees might continue to meet, hold hearings, and conduct studies, but except for treaties, nominations, or other matters for which the President requested consideration, only appropriations measures would be introduced, reported, or enacted. The bill also established the calendar year as the fiscal year, and the President was to submit his budget by July 15. Sixteen of the twenty-seven senators on Appropriations opposed the special session, though most favored changing the fiscal year to coincide with the calendar year. Some felt it would be difficult to keep noncommittee members in Washington for a session devoted almost exclusively to appropriations. Others recognized that every second year, a few senators repudiated in the November election would return to act on the budget.

Figure C–7. Should All Appropriation Bills Be Combined into a Single Omnibus Measure?

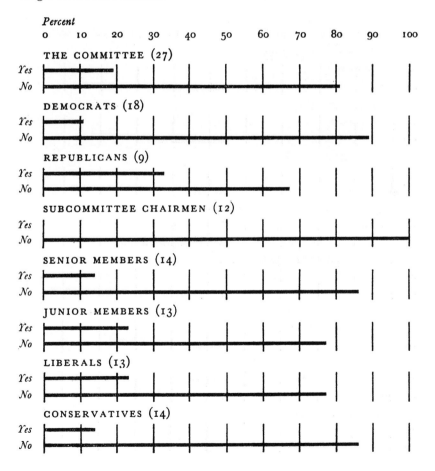

Beginning in the mid-1940s, the late Senator Harry F. Byrd urged the consolidation of all appropriation measures into a single annual bill so that each house could secure an overall view of the budget. Chairman Cannon insisted that House Appropriations try the procedure for the 1950 session. A bill of 425 pages was the result. Members complained that there was insufficient time in full committee to weigh different programs, with the result that each subcommittee's recommendations were uncritically accepted. In 1951, by a vote of 31 to 18, the House committee abandoned the experiment. The Senate committee, which traditionally waited for House action to be completed before taking up a measure, also found it difficult to handle the omnibus bill in the limited time remaining in the session. As a result, ten of the Senate Appropriations subcommittee chairmen also objected to the omnibus approach, and it was dropped.

Figure C–8. Should the President Be Granted an Item Veto on Appropriation Bills?

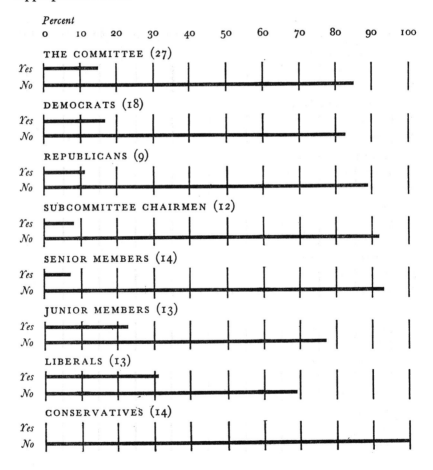

The reason for the overwhelmingly negative response to this question is clear. Many of the other suggestions affected the balance of power within the committee, or between the committee and the Senate, or between the House and the Senate; this proposal would change the balance of power between the legislative and executive branches. As one member put it, "The President already has too much power." Another commented: "If the President had the item veto, you might as well forget about Congress meeting."[2]

2. The item veto first appeared in the Provisional Constitution of the Confederate States of America. Since the 1870s, when President Grant first asked Congress to give him an item veto, various constitutional amendments and statutes have been proposed granting the chief executive this power. By the 1960s, more than forty states had permitted their governors some form of item veto. An excellent summary of the arguments for and against the item veto can be found in Robert Ash Wallace, *Congressional Control of Federal Spending* (Wayne State University Press, 1960), pp. 136–50.

APPENDIX D

Proposed Reassignment of Appropriation Bills

A fundamental need of the Senate Committee on Appropriations is to consolidate the fragments of agency programs now spread over fourteen subcommittees into fewer, more cohesive groupings. Five bills, generally corresponding to the existing program divisions within the Bureau of the Budget,[1] and each the responsibility of a subcommittee of the same title as the bill, would mean greater responsibility and a more nearly balanced workload within the committee than now exists. Table D–1 identifies the appropriation bill to which a particular agency was assigned during the Ninetieth Congress (1967–68), and specifies one of the five proposed bills—or subcommittees—to which it should be assigned to attain a more comprehensive review. The symbols used in Table D–1 are defined as follows:

Appropriation Bills	*Symbol*
Agriculture and Related Agencies	AG
Defense	DOD
District of Columbia	DC
Foreign Assistance and Related Agencies	FA
Independent Offices and Department of Housing and Urban Development	IND
Interior and Related Agencies	INT
Labor, and Health, Education, and Welfare, and Related Agencies	L-HEW
Legislative	LEG
Military Construction	MC
Public Works and Atomic Energy Commission	PW-AEC
State, Justice, Commerce, the Judiciary, and Related Agencies	S-J-C-J
Transportation	T
Treasury, Post Office, and Executive Office	T-PO-EO

1. After July 1, 1970, the Office of Management and Budget.

Bureau of the Budget Divisions	Symbol
Economics, Science, and Technology Programs	ESTP
General Government Management	GGM
Human Resources Programs	HRP
International Programs	IP
National Security Programs	NSP
Natural Resources Programs	NRP

Recommended Appropriation Bills	
Agricultural and Natural Resources	ANR
General Government	GG
Human Resources	HR
National Security	NS
Science and Technology	ST

Table D–1. Assignments of Federal Agencies to Appropriation Bills During the Ninetieth Congress, Corresponding Bureau of the Budget Program Divisions, and Proposed Reassignments

Agency	Appropriation bill	Bureau of the Budget division	Recommended appropriation bill
Administrative Conference of the U.S.	T-PO-EO	ESTP	GG
Administrative Office of the U.S. Courts (Judiciary)	S-J-C-J	GGM	GG
Advisory Commission on Intergovernmental Relations	T-PO-EO	HRP	GG
Agency for International Development	FA	1P	NS
Aging, Administration on (HEW)	L-HEW	HRP	HR
Agriculture, Department of (general, except Forest Service)	AG	NRP	ANR
Agricultural Research Service (Agriculture)	AG	NRP	ANR
Agricultural Stabilization and Conservation Service (Agriculture)	AG	NRP	ANR
Air Force, Department of the	DOD	NSP	NS
Alaska Power Administration	PW-AEC	NRP	ANR
Alaska Railroad (Transportation)	T	ESTP	ST
American Battle Monuments Commission	S-J-C-J	NSP	NS
American Printing House for the Blind (HEW)	L-HEW	HRP	HR
American Revolution Bicentennial Commission	INT	NRP	ANR
Appalachian Regional Commission	IND	ESTP	ST
Apprenticeship and Training, Bureau of (Labor)	L-HEW	HRP	HR
Architect of the Capitol (Legislative Branch)	LEG	GGM	GG
Arms Control and Disarmament Agency, United States	S-J-C-J	IP	NS
Army, Department of the			
Military functions	DOD	NSP	NS
Rivers, harbors, and flood control	PW-AEC	NRP	ANR
Panama Canal	PW-AEC	NRP	ANR

Table D–1 *(Continued)*

Agency	Appropriation bill	Bureau of the Budget division	Recommended appropriation bill
Atlantic-Pacific Interoceanic Canal Study Commission	PW-AEC	NRP	ANR
Atomic Energy Commission	PW-AEC	ESTP	NS
Bonneville Power Administration (Interior)	PW-AEC	NRP	ANR
Botanic Garden (Legislative Branch)	LEG	GGM	GG
Budget, Bureau of the	T-PO-EO	GGM	GG
Bureau of (see other part of title)			
Business and Defense Services Administration (Commerce)	S-J-C-J	ESTP	ST
Business Economics, Office of (Commerce)	S-J-C-J	ESTP	ST
Canal Zone Government	PW-AEC	NRP	GG
Census, Bureau of the (Commerce)	S-J-C-J	ESTP	HR
Central Intelligence Agency	. . .ᵃ	IP	NS
Children's Bureau (HEW)	L-HEW	HRP	HR
Civil Aeronautics Board	IND	ESTP	ST
Civil Defense (Department of Defense)	IND	NSP	NS
Civil Rights, Commission on	S-J-C-J	GGM	HR
Civil Service Commission	IND	GGM	GG
Civil War Centennial Commission	INT	NRP	ANR
Coal Research, Office of (Interior)	INT	NRP	ANR
Coast and Geodetic Survey (Commerce)	S-J-C-J	ESTP	ST
Coast Guard (Transportation)	T	ESTP	GG
Coastal Plains Regional Commission	S-J-C-J	ESTP	ST
Commerce, Department of	S-J-C-J	ESTP	ST
Commercial Fisheries, Bureau of (Interior)	INT	NRP	ANR
Commissions (see other part of title)			
Commodity Credit Corporation (Agriculture)	AG	NRP	ANR
Commodity Exchange Authority (Agriculture)	AG	NRP	ANR
Communications Satellite Corporation	. . .	ESTP	ST
Consumer and Marketing Service (Agriculture)	AG	NRP	ANR
Cooperative State Research Service (Agriculture)	AG	NRP	ANR
Coordinator for Meteorology, Office of	S-J-C-J	ESTP	ST
Council of Economic Advisers	T-PO-EO	ESTP	GG
Defense, Department of (except Civil Defense, Civil Works, Military Construction, and Office of Assistant Secretary for International Security Affairs)	DOD	NSP	NS
Civil Defense	IND	IP	NS
Civil Works	PW-AEC	NRP	ANR
Military Construction	MC	NSP	NS
Office of Assistant Secretary for International Security Affairs	FA	IP	NS

Table **D–1** *(Continued)*

Agency	Appropriation bill	Bureau of the Budget division	Recommended appropriation bill
Defense Intelligence Agency	DOD	IP	NS
Delaware River Basin Commission	PW-AEC	NRP	ANR
Departments (see other part of title)			
District of Columbia	DC	GGM	HR
Economic and Market Analysis, Office of (HUD)	IND	HRP	HR
Economic Development Administration (Commerce)	S-J-C-J	ESTP	ST
Economic Opportunity, Office of	L-HEW	HRP	HR
Economic Research Service (Agriculture)	AG	NRP	ANR
Education, Office of (HEW)	L-HEW	HRP	HR
Arts and Humanities Educational Activities	INT	HRP	HR
Civil Rights Educational Activities	S-J-C-J	HRP	HR
Emergency Fund for the President	T-PO-EO	GGM	GG
Emergency Planning, Office of	IND	ESTP	NS
Employees Compensation, Bureau of (Labor)	L-HEW	HRP	HR
Employment Security, Bureau of (Labor)	L-HEW	HRP	HR
Engineers, Corps of (Army)	PW-AEC	NRP	ANR
Environmental Science Services Administration	S-J-C-J	ESTP	ST
Equal Employment Opportunity Commission	S-J-C-J	HRP	HR
Executive, Legislative, and Judicial Salaries, Commission on	IND	GGM	GG
Executive Mansion	T-PO-EO	GGM	GG
Executive Office of the President	T-PO-EO	GGM	GG
Expenses of Management Improvement	T-PO-EO	GGM	GG
Export-Import Bank of the United States	FA	IP	NS
Export Control, Office of (Commerce)	S-J-C-J	ESTP	NS
Extension Service (Agriculture)	AG	NRP	ANR
Farm Credit Administration	AG	NRP	ANR
Farmer Cooperative Service (Agriculture)	AG	NRP	ANR
Farmers Home Administration (Agriculture)	AG	NRP	ANR
Federal Aviation Administration (Transportation)	T	ESTP	ST
Federal Bureau of Investigation (Justice)	S-J-C-J	GGM	GG
Federal Coal Mine Safety Board of Review	INT	NRP	ANR
Federal Communications Commission	IND	ESTP	ST
Federal Crop Insurance Corporation (Agriculture)	AG	NRP	ANR
Federal Deposit Insurance Corporation	IND[b]	GGM	GG
Federal Field Committee for Development Planning in Alaska	INT	ESTP	ANR
Federal Highway Administration (Transportation)	T	ESTP	ST
Federal Home Loan Bank Board	IND	HRP	HR

Table D-1 (*Continued*)

Agency	Appropriation bill	Bureau of the Budget division	Recommended appropriation bill
Federal Housing Administration (HUD)	IND	HRP	HR
Federal Interagency Committee on Education	L-HEW	HRP	HR
Federal Maritime Commission	S-J-C-J	ESTP	ST
Federal Mediation and Conciliation Service	L-HEW	HRP	HR
Federal National Mortgage Association (HUD)	IND	HRP	HR
Federal Power Commission	IND	NRP	ANR
Federal Prison Industries, Inc. (Justice)	S-J-C-J	GGM	GG
Federal Radiation Council	L-HEW	HRP	ST
Federal Railroad Administration (Transportation)	T	ESTP	ST
Federal Savings and Loan Insurance Corporation (FHLBB)	IND	HRP	HR
Federal Supply Service (GSA)	IND	GGM	GG
Federal Trade Commission	IND	ESTP	ST
Federal Water Pollution Control Administration (Interior)	PW-AEC	NRP	ANR
Field Services, Office of (Commerce)	S-J-C-J	ESTP	GG
Fine Arts, Commission of	INT	GGM	GG
Food and Drug Administration (HEW)	L-HEW	HRP	HR
Foreign Agricultural Service (Agriculture)	AG	NRP	NS
Foreign Claims Settlement Commission	S-J-C-J	IP	NS
Forest Service (Agriculture)	INT	NRP	ANR
Four Corners Regional Commission	S-J-C-J	ESTP	HR
Franklin Delano Roosevelt Memorial Commission	INT	NRP	ANR
Freedmen's Hospital (HEW)	L-HEW	HRP	HR
Gallaudet College (HEW)	L-HEW	HRP	HR
General Accounting Office	IND	GGM	GG
General Services Administration	IND	GGM	GG
Geological Survey (Interior)	INT	NRP	ANR
Government Printing Office (Legislative Branch)	LEG	GGM	GG
Health, Education, and Welfare, Department of (general)	L-HEW	HRP	HR
Assistance to Refugees in the U.S.	FA	· · ·	HR
House of Representatives	LEG	GGM	GG
Housing and Urban Development, Department of	IND	HRP	HR
Housing Assistance Administration (HUD)	IND	HRP	HR
Howard University (HEW)	L-HEW	HRP	HR
Immigration and Naturalization Service (Justice)	S-J-C-J	GGM	GG

Table D–1 *(Continued)*

Agency	Appropriation bill	Bureau of the Budget division	Recommended appropriation bill
Indian Affairs, Bureau of (Interior)	INT	NRP	HR
Indian Claims Commission	INT	NRP	HR
Information Agency, United States	S-J-C-J	IP	NS
Interagency Committee on Mexican-American Affairs	. . .ᵉ	GGM	NS
Intergovernmental Relations and Urban Program Coordination, Office of (HUD)	IND	HRP	HR
Interior, Department of the (except Bureau of Reclamation and power marketing agencies)	INT	NRP	ANR
International Agricultural Development Service (Agriculture)	AG	NRP	NS
International Boundary and Water Commission, U.S. and Mexico (State)	S-J-C-J	NRP	ANR
International Commerce, Bureau of (Commerce)	S-J-C-J	ESTP	NS
International Labor Affairs, Bureau of (Labor)	L-HEW	HRP	NS
International Monetary Fund	T-PO-EO	IP	NS
Interstate Commerce Commission	IND	ESTP	ST
Interstate Commission on the Potomac River Basin	PW-AEC	GGM	ANR
James Madison Memorial Commission	INT	NRP	ANR
John F. Kennedy Center for the Performing Arts	INT	ESTP	HR
Judiciary, The	S-J-C-J	GGM	GG
Justice, Department of	S-J-C-J	GGM	GG
Labor, Department of (except Bureau of International Labor Affairs)	L-HEW	HRP	HR
Labor Management Services Administration (Labor)	L-HEW	HRP	HR
Labor Standards, Bureau of (Labor)	L-HEW	HRP	HR
Labor Statistics, Bureau of (Labor)	L-HEW	HRP	HR
Land and Facilities Development Administration (HUD)	IND	HRP	HR
Land Management, Bureau of (Interior)	INT	NRP	ANR
Legislative Branch	LEG	GGM	GG
Lewis and Clark Trail Commission	INT	NRP	ANR
Library of Congress (Legislative Branch)	LEG	GGM	GG
Manpower Administration (Labor)	L-HEW	HRP	HR
Marine Science, Engineering, and Resources, Commission on	INT	ESTP	ST
Maritime Administration (Commerce)	S-J-C-J	ESTP	ST
Maritime Commission, Federal	S-J-C-J	ESTP	ST

Table D–1 (*Continued*)

Agency	Appropriation bill	Bureau of the Budget division	Recommended appropriation bill
Medical Services Administration (HEW)	L-HEW	HRP	HR
Meteorology, Office of Coordinator for	S-J-C-J	ESTP	ST
Mineral Exploration, Office of (Interior)	INT	NRP	ANR
Minerals Mobilization, Office of (Interior)	INT	NRP	ANR
Mines, Bureau of (Interior)	INT	NRP	ANR
Model Cities Administration (HUD)	IND	HRP	HR
National Aeronautics and Space Administration	IND	ESTP	ST
National Aeronautics and Space Council	IND	ESTP	ST
National Agricultural Library (Agriculture)	AG	NRP	ANR
National Archives and Records Service (GSA)	IND	GGM	GG
National Capital Planning Commission	INT	GGM	HR
National Capital Transportation Agency	INT	GGM	HR
National Council on Marine Resources and Engineering Development	INT	ESTP	ST
National Foundation on the Arts and Humanities	INT	HRP	HR
National Gallery of Art	INT	ESTP	ST
National Highway Safety Bureau (Transportation)	T	ESTP	ST
National Institutes of Health (PHS-HEW)	L-HEW	HRP	HR
National Labor Relations Board	L-HEW	HRP	HR
National Library of Medicine (PHS-HEW)	L-HEW	HRP	HR
National Mediation Board	L-HEW	HRP	HR
National Park Service (Interior)	INT	NRP	ANR
National Railroad Adjustment Board	L-HEW	HRP	HR
National Science Foundation	IND	ESTP	ST
National Security Agency	. . .ª	IP	NS
National Security Council	T-PO-EO	NSP	GG
National Transportation Safety Board (Transportation)	T	ESTP	ST
Navy, Department of the	DOD	NSP	NS
New England Regional Commission	S-J-C-J	ESTP	ST
North Atlantic Treaty Organization	FA	NSP	NS
Obscenity and Pornography, Commission on	T-PO-EO	GGM	GG
Office of (see other part of title)			
Oil and Gas, Office of (Interior)	INT	NRP	ANR
Oil Import Administration (Interior)	INT	NRP	ANR
Outdoor Recreation, Bureau of (Interior)	INT	NRP	ANR
Ozarks Regional Commission	S-J-C-J	ESTP	ST
Panama Canal Company	PW-AEC	NRP	ANR
Patent Office (Commerce)	S-J-C-J	ESTP	ST
Peace Corps	FA	IP	NS

Table **D**–1 *(Continued)*

Agency	Appropriation bill	Bureau of the Budget division	Recommended appropriation bill
Permanent Committee for the Oliver Wendell Holmes Devise Fund	LEG	GGM	GM
Planning Standards and Coordination, Office of (HUD)	IND	HRP	HR
Post Office Department	T-PO-EO	GGM	GG
President's Advisory Committee on Labor-Management Policy	T-PO-EO	HRP	HR
President's Commission on Law Enforcement and Administration of Justice	S-J-C-J^d	GGM	GG
President's Committee on Consumer Interests	L-HEW	HRP	HR
President's Committee on Employment of the Handicapped	L-HEW	HRP	HR
President's Committee on Equal Opportunity in Housing	. . .º	HRP	HR
President's Committee on Manpower	L-HEW	HRP	HR
President's Committee on Mental Retardation	L-HEW	HRP	HR
President's Council on Recreation and Natural Beauty	INT	NRP	ANR
President's Council on Youth Opportunity	. . .º	HRP	HR
Property Management and Disposal Service (GSA)	IND	GGM	GG
Public Buildings Service (GSA)	IND	GGM	GG
Public Health Service (HEW)	L-HEW	HRP	HR
Emergency Health Activities	IND	HRP	NS
Indian Health Activities	INT	HRP	HR
Public Land Law Review Commission	INT	NRP	ANR
Public Roads, Bureau of (Transportation)	T	ESTP	ST
Railroad Retirement Board	L-HEW	HRP	HR
Reclamation, Bureau of, and power marketing agencies (Interior)	PW-AEC	NRP	ANR
Rehabilitation Service Administration (HEW)	L-HEW	HRP	HR
Renegotiation Board	IND	ESTP	NS
Renewal Projects Administration (HUD)	IND	HRP	HR
Rural Community Development Service (Agriculture)	AG	NRP	ANR
Rural Electrification Administration (Agriculture)	AG	NRP	ANR
Ryukyu Islands (Army)	FA	NSP	NS
Saint Elizabeth's Hospital (HEW)	L-HEW	HRP	HR
Saline Water, Office of (Interior)	INT	NRP	ANR
Science and Technology, Office of	IND	ESTP	ST
Securities and Exchange Commission	IND	ESTP	GG
Selective Service System	IND	HRP	NS

Table D–1 (*Continued*)

Agency	Appropriation bill	Bureau of the Budget division	Recommended appropriation bill
Senate	LEG	GGM	GG
Small Business Administration	S-J-C-J	ESTP	ST
Smithsonian Institution	INT	ESTP	ST
Social and Rehabilitation Service (HEW)	L-HEW	HRP	HR
Social Security Administration (HEW)	L-HEW	HRP	HR
Soil Conservation Service (Agriculture)	AG	NRP	ANR
Soldiers' Home, United States	L-HEW	NSP	HR
Southeastern and Southwestern Power Administrations (Interior)	PW-AEC	NRP	ANR
Special Representative for Trade Negotiations	S-J-C-J	IP	NS
Sport Fisheries and Wildlife, Bureau of (Interior)	INT	NRP	ANR
St. Lawrence Seaway Development Corporation (Transportation)	T	ESTP	ST
Standards, National Bureau of (Commerce)	S-J-C-J	ESTP	ST
State, Department of (general)	S-J-C-J	IP	NS
International Boundary and Water Commission	S-J-C-J	NRP	ANR
Migration and Refugee Assistance	FA	IP	HR
Passamaquoddy tidal power project	PW-AEC	NRP	ANR
State Technical Services, Office of (Commerce)	S-J-C-J	ESTP	ST
Statistical Reporting Service (Agriculture)	AG	NRP	ANR
Stockpiling (GSA-OEP)	IND	GGM	NS
Subversive Activities Control Board	S-J-C-J	GGM	GG
Supreme Court of the United States (Judiciary)	S-J-C-J	GGM	GG
Tariff Commission, United States	S-J-C-J	IP	NS
Tax Court of the United States	T-PO-EO	GGM	GG
Telecommunications Management, Office of (OEP)	T-PO-EO	ESTP	ST
Tennessee Valley Authority	PW-AEC	NRP	ANR
Territories, Office of (Interior)	INT	NRP	ANR
Territorial Expansion Memorial Commission, United States	INT	NRP	ANR
Trade Negotiations, Special Representative for	S-J-C-J	IP	NS
Transportation, Department of	T	ESTP	ST
Transportation and Communication Service (GSA)	IND	GGM	GG
Travel Service, U.S. (Commerce)	S-J-C-J	ESTP	ST
Treasury Department	T-PO-EO	GGM	GG
Trust Territory of the Pacific (Interior)	INT	NRP	NS
Upper Great Lakes Regional Commission	S-J-C-J	ESTP	ST
Urban Technology and Research, Office of (HUD)	IND	HRP	HR

Table **D-1** *(Continued)*

Agency	Appropriation bill	Bureau of the Budget division	Recommended appropriation bill
Urban Transportation Administration (HUD)	IND	HRP	HR
Veterans Administration	IND	HRP	HR
Virgin Islands Corporation	INT	NRP	GG
Vocational Rehabilitation Administration (HEW)	L-HEW	HRP	HR
Wage and Hour Division (Labor)	L-HEW	HRP	HR
Washington Metropolitan Area Transit Authority	IND	GGM	HR
Water Resources Council	PW-AEC	NRP	ANR
Water Resources Research, Office of (Interior)	INT	NRP	ANR
Weather Bureau (Commerce)	S-J-C-J	ESTP	ST
Welfare Administration (HEW)	L-HEW	HRP	HR
White House Office	T-PO-EO	GGM	GG
Women's Bureau (Labor)	L-HEW	HRP	HR
Woodrow Wilson Memorial Commission	INT	NRP	ANR

Definitions of symbols appear on pp. 264–65.

a. Classified.

b. No funds derived from taxes or federal appropriations are allocated to or used by the FDIC; income is derived from insurance assessments paid by insured banks and from interest on investments in U.S. government securities.

c. Interagency contributions.

d. Supplemental.

Index

PRINTED IN U.S.A.